Helping
People
Forgive

Other Westminster John Knox books
by David W. Augsburger

Conflict Mediation across Cultures: Pathways and Patterns
Pastoral Counseling across Cultures

Helping People Forgive

David W. Augsburger

Westminster John Knox Press
Louisville, Kentucky

Acknowledgments will be found on page 180.

Book design by Jennifer K. Cox
Cover design by Kim Wohlenhaus
Cover illustration. La Cathédrale, *Auguste Rodin, 1840–1917. French. Courtesy of SuperStock*

First edition

Published by Westminster John Knox Press
Louisville, Kentucky

This book is printed on acid-free paper that meets the American National Standards Institute Z39.48 standard. ♾

PRINTED IN THE UNITED STATES OF AMERICA

00 01 02 03 04 05 — 10 9 8 7 6 5 4 3

Library of Congress Cataloging-in-Publication Data

Augsburger, David W
Helping people forgive / David W. Augsburger — 1st ed.
p. cm.
Includes bibliographical references (p.)
ISBN 0-664-25686-4 (alk paper)
1. Forgiveness—Religious aspects—Christianity.
2. Visualization—Therapeutic use. I. Title.
BV4647.F55A96 1996
234' 5—dc20 96-21400

Contents

Illustrations

Preface

Forgiveness has always had its detractors.

From the one side it is seen as too easy, too simple, too quick a fix for any significant injury.

From the other, it is viewed as too difficult, too complex, too long and tortuous a road when revenge or retaliation would get to the point more economically.

These two perspectives struggle in the clash of "the therapeutic society" with "the civil society." The one seeks to find substitute forms of forgiveness to make ourselves and our significant others feel better; the other looks for means of improving relationships, creating a better community, finding the healing that makes better people of us. Compassion and justice will wrestle forever.

The many novels, movies, and plays that focus on the desperate search for reconciliation reveal the yearning, often latent but ultimately making its tortured appearance, of persons groping for connection or reconnection. And those things which make up the soul of the behavioral sciences—the spirit of ethics, philosophy, and theology, the heart of all effective therapy— are revealed in their attempts at healing the ruptured, bridging the alienated, restoring the estranged.

Yet our metaphors have become tired, our images of healing eroded down to the bare threads of perceptions and attributions entwined with communication and tolerance, and there are occasional loose threads of forgetfulness and fatigue. *Forgo* has come to mean "let go"; *forgive* has been reduced to "give up"; *forget* is to "get free."

In privatizing the experience, individualizing the goal, treating the intrapsychic, we have drained forgiveness of its power to reknit the torn, rekindle the cold.

Can the leaf return to the tree, or the branch green again?

Can the wrenched arm return to the socket and embrace again?

Can we find new metaphors of restoration, new maps of the circulatory systems of the soul that nourish troubled relationships into trembling friendships?

Helping people forgive is our calling, our vocation as persons, whether we are in the "helping professions" formally, or offering help informally in the daily brushes and abrasions. In each effort to "help another to" we find help for ourselves, for the pain we have inflicted, for the pain we have suffered. And in this healing journey, we discover the trajectory of the soul. It is an arrow shot Godward, which inevitably falls earthward again, but in the flight feels the wind of the spirit on its fletching and the upward call of grace.

This, my third book on forgiveness, will not be my last. Forgiveness has been the inner theme of a dozen of my efforts on counseling, conflict, communication, and conciliation. Perhaps every life has a theme, a discernible motif, connected unquestionably to its central weakness, injury, or inability, and the more deeply we pursue it, the closer we come to each other. We touch one another's truth. The ancient philosophers suggested that there are only seven truths and all else is elaboration. They did not name forgiveness as one of them. Perhaps that is because it embraces and enables justice, prudence, temperance, and above all charity.

D.W.A.

Claremont, California

Helping People Forgive

1

New Metaphors, Models, and Images of Reconciliation

> Many promising reconciliations have broken down because, while both parties came prepared to forgive, neither party came prepared to be forgiven
>
> —Charles Williams (1886–1945)

> Now the ears of our ears awake,
> And now the eyes of our eyes are opened.
>
> —e. e cummings

> Thou shalt not nail another to his past.

Do I Have to Forgive?

The following account by Richard Lord vividly illustrates the question of whether one must always forgive:

> I was asked by Betty Jane Spencer, "Preacher, do I have to forgive a man who murdered my four sons?"
>
> A few years earlier, a group of young men had gotten high on drugs and broken into her Indiana farmhouse and committed mass murder. Betty Jane's sons were killed. She was shot and left for dead. Since beginning his prison sentence, one of the convicted criminals wrote to tell her he had "found Christ" and asked her forgiveness.
>
> When she said "Preacher," I knew she wanted more than my opinion. She wanted a statement that represented the Christian tradition. "Am I obligated as a Christian to forgive in this situation? Just what does the church mean by 'forgiveness'? He did not say 'I'm sorry,' . . . just 'Forgive me,'" she continued. "What am I to do?"
>
> I told her to give me six months and I would try to give her an answer. During that time I sought out victims of violent crimes, and those whose loved ones had been shattered by crimes. I studied the Jewish tradition and looked at what the church has said.

The victims who talked with me were very disturbed by the issue of forgiveness. They were constantly being told they must forgive, but most could not. . . . Victims' resistance to forgiveness seems to focus on two elements: forgiveness as forgetting and forgiveness as excuse. . . .Victims of violence are deeply concerned that their loved ones not be forgotten.

Forgiving may also imply excusing. . . . Does finding Christ excuse what was done? . . . Leaders of the prison ministry say that man should be released so he can witness for Christ. Betty Jane wonders why he can't witness for Christ in prison.

What can we learn from the Judeo-Christian tradition about forgiveness which does not imply forgetting or excusing? On Yom Kippur, sins against God are forgiven. But if you have sinned against your neighbor, you must go to him or her and seek forgiveness. Not even God forgives what you have done to another. . . .

I remembered the times I have proclaimed, "Your sins are forgiven." I now imagine a battered wife thinking to herself, "Who gave you the right to forgive the one who beats me?" I no longer say in a general or public way, "Your sins are forgiven." . . .

Victims ask us not to demand that they themselves pronounce absolution. Those of us who speak on behalf of the Christian community can speak of God's mercy to the truly repentant, but we have no right to insist that the victim establish a relationship with his or her victimizer to effect a reconciliation. Even without some reconciliation with the perpetrator, most victims gradually "let go" of their hate, anger, rage, or despair. Their negative energy becomes channeled into constructive activity such as working for victim causes or supporting other victims.

Betty Jane Spencer is open to a future without her sons. She is a prominent national leader in the victim rights movement. But she is not open to a future with those who killed her children. She had no relationship with them before the murders and she desires none now. She hopes they create for themselves a positive future, but one that does not include her.

Betty Jane is quite ready to affirm that God is merciful and is hopeful that the murderers of her sons will find a genuine relationship with God. But don't ask her to be responsible for their salvation. Don't ask her to go to them and judge their hearts. Let a representative of the church assume that burden.

When I saw Betty Jane six months later, I told her No (Lord 1991, 902–3).

Is Forgiveness Optional?

Betty Jane Spencer's story stimulates a rushing stream of questions. What else, given his reliance on therapeutic empathy, could Pastor Lord answer? Where else might he have turned for help? To the tradition of scripture? To the support of Christian community? To a theology of mediation, reconciliation, and victim-offender transformation?

What of Mary Jane Spencer's pain? Is forgiveness possible in such tragedy? Is it a desirable outcome or should retributive justice run its course?

What kind of forgiveness is being requested here? Remission of punishment? Release from guilt? Return to the innocence of denial? Memory fatigue? Or the creation of a relationship? If so, on whose terms, for whose sake, for what ends?

Does anyone have the right to ask for forgiveness? Or can one only offer genuine repentance and wait patiently for the gift of forgiveness if the other chooses to give it?

What of the pastor in this example, what of his theology and pastoral response? Is he hearing the real question of the parishioner or struggling with his own dilemma? How does he decide that this is a yes–no issue to be adjudicated? What if it is a profoundly emotional issue to be explored?

What if he facilitated the long, slow process of dialogue between the offended and the offender? Certainly the murderer's first request seems cavalier in terms of the heinousness of the crimes committed. But what if it is a first opening toward an eventual repentance that might recognize the full seriousness of the evil done?

Would forgiveness—truly human forgiveness—ever be possible? If so, on what terms, to what extent, by what steps?

This is only the beginning of the questions, the quandaries, evoked by this heartrending story. In his commentary on this same story, William Willimon is less than appreciative of Lord's solution to the parishioner's question.

> Lord presents himself as a pastor who, confronted by a specific, suffering parishioner, empathetically struggled with her situation in a caring, compassionate way. Some pastors, when asked by this woman, "Do I have to forgive?" might have quoted scripture to her, not because Jesus was an "expert," but because Jesus is the one who brought Pastor Lord and Betty Jane Spencer together in the first place. Jesus certainly had much to say on the subject of forgiveness, much of which was very straightforward and specific: "And forgive us our debts, as we have also forgiven our debtors" (Matt. 6:12).

> Lord was too deeply concerned for this woman to quote any Jesus to her. So he went rummaging in the "Judeo-Christian tradition" for answers and, after six months, found the answer that she really need not try to forgive the young killer who asked her forgiveness. That was not her vocation as a Christian, nor was it Pastor Lord's "right" to urge her to do so (Willimon 1991, 165).

Willimon's words, ironic though they may be, address the ubiquitous tendency to do the pragmatic rather than the principled, to seek congruence with oneself rather than with moral virtue. It may well be that Lord represents what Willimon calls "rebellious ethics," which refuses the expectations of tradition and the ministerial role and dismisses scripture, Jesus, church tradition, and the liturgy of the church in favor of the freedom to do what one thinks personally to be right (Willimon 1991, 170).

This is a crucial moment in her life, a moment that deserves not an answer but a co-exploration. "What does forgiveness mean to you?" "What step could you take to begin conversation with the offender, since such dialogue is necessary to healing for both of you?" How could he step back from defining her situation for her and resolving it for her in a clear negative answer in order to join her in a deeper struggle to go as far in forgiving as is possible in this difficult circumstance? Are there levels of forgiveness? Do we long for more than we may be able to achieve? Do we settle for less than might be possible?

If empathy is our primary value; if emotivism serves as our ethical process; if tradition, scripture, and the resources of the church are no longer of use, what does forgiveness mean? We may fall back on the popular therapeutic values of our culture—utilitarian guidelines for stress reduction—and forgive if it sets *us* free or not forgive if it requires too much pain.

If, however, the interpersonal bridge (reconciliation) is to have any structural integrity; if it can be suspended across deep and abysmal injuries; if it is to be sound enough to bear the weight of persons traveling to the other side once more, then forgiveness must be more than a social lubricant, a survival technique, a relational strategy, a memory fatigue, an individual escape, a dismissal of hurt or anger or a ritual of denial.

The Interpersonal Bridge

A bridge must bear weight; forgiveness must hold up under the coming and going of life. A bridge must be connected at both ends; forgiveness must show some measure of movement from both offended and offender. A bridge must stretch, unsupported, across vast emptiness; forgiveness must risk the unknown, the unsupported, the unpredictable. A bridge must join the separated, connect the severed; forgiveness rejoins, reconnects, or constructs a new path. The bridges of human relationship are not easy to build; and once built, they are not simple to maintain; and if they endure, a costly toll is charged for each crossing. There's nothing easy about it, nothing simple, nothing cheap about the grace of renewing broken relationships.

A bridge, though only one metaphor among many we shall use, represents a particular paradigm of reconciliation. Multiple paradigms are available to be employed, new paradigms wait to be explored, and unknown paradigms need to be discovered. A paradigm is a model or a map of one's way of seeing one's world. This map shapes our perceptions, guides our explorations, labels our interpretations, and selects our retentions. If one seeks to find one's way in downtown Los Angeles using a map of Manhattan, one will find Broadway but will still be wrong. The frustration has nothing to do with behavior—one is reading the map and seeking the street signs. Nor is it due to one's attitude or sincerity. It comes from having the wrong map.

Some of our traditional maps of reconciliation are trustworthy; they have not failed us; we have failed to follow them. Others have led us astray, misguided us into unfamiliar streets, and we have lost our way.

We are in a constant search for new metaphors of reconciliation, better maps of mediation, a clearer cartography of human relationships—both broken and mended, ruptured and healed. But what is needed is an alternative paradigm, a model or map that will free us to see new aspects of the reconciling process and arrive at a new configuration of the healing reality.

Perhaps by following a fresh trail of metaphors, like those of Melanie Klein, Heinz Kohut, Murray Bowen, René Girard, Alasdair MacIntyre, John Howard Yoder, and Stanley Hauerwas, we can find our way toward a shift in paradigms, a much-needed shift that may open possibilities for bridging the rifts that plague humankind and human society.

The Nature of Paradigms

The use of the word *paradigm* to describe major shifts in ways of perceiving and construing the world emerges from the thesis of Thomas Kuhn, physicist and historian of science. Although Kuhn limited his theories to the natural sciences, which he considered "mature sciences," those of us in the social sciences (proto-sciences, according to him) also make use of his concepts.

Kuhn's proposition is that science does not grow cumulatively with increasing knowledge and research, moving us ever closer to solutions. Instead, it moves forward by way of "revolutions." A group begins to perceive reality in ways qualitatively different from the prevailing views. A new model or theoretical structure, a new paradigm, is gradually forming, attracting adherents and revolutionizing thought. This is a protracted process, with adherents to the older paradigm fighting a rear-guard action. Finally the two paradigms separate sufficiently so that persons speaking from the rival constructs no longer understand each other. Metaphorically, the situation is then like two persons sitting at the same checkered board, one playing chess and the other checkers. Or, in the social sciences, it is like two divorced people discussing the common past in their former marriage, although each has rewritten the story on the basis of pain and pride, loss and reconstruction.

The Copernican paradigm yielded to the Newtonian, which was replaced by the Einsteinian. Abandoning one and embracing another is not simply a rational choice; the scholar is personally involved in this leap from one framework to another. It is, in Kuhn's words, like a religious experience, a "conversion," "a flash of intuition," and "scales fall from the eyes" (Kuhn 1970, 122–23).

The meaning of the word *paradigm* is not simple. Kuhn has been credited with using the term in at least twenty-two different ways. His final definition is "the entire constellation of beliefs, values, techniques, and so on shared by the members of a given community" (Kuhn 1970, 175). More simply, it is often used to refer to models of interpretation, frames of reference, or belief systems.

> The proponents of competing paradigms practice their trades in different worlds . . . see different things when they look from the same point in the same direction . . . see them in different relations one to the other. . . . The transition between competing paradigms cannot be made a step at a time, forced by logic and neutral experience. Like the gestalt switch, it must occur all at once (though not necessarily in an instant) or not at all (Kuhn 1970, 150).

In theology, psychology, philosophy, or the arts, "old" paradigms can live on, reappearing in changing forms. Or a former and now forgotten paradigm may be "rediscovered," for example, Saint Paul's letter to the Romans—recovered by Augustine in the fourth century, Luther in the sixteenth, Barth in the twentieth. An old paradigm rarely disappears totally. Hans Küng notes that the Hellenistic paradigm of the second century still lives on in segments of the Orthodox churches, the medieval Roman Catholic paradigm continues in Catholic traditions, the Protestant Reformation paradigm of the sixteenth century exists in Protestant confessionalism, the Enlightenment paradigm in liberal theology.

Each group uses its own paradigm to argue in that particular paradigm's defense. One comes to accept a paradigm's validity by stepping into its circle, and it is not logically compelling to those who refuse to step into that circle. Paradigm choice is a choice of community, and since each community's perspective is partial, culturally located, and socially biased, it can never claim absolute status.

We each speak from a particular social location; we utilize its metaphors and rely on its basic assumptions for the framework of our worldview. I write from a social location of a Euro-American male who addresses the community of pastoral counselors from a position that is Christian, neither Catholic nor Protestant, but Anabaptist in heritage and commitment. This offers a minority perspective—pacifist from the historic peace church tradition, multicultural from a bias against mainstream Western Christianity with its merger of faith with national allegiances and nationalism, and countercultural in its view of Christian believers as resident aliens in any and every culture. This central metaphor of peacemaking, bridgebuilding, and reconciling the alienated shapes my theology, my psychology, my practice as a therapist. Every reader critiques from a particular social location using metaphor, employing basic assumptions that combine to express a functional if not compelling vision of reality.

Paradigm: The Remedy for Irreversibility

A major paradigmatic shift occurred two thousand years ago in the philosophical breakthrough that allowed persons to disavow their past and alter their future through "forgiveness." Forgiveness is "the remedy against the irreversibility and unpredictability" of our human actions, argues Hannah Arendt, and it is an act that can correct previous actions or release persons from the consequences of those actions. The knowledge that release through forgiveness is constantly available allows us to remain free agents. Forgiveness allows us to change our minds, begin again, and risk further relationship.

Jesus' teaching about forgiveness, Arendt maintains, has been neglected in philosophical and political thought because of its close association with the Christian tradition, but it is a major philosophical breakthrough. "Jesus maintains against the 'scribes and pharisees' first that it is not true that only God has the power to forgive, and second that this power does not derive from God—as though God, not men, would forgive through the medium of human beings—but on the contrary must be mobilized by men toward each other before they can hope to be forgiven by God also" (Arendt 1958, 238). Arendt's analysis, which takes great pains to remain secular while drawing from one of the greatest religious thinkers of all time, is directed toward showing the dignity of the human person and the innate capacity for reflective, goal-oriented choice. Forgiveness, she argues, is a central part of this capacity for meaning and significance in existence. "Without being forgiven, released from the consequences of what we have done, our capacity to act would, as it were, be confined to one single deed from which we could never recover; we would remain the victims of consequence forever" (Arendt 1958, 238). Jesus made the discovery of the function and role of forgiveness in the realm of human affairs, "and the fact that he made this discovery in a religious context [is there any other?] and articulated it in religious language [is there any more deep?] is no reason to take it less seriously in a strictly secular sense" (my parenthetical comments).

This breaking of the cycle of blind retaliation or judicial retribution allows persons, relationships, or institutions to start over, to begin again. Russian writer Aleksandr Solzhenitsyn observed after his own great suffering in the labor camps, "In this way we differ from all animals. It is not our capacity to think that makes us different, but our capacity to repent, and to forgive. Only humans can perform that most unnatural act, and by doing so only they can develop relationships that transcend the relentless law of nature" (quoted in Yancey 1991, 37).

Paradigm: The True Location for Worship

A second paradigmatic shift in Jesus' teaching is the rejection of geographical place as the blessed location for effective prayer and the substitution of a spiritual location. In the dialogue with the Samaritan woman, Jesus reports that a physical place of pilgrimage, worship, or prayer is irrelevant; the true worship is offered in spirit and reality, with inner depth and relational integrity (John 4:19–24). The spiritual location is the place of experienced forgiveness where spirituality and integrity of relationships become one.

In challenging the temple cult, Jesus is undermining a paradigm that has guided religious practice in virtually all the surrounding cultures for centuries and has ruled the practices of his own people for over a thousand years since Solomon. Place, the holy location; space, the holy edifice; and liturgy, the holy ritual, are not what matters in the eyes of God. Instead, it is the ethical, relational, covenantal location in the midst of persons that is the holy place-space-worship. Forgiveness, in the teaching of Jesus, becomes the sole condition for prayer.

As the meaning of this paradigm shift invalidates the old assumptions about sacred places and holy turf, a new understanding of the ethical location for true prayer and spirituality unfolds. Although the followers of Jesus soon return to the practice of revering holy places, objects, buildings, and altars, the radical understanding of the forgiving community and the necessity for prayer (the love of God) to be indivisibly united with moral integrity (the love of neighbor) continue to disturb the consciences and the practice of all who follow him.

Philosophical Metaphors

We are metaphor-motivated persons. Our metaphors create images that reach deep into the primary-process thought of the unconscious and thus strongly influence thoughts and emotions. A change in metaphor is the most radical way of altering perceptions, feelings, and behavior. It alters the image that links primary impulses, fears, hopes, and wishes attached to the basic core of trust. Enlarging our vision of the reconciling process requires, at the outset, that we reexamine our metaphors, re-envision our images, realize our parables, and explore how these combine to shape our stories as persons and the stories of the communities that guide us.

Obviously, our present understandings of forgiveness grow from the models and metaphors that guide our perceptions and practices. Many of these work in tandem, as do the multiple strands in a rope. This image is from the philosopher Wittgenstein, who suggests, consider a rope with at least five strands. No single strand is the rope, nor is the central strand around which the others are formed. No strand serves as the central element, the core. All together constitute a rope, and intertwined they are able to do what no strand could bear or support (Wittgenstein 1952, 67).

Our metaphors are multistrand: philosophical, psychological, theological, biblical, and cultural strands that blend into the composite whole. To illustrate, let's examine a first strand, the philosophical, by exploring multiple metaphors that form our thought. These may include the following:

Forgiveness is a reversal of moral judgment—a retraction or modification of a previous moral judgment made about a wrongful act. One comes to see that an act that one had judged as wrong is in fact not so. But, when the act is unquestionably wrong, such a model is untenable (Haber 1991, 13).

Forgiveness is a reversal of moral attitude—the act committed may be seen as wrong while the agent who committed the act is seen in a new, more favorable light (Murphy and Hampton 1988, 37). This divides an ethics of being from an ethics of doing, and the decision to see another in a new, more favorable light in spite of unrepentant wrongdoing is an exercise in self-deception (Haber 1991, 14).

Forgiveness is a remission of punishment—to remit, to let off, to pardon, to cancel punishment. However, forgiveness may be given when no idea of punishment had occurred, in fact, forgiveness and the consequences of punishment are two separate concepts that are logically independent.

Forgiveness is the overcoming of resentment—to overcome resentment, not simply by forgetting or ignoring, but on moral grounds (Murphy 1982, 508). This may be an act of the will, or a process over a long time which has both volitional and emotional aspects. However, resentment has positive (a passion for justice) and negative (a desire for revenge) aspects, and the nature of the emotion, volition, and intention must be considered in any such definition.

Forgiveness is an exchange of a commodity, a transaction—to "give" forgiveness, to grant, to ask for, to receive forgiveness is not to visualize a thing that is exchanged, yet something is given and received which can be named. One gives up charges of offense and gives the other a word, an act, a statement of release. One gives the other a request, an act of seeking forgiveness, and the other gives it back again.

Forgiveness is a performative utterance—the actual occasion of forgiveness is performed by a recognized verbal formula. "A performative utterance" offers a (1) conventional procedure (2) with a ritual effect (3) through certain words (4) by certain appropriate persons (5) in certain appropriate and particular circumstances; (6) the procedure is executed by all participants correctly and (7) completely, (8) with congruent and sincere thoughts and feelings (9) resulting in their so conducting themselves subsequently. Such performative utterances include rituals from "I take this woman to be . . ." to "I bet ten thousand on Dan Patch in . . ." (Austin 1962, 13–16; Haber 1991, 40–45).

Each of these philosophical models operates out of a different metaphor—moral, ethical, legal, psychological, economical, or ritual—and each represents a particular paradigm of human selfhood and community. Persons, relationships, and communities change as we give birth to new paradigms.

Biblical Metaphors of Forgiveness

Many of the metaphors employed by Jesus in his subversive teaching, storytelling, and symbolic actions expressed aspects of forgiveness. Fifteen of the most vivid are highlighted here.

A debt (Matt. 18:21–35). The cancellation of a debt, small and forgettable or large and unpayable, symbolizes forgiving.

A stone (John 8:2–11). The stone of execution that no one has the right to throw because no one is without sin.

A robe, ring, sandals, and a feast (Luke 15:22–24). The prodigal returning home receives these four symbols as signs of acceptance—clothing, status, dignity, and celebration.

A hug, a kiss (Luke 15:20). The returning son is received by his father with pity. "He ran [to the boy] and put his arms around him and kissed him."

Paralysis ended (Matt. 9:1–8; Mark 2:10; Luke 5:17–26). The paralyzed muscles renew. The arms and legs respond in action and health through forgiveness.

Illness healed (Luke 5:17–26). Illness is metaphor for our brokenness and healing is equated with experiencing forgiveness.

Blindness cured (Mark 4:10–12). The ability to see another again, hear another once more, turns one toward reality and in "turning" to "receive" God's forgiveness.

Table manners (Matt. 6:11–12; John 13:18; Matt. 26:26–29). In line with the Aramaic word for forgiveness, which has the root "table," Jesus transforms the sharing of food at the table into a metaphor for realized forgiveness. The older brother of the prodigal will not come in to the table (will not forgive). In the Lord's Prayer the conjunction *and* joins the phrases "Give us this day our daily bread *and* forgive us our debts as we forgive our debtors." And the sacrament of forgiveness is bread and wine shared at the table of the Lord.

Erotic perfume, tears, kisses (Luke 7:36–50). These symbols of repentance and gratitude are recast as metaphors of realized forgiveness, as the evidence of a woman's deep love after she was accepted in spite of her past behavior.

This is a partial listing. Some might add those metaphors traditionally utilized—cross, whip, thorns, nails, tomb—as symbols of suffering accepted in forgiving love. These metaphors, interpreted as they are by theological, historical, and philosophical perspectives that direct the reader's vision, can still explode with new power in the re-creation of our paradigms. The recovery of the original metaphor or the re-creation of further images requires the use of story. Parables, told with apologies to the master parable maker, may reveal the metaphors we have come to use to interpret the meanings of forgiving and being forgiven.

Unilateral or Mutual?

Can we speak equally of forgiveness as a unilateral act from an individual paradigm or as a mutual transaction from an interpersonal paradigm? The first sets the offended person free by releasing all resentment, all claims for recognition of the injury by the offender, all demands for repentance and restitution; the second is a mutual recognition that repentance is genuine (repentance by one or both parties) and right relationships have been restored or achieved.

The most common usage—forgive and forget—tends toward the first of these options. In a Western, individualist culture, unilateral "forgiveness" becomes the norm for a number of significant psychological and sociological reasons. (1) The individual's foothold on reality has moved from external relationships with significant others to an internal base grounded in self-love. (2) The institutions of family, marriage, community, vocation have become multiple, unrelated circles with little overlap, connection, or accountability and consequently are relativized. (3) Conflicts and broken relationships become the private property of the disputants (rather than jointly owned by the community). (4) The resolution of differences, alienations, or injuries moves inward to intrapsychic mechanisms rather than being an interpersonal issue. In more collective cultures—traditional cultures, the biblical worldview, the contemporary two-thirds world—the understanding of forgiveness is that it is not a private act of intrapsychic release but instead a truly social transaction of interpersonal reconciliation. The conflict belongs to the community as well as to the disputants; the responsibility to seek reconciliation is shared; and the understanding of forgiveness is focused on regaining the other as sister or brother.

In the diagram of unilateral or mutual forgiveness (figure 1.1), the first column, unilateral restoration of respect and equal regard, contains the dominant definition of forgiving used in Western culture. It is essentially a return to mutual goodwill, or to neighbor-love that cancels conditions

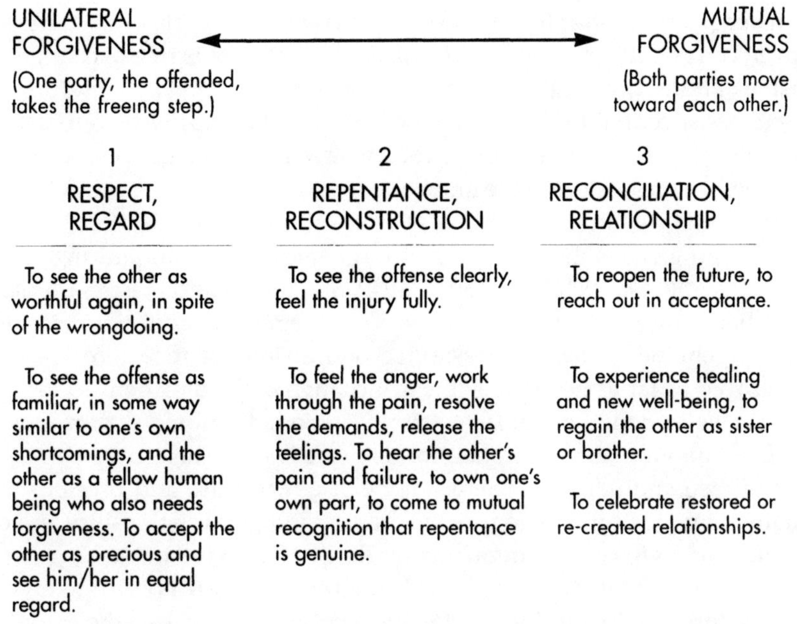

UNILATERAL FORGIVENESS
(One party, the offended, takes the freeing step.)
MUTUAL FORGIVENESS
(Both parties move toward each other.)
1
RESPECT, REGARD
2
REPENTANCE, RECONSTRUCTION
3
RECONCILIATION, RELATIONSHIP
To see the other as worthful again, in spite of the wrongdoing.
To see the offense as familiar, in some way similar to one's own shortcomings, and the other as a fellow human being who also needs forgiveness. To accept the other as precious and see him/her in equal regard.
To see the offense clearly, feel the injury fully.
To feel the anger, work through the pain, resolve the demands, release the feelings. To hear the other's pain and failure, to own one's own part, to come to mutual recognition that repentance is genuine.
To reopen the future, to reach out in acceptance.
To experience healing and new well-being, to regain the other as sister or brother.
To celebrate restored or re-created relationships.

Figure 1.1

Continuum from Unilateral to Mutual Forgiveness

for seeing the other as a worthy human being, and in the level of unconditional regard appropriate to the relationship, sets the self free from demands and in so doing, frees the other. It asks for nothing as prerequisite, it expects nothing in consequence. If further reconciliation follows, it is seen as a separate, fortuitous, surprising gift.

In the second column, repentance and reconstruction, is a definition of a forgiveness that faces the injury done, feels the impact on the person and community, and works toward a goal of mutual justice. In more collective and communal societies, such as the biblical world of both the Hebrew and the Christian scriptures, this is the primary understanding of what forgiveness is about in the restoration of right relationships. Whereas the forgiveness in the first column may be virtually unconditional, as love is without conditions, that of the second is conditional, with substantive expectations that must be met in mutual negotiation and appropriate repentance.

When a wrongdoer repents, she or he is no longer the same person as the offender—she or he now has disavowed the old behavior, affirmed a new principle of moral action and pledged to follow it. This disavows identity with the wrongdoer so the reason for resentment no longer remains.

The forgiver can offer forgiveness without sacrificing self-respect; the forgiven can receive forgiveness by affirming a self that is free to change, capable of transcending the past, worthy of being accepted in the future. Repentance is central to the process of forgiving. Perhaps we can forgive in the absence of repentance. But if it is to have moral integrity—for the forgiveness to mean more in the moral universe than denial or forgetfulness—there must be genuine encounter with the offender and the offense.

"Cheap grace is the preaching of forgiveness without requiring repentance," wrote Dietrich Bonhoeffer (1949, 36). Repentance has, in Christian tradition, consisted of three dimensions—remorse, restitution, renewal. First, a genuine sorrow is necessary; second, an attempt to restore what was destroyed as far as is possible; third, a change in life direction. So forgiveness is the recognition that repentance is intended, embraced, pursued.

Love may be unconditional, forgiveness is not. There may be no demands as conditions for seeing the other as worthful and precious, but many demands for trusting, risking, and joining in relationship—no demands for loving; many demands for living. The familiar teaching of unconditional, unilateral forgiveness is not forgiving but a return to loving.

The forgiveness outlined in the third column recognizes the complexity of reopening the future in risk, restoring relationship in trust, and recreating the nature of that alliance in justice. As this process progresses, conditions are again reduced, expectations are jointly contracted and, when mutual, come to be understood as the basis of life in community. The movement of these conditions—the demands for justice—from foreground (figure) to background (ground) signals the opening of the ongoing give-and-take of mutuality. The forgiveness in this column matches, most closely, the concept of forgiveness taught in the central passage of Matthew's Gospel (chapter 18), where Jesus' goal for and definition of forgiveness is "regaining the brother."

This concept of forgiveness raises many issues. Is it appropriate to speak of unconditional forgiveness, or should we more correctly refer to this as acceptance or love? Is repentance essential, indispensable, central to the work of forgiving? What forgiveness is possible for the offended when there is no repentance by the offender? Is forgiveness ever morally justified in such circumstances? Would it be better to speak of a "willingness to forgive" that emerges from a restoration of love rather than "unilateral forgiveness"? If there is no repentance by the offender, is it not necessary for the offended to move into a position of loving openness and then grieve the failure of the relationship, the pain of the injury, the absence of resolution? Is not the process of grief and healing the appropriate process rather than the mechanisms of an intrapsychic release? When there is repentance, will this inevitably lead to an openness to covenant a new justice? Does reconciliation imply a return to the prior relationship or the courage to re-create relationship?

Requesting Forgiveness

The appeal for forgiveness, whether a direct request or an indirect request through offering sincere repentance, takes one down an intriguing series of pathways. Does the request give an account and plead innocence or extenuating circumstances? Or does the wrongdoer accept responsibility for actual consequences? If the latter, is the request for release (negative) or readmission (positive)? If the second, is the goal the restoration of relationship or the achievement of a new shared context in the moral community? The model that follows is developed from the work of Carl-Reinhold Brakenhielm on forgiveness (1993).

These options and their interrelationships can be mapped on a flow chart (see figure 1.2).

1. *Nonresponsible forgiveness.* If the offender is seen as immature, unaware, mentally incompetent, psychologically ill, morally incapable, or in some other way outside moral responsibility for the injury, one offers a forgiveness that is a blend of patience, forbearance, and understanding. "Father, forgive them for they know not what they do," was Jesus' first word from the cross (Luke 23:34). He is not holding his executioners responsible for the heinous act they are performing in carrying out a sentence of death oblivious to the innocence of the victim. Philosopher Jeffrie Murphy asks, concerning this first word from the cross, Should it read, "Father, *excuse* them for they know not what they do"? (Murphy 1988, 20). Is it not response to nonresponsible wrongdoing?

"One is angry at malice but not at weakness," the proverb suggests, differentiating between falseness and frailty. When the person is seen as nonculpable, as excusable, as understandable, the injury can be accepted. Or, if there are sufficient mitigating circumstances—anxiety in crisis, illness, ignorance, other's failure, which set off a domino effect—the extenuating account may reduce or erase the person's final responsibility. The account given often includes "my intentions were good," "I had no choice," "I meant no harm," or "I didn't know."

2. *Responsible forgiveness.* If the offender is fully aware of the act and recognizes its impact, injury, or other consequences, a request for forgiveness must begin with an admission of responsibility, a confession that one is culpable, an intention to change behavior. Responsible forgiveness has at least two aspects (looking backward and forward): admission that the act was morally or relationally indefensible and intention to not repeat it again.

On the deeper level of attitude or emotions, responsible forgiveness

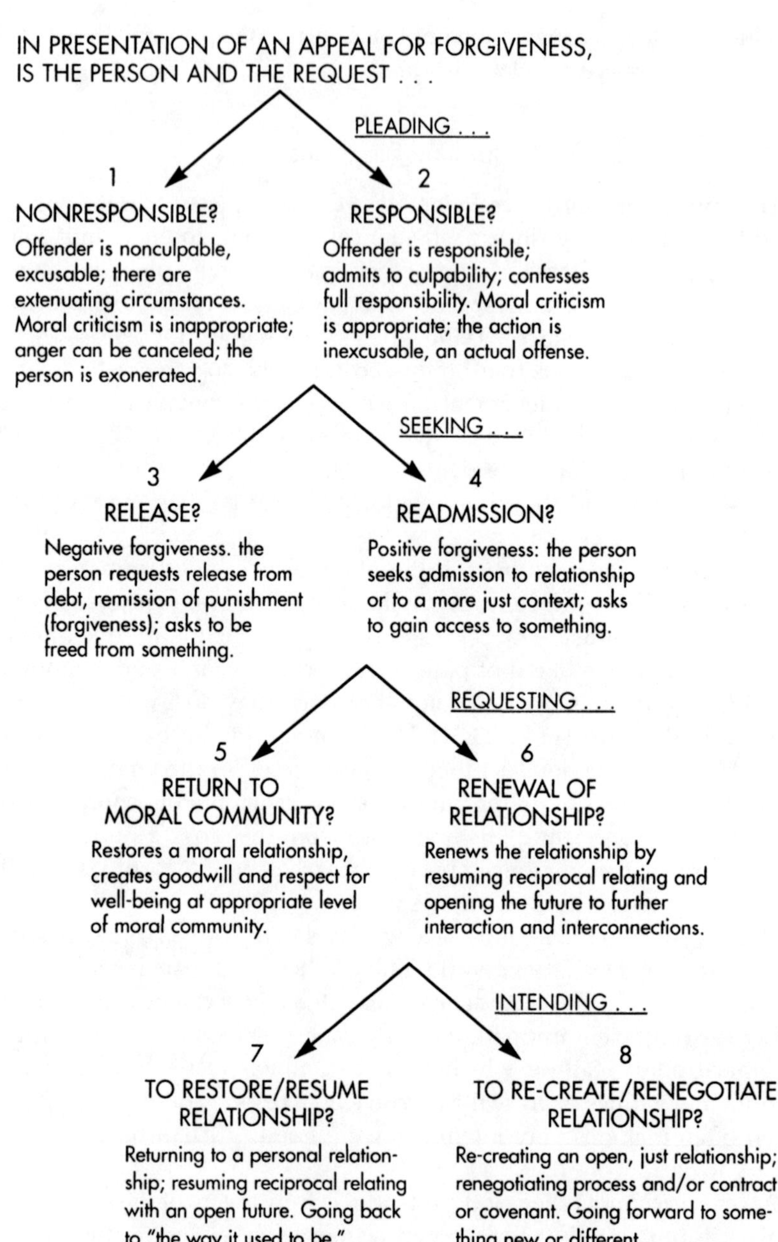

IN PRESENTATION OF AN APPEAL FOR FORGIVENESS,
IS THE PERSON AND THE REQUEST . . .
PLEADING . . .
1
NONRESPONSIBLE?
Offender is nonculpable, excusable; there are extenuating circumstances. Moral criticism is inappropriate; anger can be canceled; the person is exonerated.
2
RESPONSIBLE?
Offender is responsible; admits to culpability; confesses full responsibility. Moral criticism is appropriate; the action is inexcusable, an actual offense.
SEEKING . . .
3
RELEASE?
Negative forgiveness. the person requests release from debt, remission of punishment (forgiveness); asks to be freed from something.
4
READMISSION?
Positive forgiveness: the person seeks admission to relationship or to a more just context; asks to gain access to something.
REQUESTING . . .
5
RETURN TO MORAL COMMUNITY?
Restores a moral relationship, creates goodwill and respect for well-being at appropriate level of moral community.
6
RENEWAL OF RELATIONSHIP?
Renews the relationship by resuming reciprocal relating and opening the future to further interaction and interconnections.
INTENDING . . .
7
TO RESTORE/RESUME RELATIONSHIP?
Returning to a personal relationship; resuming reciprocal relating with an open future. Going back to "the way it used to be."
8
TO RE-CREATE/RENEGOTIATE RELATIONSHIP?
Re-creating an open, just relationship; renegotiating process and/or contract or covenant. Going forward to something new or different.

Figure 1.2

Forgiveness Decision Tree

does not plead ignorance or innocence even though there are often circumstances that could be cited, past history that could be recited, or intentions that can be affirmed. Responsible forgiveness is defined by philosopher P. F. Strawson: "To ask to be forgiven is in part to acknowledge that the attitude displayed in our actions was such as might properly be resented and in part to repudiate that attitude for the future (or at least for the immediate future); and to forgive is to accept the repudiation and to forswear the resentment" (1974, 6). The action deserves repudiation and can appropriately be resented, but the forgiver releases both. The actor recognizes the other's right to resentment and chooses to repudiate the offending action as a request for reconciliation.

Responsible forgiveness views the offender as an agent of choice who is only respected when confronted with the reality of just relationships. As Bishop Stephen Neill writes:

> Forgiveness is sternly and ruthlessly realistic. It starts from an unemotional and factual consideration of just what has happened, of the consequences that have flowed from it, and of the responsibilities of those concerned. Being akin to justice, it makes full allowance for ignorance and inexperience, for the strength of temptation and the confusion of human motives. But being realistic, it insists on treating responsible beings as responsible and will not palter with any attempt to assist them in evading their responsibilities. When every allowance has been made, when every legitimate excuse has been accepted, the verdict still may be, "This was wrong; they knew, or if they had thought for a moment, they would have known that it was wrong; and still they did it" (Neill 1959, 210).

3. *Negative forgiveness; release.* The forgiveness sought by children, which we are capable of seeking all life long, is a request for remission of punishment. The appeal is a plea to be released from consequences, from the other's anger and resentment, or from one's own feelings of guilt. The confession of an infidelity, in some circumstances, may be wholly negative: the guilt ventilated and released is now a burden for the spouse, the affair reported is an angry message of devaluation or revenge, the request for forgiveness a second and even more confusing injury.

Negative forgiveness may also be an escape from retribution, motivated by the fear that another will "get even" in some way, or that retribution may come through rejection of the community as well as retaliation by the offended.

> Four different forms of negative forgiveness: release from bitterness and hatred, freedom from guilt, liberation from a wrongful life-style, and remission of punishment often overlap and even

> flow together into what one can call positive forgiveness. A person who pleads for forgiveness not only asks to escape or avoid something but also often seeks to gain access to something (Brakenhielm 1993, 27).

4. *Positive forgiveness; readmission.* When the object of the offender's request for forgiveness is restoration of relationship, the interaction is a forward, futuristic, positive transaction of healing.

The offender seeks not just release but restoration, not just relief but reconciliation on whatever level is appropriate or possible. Although the first word from the cross offered a nonresponsible expression of Jesus' willingness to forgive his executioners, his teaching on forgiveness focuses almost exclusively on positive forgiveness. The goal is "the regaining of the brother" (Matt. 5:23–24; 18:15), and nothing, not even a sevenfold repetition in one day is to block the disciple's acceptance of the offender's word of repentance as genuine and the relationship resumed.

Positive forgiveness reopens the future to ongoing mutuality and reciprocity. It does not negate the need for justice and for the caring renegotiation of the restored relationship in ways that support healing, change, and increasing integrity. It seeks to be constructive and recreative in renewing the relationship at the level now appropriate to the new experiences just expressed and integrated into the parties' common life.

5. *Return to moral community.* No personal relationship may have existed between the parties, and no act of forgiveness guarantees that such will automatically follow. The participation in the larger moral community that they share is reaffirmed by forgiveness, and this may be the appropriate level for the parties in the future. The breakdown of an intense personal relationship will require profound forgiveness from both sides, and the outcome of the conciliation may be the return to civility in the moral context of the larger community that embraces them without the resumption of the special relationship that existed before the rupture.

When a marriage covenant is broken, both parties in the loss, and in particular the one more betrayed or abandoned, may work actively at finding the best reconciliation possible. When the resumption of the covenant and commitment is not possible, each can commit the self to seek respect for the well-being of the other with an attitude of goodwill that restores an appropriate moral relationship within the larger moral community. This too is positive forgiveness although the bonding has been severed and the union no longer exists. Nevertheless, it is desirable for both, requisite of each, that a moral resolution congruent with their ongoing existence in community be achieved in positive forgiveness. Differing ratios of responsibility and ability to respond frequently frustrate the desired return to such civility in moral community.

6. *Renewal of relationship.* Personal relationships can be restored, or for the first time experienced with depth and integrity, through the healing of the injury or the bridging of the breach. A return to open communication, open trust and risk in increasing increments, open spontaneity, and the freedom to fail again allows people to resume the slow evolution of friendship or loving commitment. Relationships have histories and continuities that enrich them, depths that intensify them, heights of peak experiences that celebrate intimacy or collaboration, and lengths that promise to reach into the future. Forgiveness may renew one, several, or all four of these dimensions.

7. *Restoring or resuming relationship.* Restoration or resumption of the relationship presumes that a level of justice and equity existed prior to the injury. The offended and the offender, through appropriate mutual repentance, restore the relationship and seek to live out its deeper intentions and understandings. These shared elements of trust, friendship, or covenant will be deepened, perhaps corrected or clarified by the incident, but the continuity with the past is reaffirmed by both as they rejoin, reunite, and reopen the future. If this leaves issues of injustice unrecognized, or allows oppression or repression to go unchallenged, the seeds of future conflict are either already germinating or are being poisoned by the resumption of a toxic relationship. "Most of the couples I see in conjoint therapy," a colleague told me, "show this striking contrast. He says, 'I just want things to be exactly the way they used to be.' And she says, 'No matter what, things will have to be different. I can't go back to the way it was.'"

8. *Re-creating or renegotiating relationship.* Creative forgiveness, after mutual recognition of both parties' involvement (whatever the ratio of responsibility), seeks to restructure the shared context, rebuild the floor of basic commitments, redistribute the power and resources, and re-envision the future. Forgiveness may be primarily a return, a regaining, a restitution of an old order, a backward movement, a regression to the previous situation with the old injustices that motivated the original action or injury. Or forgiveness may be a revolution, a progression into a new situation, a transformation that alters the status quo, that challenges the many compromises that create our systems—the cultural system, the religious system, the communal system, the family system, the marital system.

Forgiveness that returns has the potential of enslaving; forgiveness that turns holds the possibility of freeing. The enslavement comes from the necessity of the forgiven to yield to the definition of obligation and debt imposed by the culture's definition of justice and its contextually defined balance of distribution. The guilty one—in a position of indebtedness and obligation—is accepted once more by making amends, paying the debt, suffering the consequences. The return to favor or the granting of renewed status locks the person into the culture's prescriptions, the religion's prohibitions, the family's traditions and rules, the marriage's previous contract or covenant.

Forgiveness that turns, moves in new directions—re-creating, restructuring, radically transforming.

> The forgiveness Jesus describes and lives out is profoundly radical, one which rejects the cycle of cultural transaction. Jesus does not forgive as a means of returning people to the *status quo*. His actions are directed at transforming them, at breaking them out of the limited vision of culture and idol so that they catch a glimpse of the true God beyond culture and the culture's moral system (who is right and who is wrong). This glimpse of the true God beyond culture shows that the reign of God is a world free of the distinction of status (rich/poor, slave/free, innocent/guilty) on which culture and idol thrive (Hinkle 1993, 325).

Such forgiveness moves from the old domination system of cultural-political-religious control with its claims to entitlement and participates in God's "kin-dom," in a royal reign of transforming justice. It sees forgiveness as joining in solidarity with those who differ with us. Our own assumptive world is no longer absolute—what John Hinkle calls the essence of idolatry—but is related by love and justice into a passionate community of authentic engagement. Such a community is formed by the new values of the reign of God, which are shaped, most of all, by a loving, forgiving, justice-seeking passion (passion springing from the encounter with the passion of Christ and empowering with compassion).

It is intriguing to examine the Gospels to observe the varieties of forgiveness recorded in the life of Jesus.

The most-quoted words of forgiveness, "Father, forgive them; for they know not what they do" (Luke 23:34, RSV), offer option 1 (see figure 1.2), nonresponsible forgiveness. Jesus recognizes the ignorance and blind obedience of those carrying out the crucifixion. They are nonculpable, outside moral responsibility, "they know not what they do." Jesus' response to the woman taken in the act of adultery (John 8:1–11) recognizes her responsibility (option 2) and offers her release (option 3) and return to a moral community (option 5). In his teaching on forgiveness of repetitious failures (Luke 17:3–4), Jesus calls for confronting the repeat offender with a demand for repentance (option 2) and continuing openness to forgiving. Even when the offense is repeated the symbolic seven times (total betrayal), one is encouraged to offer release (option 3) or readmission (option 4). In Matthew 18, the more extended parallel, the issues of confrontation and responsibility (option 2), or working through to reconciliation (options 4 and 5), and of regaining the brother as brother (options

7 or 8) are taught as the real goal of reconciling action. In the parable on forgiving, which follows, the man seeks forgiveness from the king for the unpayable debt. He is seeking release (option 3); the king offers a return to moral community (option 5), which obviously the man does not choose to pursue. His own response to the friend who owes him a small debt is to refuse forgiveness. In pursuit of justice, the king reverses his action and cancels the forgiveness once given. These examples from the Gospels illustrate not only the many forms of forgiveness reported there but the impossibility of a single definition, the necessity of flexibility in dealing with the breakdown of human relationships, and the recognition of the many directions our own attempts at healing may take.

A contemporary example further illustrates varieties of forgiveness. After twenty years of mutually satisfactory marriage, Alice recovers memories of sexual abuse in her childhood that triggers rage toward all males, including the spouse she has loved in intimacy for two decades. She withdraws from all contact, rejects his affection, breaks off the marital relationship. The wrong she is doing, she insists, is necessary and inevitable in view of the wrong done to her. She admits only regret for how she has done this violation of the marriage, not that she has done it.

If Alice's husband understands the depth of her pain, and realizes it is not about him, is he justified in tendering forgiveness, since such forgiveness offers a certain moral wisdom and compassion? He sees the other as, in some sense, not responsible. The victim comes to understand the way in which he is not the victim at all in this marital tragedy. Is this insight equivalent to forgiveness even though there is no repentance? The moral wisdom evidenced is rather a recognition of how the wrongdoer may be understood, empathically accepted, and finally excused. Compassion empowers the person to excuse when excuse is clearly appropriate. One should not confuse forgiveness with excuse. Yet there are times when the first level of response to an extremely painful situation is option 1, nonresponsible forgiveness. If Alice's pain turns to malicious attack in vindictive retaliation at her husband as a substitute target, he may come to see it as mixed with nonresponsible and responsible elements, so both options 1 and 2 are necessary. His own confusion, the loss of a spouse, and the gain of a person acting like an angry adolescent may block his willingness to move to option 3 and release her from the relationship that she finds impossible to sustain because of years of transferent conditioning. Or he may hope for option 4 and patiently seek readmission. If this is rebuffed and the marriage ends in divorce, an appropriate return to moral community, option 5, may follow; if it is reciprocated, then options 6 and 8 may ensue.

The motivation in such a journey, if the forgiveness is to effectively reconnect across the injury, must be a lasting measure of mutuality, an awareness of our joint need, as well as our individual needs, for being forgiven as well as forgiving.

Parables of Human Forgiveness

The following series of parables offer metaphors of forgiveness in human relationships. These can be utilized to draw out personal metaphors of giving and receiving pardon.

> Once a father and son were locked in the dance of benevolent dictator controlling blessed child. In rebellion, the son eloped with a woman who represented all that the father hated—she was divorced, twelve years older, and of an unacceptable religious faith. "He'll have to accept me when I'm his daughter-in-law," she said publicly. "She is not my daughter; I'll never speak to her," he replied. Thirty years passed. She was in his home weekly. He never spoke her name, never looked at her. She was invisible. Then his wife died. A few months later, he began dating again. When the woman came to visit in his home community—they were dating in a Sunbelt retirement context—he went into panic. His son, retrieving him from the hospital emergency room, said, "Dad, what is this all about?" At last he told him. He was dating a woman—thrice divorced, twenty years his junior, and of his daughter-in-law's hated religion. "You're doing the same thing to me I did to you," the son said.
>
> The next week, the father called his daughter-in-law by name.
>
> *Metaphor:* Forgiveness is not something we do, it's something we discover—when one realizes the other's evil/offense/failure is one's own too.

> There was a divorce, a fanciful liberating flight for the wife, an excruciating blow to the husband. After draining the bank accounts, filing for divorce, and cutting off all communication, she attempted to destroy his reputation and job. The man, bitter at the alienation, allegations, and alimony, struggled with resentment. Feelings of forgiveness were not possible, but he found a way to reframe the situation. "I will consider each alimony check as three thousand expressions of forgiveness," he decided, "I will not be held hostage by resentment when I can view it as a creative act."
>
> *Metaphor:* Acts of kindness, not the feelings that rise from reverie or recollection, are the true measure of moral choice.

> A pastor betrayed his vocation by violating the boundaries between himself and a counselee, with whom he was sexually intimate. The congregation took away his credentials, cut off his salary, and asked him to get help. During his rehabilitation, he participated in a reconciliation process with the church's leadership, and expressions of forgiveness were exchanged. But feelings were low; little was changed.
>
> In subsequent months, stories were still told, but less frequently. Crit-

ical rumors were passed, but less often. "I have not experienced forgiveness," the pastor said. "What I experience is memory fatigue. As people become tired of the anger, tired of holding resentments, tired of the whole story, they may not accept me as a friend again, but they speak to me."

Metaphor: Ostracism until memory fatigue sets in allows eventual acceptance and re-entry into social life.

Her father is a fundamentalist preacher who knows good and evil—in others. He judges right and wrong—in others. And he condemns the guilty with little mercy. He stands on the side of God—an angry judging god who condemns sin and sinners alike. But when she was eight years old, her father began the "bedtime games" that became sexual abuse. He told her it was quite all right, of course, and since he could do no wrong, he did her wrong. She left home at sixteen to get away from him, and now, a decade later, she often longs for forgiveness to happen between them. He will not talk of the past, much less express any repentance. He wants her to come home as the prodigal daughter, apologizing for the ten-year cutoff in relationship. "Just forgive him and forget about it," her therapist says. "No," she decides, "I must find a third party who will act as go-between. I must try to break through the defenses. I will never be 'his daughter' again, but I can be a fellow adult, with a relationship based on the reality we share, whatever it will be."

Metaphor: Forgiveness requires recognition of what happened, reconstruction of what was destroyed, reopening of the future. (Genuine forgiveness is participation, reunion overcoming the power of estrangements, according to Tillich.)

The placed was trashed. The two kids who had broken into her house and stripped it of anything they could pawn had also turned the place upside down. The antiques—the priceless gifts from her mother and grandmother—lying broken on the floor pained her most deeply. When the kids were caught, she asked for the chance to meet them, one by one, with a mediator. The conversations were difficult. The young men, not the stereotypical young toughs, but high school juniors from the school she passed each day, were noncommittal. But gradually, with the help of the mediator, they began to soften. The court-sanctioned process required reparations, but nothing could restore the precious objects from her family. "I will accept the loss," she finally said. "I think that's what forgiveness is: the offended bears the cost of the offender's acts, and they go free."

Metaphor: Someone must pay—absorb the loss, bear the cost, accept the anger, pay the debt. Either the offender pays—that is justice. Or the offended pays—that is forgiveness.

The rumors were false, but only those who were close enough to know the truth dismissed them. Others believed the rumors because they came from such a trusted source, a member of the family. The defamation of character died slowly, and the ill will of her brother—who had created the scandal—became obvious to those who were close.

"There's nothing to be done but to forgive," she said. "To pursue it would only make things worse, to defend oneself only spreads the gossip. One only wins by forgiving. I will not stoop to the same level. Anyone who wrestles with a pig gets dirty, and the pig enjoys it. I will let it be known in the family that I have forgiven him; whether or not we ever speak again is not important. I've given my word to forget it."

Metaphor: Forgiveness is ritualized denial, an announcement that one has withdrawn from the situation by claiming the high ground.

Parables of Divine Forgiveness

A second series of parables provides metaphors for divine forgiveness in the relationship between God and humanity. Critiquing these parables for their choice of image may be helpful for creating one's own parables.

The kingdom of heaven is like a high school class with students rich and poor, diligent and lazy, motivated and bored, of many races and religions.

The teacher gives the final exam, then announces, "All of you have failed. There is nothing that anyone of you can do to earn a passing grade. But I will leave the room and you may grade each other. Whomever you pass, I will pass, and whoever fails anyone else, I will fail."

No sooner has the teacher left than conflict erupts. The diligent will not pass the lazy; the rich pass each other and ignore the poor; some insist that each race should pass only its own.

Groups emerge, each with its own rules and rituals for passing. Some groups remember the words of the teacher and say, "We have all already flunked. We shall pass everyone with no distinctions at all. Then we can be certain of our own forgiveness."

Metaphor: We have all flunked, but we may pass as we pass all others.

The kingdom of heaven is like a woman and a man who came to Bethlehem. She taught in Arab schools and came to be trusted by the oppressed and abused. He worked with the ruling legal community and came to know those in power. And at night they conspired on their bed and dreamed of peace accords and reconciliation. And in their union and their connections with two peoples, they became a bridge for old enemies who came to their home for tea and conversation until common humanity was nurtured. And during long evenings of conversation the representatives of enemy groups played on the floor with the couple's little son. In time the incommunicable was communicated, the unresolvable began to find resolution. And the healing that happened was taken back to each people in a plea and a plan for peace, until the Palestinian-Israeli accords were signed.

Metaphor: A go-between can embody the reconciliation that neither side can yet express with integrity or envision with parity.

The kingdom of heaven is like a man named Martin, who rose against the oppression of his people and led them in nonviolent marches of resistance, sit-ins at forbidden lunch counters, unwelcome presence in racially segregated places, and public statements to reveal the shame of racism. When the rage of the scandalized white community had reached the breaking point, Martin was tried in the conversations of a thousand barrooms, found guilty of all charges, and sentenced by common opinion to die. He was shot by a hired gun—a nondescript criminal who was found independently guilty. The rage of the white community dissipated, the outrage of the black community was repressed.

Metaphor: Guilty victims, publicly identified, sentenced, and punished, dissipate corporate rage.

The kingdom of heaven is like a father who returned to his barn at evening to find only smoking ruins. House, barn, and fields of wheat had been consumed. And he called his children together and asked, "Who has done this thing? Whoever struck the match will be punished. The fire has cost us all our living."

The five stood silently. No one would admit the deed. Then the youngest, his only daughter, stepped forward. "I am responsible. They were my matches. Punish me."

The father looked at the thin and tender back of his daughter, and his heart broke. "Someone must be punished," he said, "justice must be done." Then he stripped off his shirt and handed his belt to his oldest son. "I shall take the beating. Each of you must strike me three times with all your strength."

Metaphor: Justice is satisfied only by punishment; healing comes only by redemptive violence.

The kingdom of heaven is like a man who took his only surviving son to the top of a high mountain and prepared to slay him and offer his body as a ritual sacrifice to the God he understood. (His wife had forced the sacrifice of his other son, whom he loved, and of that boy's mother, his young and tender mistress. Now he felt commanded by mystic forces beyond his understanding to slay his wife's only son.) As the knife is lifted, he hears the voice of an angel forbidding his action. A lamb is sacrificed instead. One innocent victim is substituted for another, and the innocence of the first is revealed. God is on the side of the victim. Kierkegaard writes: "The ethical expression of what Abraham did is, that he would murder Isaac; the religious expression is, that he would sacrifice Isaac" (Kierkegaard 1954, 41).

Metaphor: One must give up that which one values most, or a substitute sacrifice that symbolizes it, to earn forgiveness.

The kingdom of heaven is like a nonviolent leader who lived in exile until the moment of his courageous and foolhardy homecoming to the land of the dictator. As he descended from the plane, soldiers surrounded him and only a few yards from the plane he was executed. His death changed nothing. Marcos, the dictator, and his military forces were more powerful and ruthless than ever. Their only rival was destroyed. Yet his death changed everything. He was the victor. The injustice was revealed. The aggressors were put to open shame. Two and a half years later the dictator was nonviolently removed from office. Marcos fell when Aquino dropped to the tarmac.

Metaphor: The innocent victim (the cross) exposes the powers of violent domination, the impotence of death, the truth of ultimate justice, and brings us to new beginnings.

Toward a New Paradigm of Forgiveness

1. Accepting and forgiving are different processes. We accept persons for the good that they *are* or *do.* We forgive persons for the evil that they did or caused.
2. Excusing and forgiving are different processes. We excuse people when we no longer hold them accountable. We forgive people when we hold them accountable but do not excuse.
3. Tolerating and forgiving are different processes. We tolerate what another has done when we overlook or ignore. We forgive what we cannot tolerate, will not overlook, or ignore.
4. Forgetting and forgiving are different processes. We do not need to forgive if we can simply forget—forgetting is passive, avoidant, repressive; it denies, detaches, dismisses. We do not forget when we forgive, but the meaning of the memory changes—forgiving is active and aware; it is recognizing the injury, owning the pain, and reaching out to reframe, re-create, restore, reconstruct, rebuild, reopen what can be opened.

2

The Mysteries of Change

Forgiving the unrepentant
Is like drawing pictures in water.
—Japanese proverb

Repentance is a sentiment which rarely troubles people until they begin to suffer
—Ambrose Bierce

Always forgive your enemies,
Nothing annoys them so much.
—Oscar Wilde

No act of forgiving
Goes unresented.

Ian Bedloe, the hero of Anne Tyler's novel *Saint Maybe*, wandered into a storefront church—the Church of the Second Chance—during Wednesday night prayer meeting, because he was attracted by the hymns sung by the two dozen worshipers. Once inside, he found himself responding to the time for prayer, asking them to pray for him, that he might be forgiven.

There was silence—and then prayers, many prayers on his behalf, and Ian felt sure that God would hear his request. Afterward, as he headed for the exit, he was stopped and greeted by the church people and then introduced to Reverend Emmett, who asked whether his prayer had been answered. Ian replied that it must have been answered, since he was truly sorry for what he had done.

Reverend Emmett asked what it was he had done. Ian thought this request unfairly intrusive, yet he found himself explaining the situation: He had caused his brother to kill himself. It happened because Ian had told him his wife was cheating on him, although now Ian wasn't really sure of that.

His brother drove into a wall. And not long after, his brother's wife died from an overdose of sleeping pills. So Ian may have caused that too. Now it appeared as if his parents would have to raise the children, and neither his mother nor his father was equal to it. But he himself was away at college and could not help, and his sister was busy with her own children.

Anyway, it seemed to Ian that God must have answered his prayer, and that he was forgiven. Reverend Emmett thought not, and said so. While God forgives everything, to be sure, one cannot just say "I'm sorry" and expect forgiveness. There has to be some practical reparation.

The conversation on responsibility and reparation ended with the pastor advising him that his first responsibility was to see to the children's welfare. And so Ian faced the option of dropping out of college, changing his plans—his parents' plans for his education—to stay home, raise his brother's children, and undo part of the harm done. Late that Friday night, Ian told his parents he was not going back to college, that he would become a cabinetmaker and help his parents with the children. He told them it was something he had to do for himself, to be forgiven.

Then it all came out: his part in his brother's death and his brother's wife's suicide, which left the children orphaned. And his parents just sat there, staring. Though he repeatedly said he was sorry, they could not utter a word. He left the table in the silence.

Ian reflected that there was something hard and inhuman about religion (retold from Tyler 1991, 125–41).

The Anne Tyler tale of a maybe saint raises many questions about the relationship between forgiveness and reconciliation, about individual release and interpersonal responsibility, about being forgiven and being a part of a forgiving and forgiven family, community, and church.

Above all it raises the systemic questions of how authentic forgiveness works. Where is the justice in a system? How do the ledgers of guilt and grace work? Who bears responsibility and how? If Ian, the offender, tears away from the family in a pseudo-forgiveness; if the frozen grief is denied and mourning is displaced onto subsequent generations, what will be the new shape of this system? How will the pain trickle down? With what long-range increase in enmeshment? What payments will be charged to the children, what emotional story of repetition without reparation, recapitulation without reconciliation be turned in a new direction? Tyler seeks to resolve those questions with her novel as each of us seeks to do with our—and our families'—lives.

But systems have a life of their own. Systems act to survive, to protect themselves from change, to perpetuate their accustomed patterns of behavior, to substitute an easy conciliation for the hard work of reconciliation. Is reconciliation possible in such a scenario without a profound challenge to and change in the system that surrounds and shapes their lives?

Systems and Reconciliation

A systems perspective on reconciliation offers an inclusive, interdependent means of examining the dynamics of participants, relationships, and circumstances, and their mysterious interactions. "System thought," in contrast to mechanical cause-and-effect explanations, explores the persons-in-context as a dynamically interrelated and interdependent set of functions. A system is a structure (a pattern of elements) that is in process (a pattern of events). The person is a set of elements undergoing multiple processes in cyclical patterns as an integrated system. Any situation of alienation between two parties is not only a system in itself, it is the conjunction of at least two, and often more, systems in conflict.

To explore reconciliation from the paradigm of family systems theory, we shall be using the pioneering work of Murray Bowen (1978), which has become the standard base for theory in family, community, and congregational development (Friedman 1985; Kerr and Bowen 1988). Bowen's theory offers an interdependent analysis of eight interlocking dynamics that are rooted biologically, grounded in present interpersonal relationships, and situated in specific sociocultural contexts. All three of these are crucial: the biological focuses on anxiety management in the system and symptom formation resulting from tension overload; the interpersonal illuminates how anxiety within becomes anxiety between persons, creating symptoms that link persons, dysfunctions that connect whole pieces of human group behavior; the sociocultural orientation recognizes that the family system is a subsystem of the community, the community of society, the society of the culture, the culture of humanity. All these are interrelated, interdependent, and constantly interactive.

The eight interlocking concepts (figure 2.1) of family systems theory offer a framework for understanding the dynamics of individual and group functioning in either calm or storm conditions. In times of calm, the mature person's level of differentiation (maturity) may keep "triangling" at a minimum, help the family emotional system to resolve anxiety, reduce

1
Differentiation of Self
The person becomes an increasingly complex, distinct structure with low or high degree of differentiation (maturity) shown in ability to function as a discrete self in relationship with significant others.

2
Triangles
All human relationships become triangular in stress The normal dyadic communication is overloaded so a third party is brought in to help resolve the tension. A neutral third can open the system. A "triangled" third blocks reconciliation of the two, impairs the third, creates symptoms, and spreads dysfunction throughout the system

3
Family Emotional System
Families develop patterns for managing anxiety, which focus on the marital dyad, on one of the partners, or on a child. This creates symptoms in marital conflict, in personal illness, or in a troubled child.

4
Family Projection Process
Anxiety and immaturity are projected in a family or any system to trickle down from those with greater resources and supporting systems to those with fewer.

5
Sibling Position
The rank order of persons in the family defines patterns of function. This may follow birth order, or the "level of self" possessed by the children Culture invests the order with obligations, duties, and privileges.

6
Emotional Cutoff
Born in symbiotic fusion, the person must resolve this union to become self. The greater level of reactive connectedness, the more likely a person will repeat such fusion in all other relationships. In a cutoff, the person uses distance (physical or emotional) to isolate.

7
Multigenerational Transmission Process
No symptom is only one generation deep A minimum of three are involved in any interpersonal or personal problem. These patterns or scripts direct the pieces of family or community behavior.

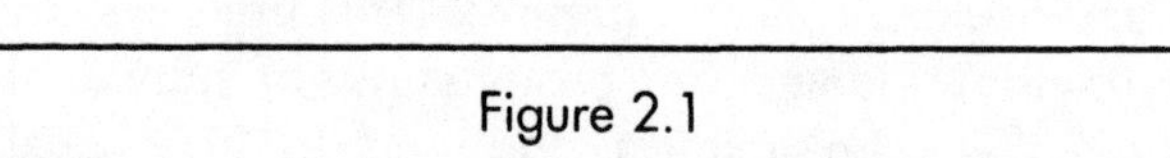

8. Societal Regression or Progression
The rise and fall of communities or societies creates the context for persons and families.

Figure 2.1
Eight Interlocking Family Systems Concepts

members' projection of past patterns and expectations, avoid emotional cutoff, and go beyond the previous generation's patterns of conflict, to act in a creative, even prophetic, way that helps transform community and society. In stormy times, any person regresses under stresses and the reverse will ensue. Functioning at a lower level of maturity, the person "triangles" others, triggering the family emotional system to overload, project its frustration onto others, and act out inherited expectations, scripts, roles, and positions. This leads to emotional cutoffs and the replication of old conflict patterns that disrupt family and community. Rage, retaliation, and resignations result. People are attacked or ignored, blamed or bypassed, worshiped and blindly obeyed or despised and discarded.

The ability to maintain one's differentiation in high-stress situations increases in the maturation process, but progress is in small increments; growth occurs in little steps and in surprisingly small movements across an entire lifetime.

To illustrate, here is a common human experience of the forces active in a family system. (The parentheses identify the eight interlocking concepts.) The good first son conceals a spiteful brat behind a conforming facade (5); he "triangles" a younger brother into his problems (2) and projects the blame for his own bad behavior (4), then cuts off all communications and relationship when confronted (6) and avoids all parental discipline in the family denial system (3). He is behaving with amazing similarity to his mother's father (a first child with an abused younger brother) who modeled after his father's eldest son's behavior (7) in a male-dominant Western individualist culture (8). Caricature that this may be, it illustrates the interplay of forces present to some degree in every human situation.

Growth and change come from, first, awareness of what has been denied and therefore replicated (we are destined by what we deny; what we resist we repeat); second, owning of one's own part in the process (focus on self-stance, not circumstance); and third, making changes by taking a new "I-position" (altering only one's own part in any two-or-more-part problem).

Reconciliation and forgiveness, since they draw their meaning from the content and the context of the difference being resolved, are not the same across relationships. Indeed, they function differently in the various systems we join—the public universe, the professional worlds, the social contexts, or the intimate systems of families. Each of these systems is, in some way, unique, and operates by its own contracts and constraints. Within the systems, each person and each relationship varies so significantly that both the character and the context of any reconciliation will differ by its role, its function, its position within that system.

Systems theory, especially family systems theory, offers us a way to understand, interact with, and intervene in these interlocking networks of relationships and to address those most puzzling of all reconciliations—those that are needed within intimate relations—marriage, siblings, parent-child or extended family. Intimate relationships are of a different order, or at least a different species, than are general social or professional relationships. In contrasting special intimate relationships with general relations, Richard Bondi writes:

> People are not interchangeable. . . . The kind and quality of the special relations I am in help shape the kind of person I am. The "other" in a special relation . . . is in a real and inescapable sense, a part of myself and I in turn am a part of the other. The real specialness is in how they reveal some essential characteristics of what it means to be human. . . . What they particularly reveal is one of the central paradoxes of human existence: that we are both bound and free (Bondi 1986, 38).

We may learn to function with high professional skills as a teacher, therapist, attorney, or doctor, and our communication and management of differences may show advanced levels of social competence, but intimate relationships reveal that we are habitual, determined, creatures of our pasts as well as the open, free, experimental persons we are capable of offering to the public. Special relationships in the intimate systems of our lives make this paradox frighteningly transparent. Our special relations contain deep involvements, profound loyalties, intimate feelings, and covenantal obligations that connect us to inner layers of the soul, former selves in the developmental process, and other persons in our family systems who served as admired models or feared villains. Intimate relations with another person are woven of affective commitments to the special needs and nuances of personality that create the chemistry of interpersonal attachments. This involves both persons rationally and emotionally, cognitively and affectively, in the public and social zone as well as the private and deeply personal, in the general and universal moral values as well as the specific and the particular honoring of what is good and right for this one special person. In intimate relations, these paradoxical elements cannot be split. We are involved in both sides of each of these polarities. We care about the other as a whole, full human being; we become systemically interrelated with the whole person, and the other, as a totality, is connected with us. This brings out levels of immaturity, depths of unconscious processes, riches of mythic interweaving, areas of denied or unrecognized toxicity, dramas of unsuspected complexity from both families of origin.

In special relations—those within intimate systems—or in normal social relations, systems theory offers a unique series of insights about reconciliation. To understand these insights, we must tease out the unique understandings of maturity, differentiation, centeredness between union and separation, and the clarity of one's selfhood shown in the "I-position." And these four elements are aspects of one and the same thing.

Finding the Center

Maturation, for many theorists and therapists, is the journey from infant union to adult separation, from dependency to independence, from closeness to distance, from relatedness to individualism. The assumption that the person becomes authentic by growing from the symbiosis of the womb to the autonomy of youth and the heteronomy of adulthood shapes the goals of therapy and the larger vision of humanness, health, and healing.

Bowen's theory stands in sharp disagreement with such assumptions of the necessity of the isolated self. Although Bowen's work brought the language of differentiation of self to the center of psychological consciousness, his meaning for this central concept is in clear contrast to the prevailing ideas of individuation, separation, and autonomy as maturity. For Bowen, all movement toward maturity, toward differentiation, is centered between union and separation. All growth is balanced between increased distinctness of self (distance) and relationship with others (closeness). Each increase in differentiation requires a more clearly defined "I-position" that clarifies and connects, that strengthens the stance and deepens the connection. Growth happens on the line, at the balance point, in the center. To move toward separation is to cut off, to run away.

No one solves a fused relationship (overattachment) or reduces enmeshment (confused boundaries) by running away. To move toward union is to intensify the fusion, to return to the enmeshment. No one deals constructively with anxiety by giving up self in union and absorption in another.

The secret of growth is to stay clear, stay centered, and stay connected. Each return to the center that extends both union and separation accelerates growth. Intrapersonal growth requires this same balance within (1) a center point between flooding of affect and isolation of affect, which allows awareness of feeling without being either overwhelmed or uninvolved; and within (2) a center point between obsessive thought or detachment. Interpersonal growth necessitates finding a center point between absorption and abandonment, between over-attached and severed relationships, between enmeshment and aloofness.

Movement, in degree of differentiation of self, is limited for most persons. Intensive therapy may enable one to function at a higher level during calm periods, but in storm there is a strong tendency to return to the level of fused interaction gained in family of origin. In spite of our best intentions of functioning at a higher level of clarity, we are all subject to early learning, conditioning, models, and expectations.

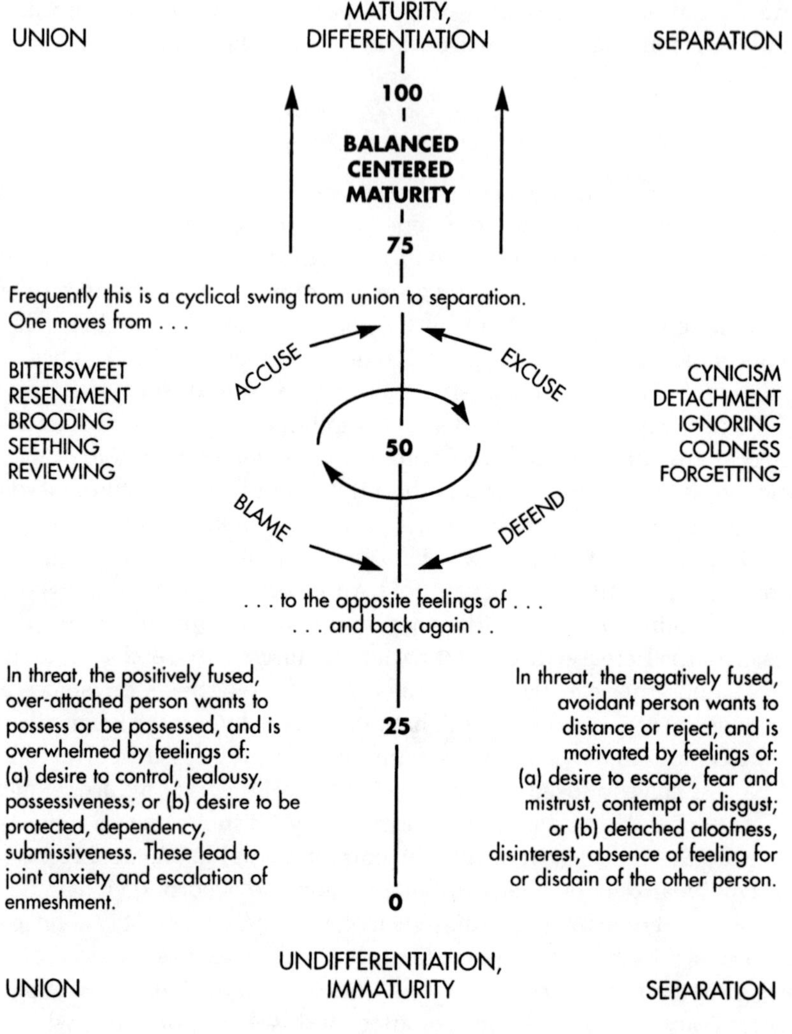

Figure 2.2

Differentiation and Cyclical Conflict

Behavior, on the lower third of the differentiation of self scale, tends to be cyclical, swinging pendulum-like from union to separation, from fusion in anger to cutoff in rejection. Figure 2.2 illustrates the cyclical mood swing from bitterness to cynicism, resentment to ignoring, brooding to detachment, seething to coldness, reviewing grievances to forgetting the impact. Each side is energized by deep needs—on the one side to possess in security and solidarity, on the other to reject for safety and separateness. The hope of union is the hope that one may possess what is desired, control what is jealously sought, all of which leads to joint anxiety between the possessor and the possessed. The goal of separation is to distance oneself from the anxiety field even at the cost of rejecting the other. The negative feelings—contempt, disgust, loathing—press toward a vindictive triumph through revenge or annihilation.

Although actual movement on the scale is in small increments, one can learn to function at a much higher level than one's natural instincts would dictate. The old automatic patterns of family of origin remain alive and active in our unconscious processes, and in stress or storm they are the immediate reactive responses. But one can learn to slow down twitchy reactivity, or thaw out where one is frozen or stuck in the ice of old withdrawal. One can learn to reduce anxiety, to be a nonanxious presence for increasing lengths of time; one can develop a resilience of thought and feeling that neutralizes increasing amounts of toxic anxiety and develops a capacity for reflective wisdom and humorous appreciation of the ironies of life. The old patterns remain in one's repertoire, and in storm will still appear as impulses to action, but new learnings that are more adaptive become increasingly available and authentic for the person.

Centered in Stress or Storm

In alienation, parties take positions, positions shaped by past history in the family of origin as well as by present capacities and choices. The crucial determinant of the position chosen is the level of maturity—differentiation—possessed by the disputant.

In reconciliation, the positions range from the heated union of fusing with the other in attack or attachment to the cool separation of avoidance and distance. Across the spectrum of options, (1) attack / attach, (2) appease, (3) apologize, (4) explain, and (5) avoid, are spread the many contrasting and complementary positions that keep us embroiled in conflict. The most common combinations—attack-attack, avoid-avoid, attach-account—all allow the disputants to continue their dance of dealing with differences in the old family patterns without needing to take a new stance. Authentic reconciliation rarely happens in any of these positions or at any of these levels of differentiation of self. Superficial resolution may occur, with someone offering an appeasement to gain reacceptance or release or someone articulately and persuasively giving an account in self-justification. But lasting reconciliation results from the centered act of giving a full and complete (though brief and focused) apology (figure 2.3).

In stress, even those who are capable of working at authentic reconciliation for others (pastors, therapists, attorneys, mediators) are incapable of

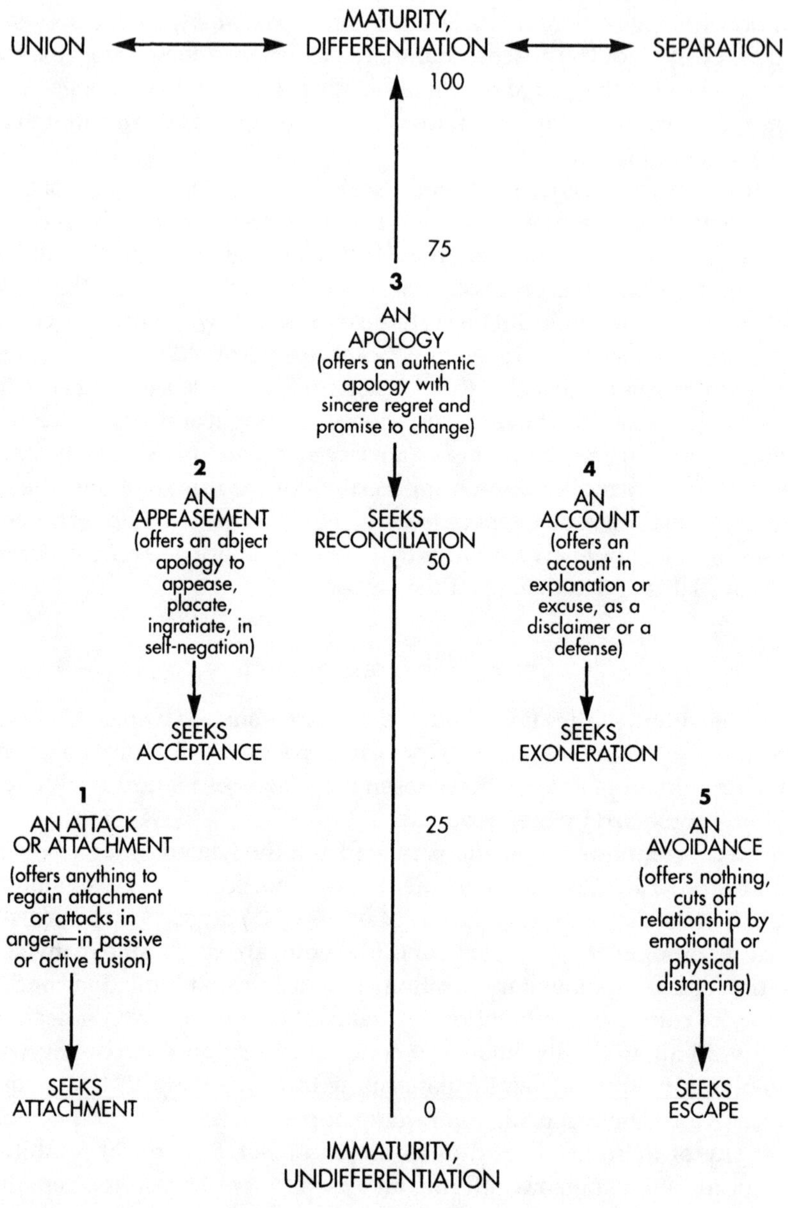
UNION
MATURITY, DIFFERENTIATION
SEPARATION
100
75
3
AN APOLOGY
(offers an authentic apology with sincere regret and promise to change)
SEEKS RECONCILIATION
50
2
AN APPEASEMENT
(offers an abject apology to appease, placate, ingratiate, in self-negation)
SEEKS ACCEPTANCE
4
AN ACCOUNT
(offers an account in explanation or excuse, as a disclaimer or a defense)
SEEKS EXONERATION
1
AN ATTACK OR ATTACHMENT
(offers anything to regain attachment or attacks in anger—in passive or active fusion)
SEEKS ATTACHMENT
25
5
AN AVOIDANCE
(offers nothing, cuts off relationship by emotional or physical distancing)
SEEKS ESCAPE
0
IMMATURITY, UNDIFFERENTIATION

Figure 2.3

Mature and Immature Approaches to Reconciliation

taking clear, healthy positions in their own conflicts. Personal involvement and emotional flooding draw the clean-professional-for-others back into acting as the unclean-protagonist-for-the-threatened-self. The brilliant therapeutic work, done all day at the prevailing rate per hour and published in well-reviewed case studies, all evaporates as the person crosses the threshold of home and encounters the unfinished agenda of family of origin being unconsciously replicated in the family of the present. The more skilled the person, the more sophisticated the behaviors become, but the basic positions remain the same. The angry child or teen who regressed to attacking the other now subtly undermines the other's self-esteem by offering analysis or helpful reinforcement to change the other. Little or no enduring growth comes from changing another person to fit one's own expectations or demands; lasting change comes solely from changes made in oneself, in one's own position, in one's own responses. Any position of attack, no matter how sophisticated, increases fusion; any strategy for appeasement leading to renewed dependent or controlling attachment increases enmeshment. On the other side—separation—the offering of an account in explanation refuses to acknowledge involvement or accept responsibility and leads toward avoidance and emotional cutoff. Authentic growth, healing, and reconciliation come from the center, from clear owning, from clean acting, and from claiming a new I-position.

Appeasement, Apology, Account

The immediate offering of an account is the most common response to seeing oneself as a wrongdoer. The instant activation of inner defenses in justification, explanation, exoneration stimulate the writing of mental scenarios, the rewriting of shared history until the least incriminating, most plausible account of the situation, congruent with one's pride structure, is created. In taking the account position, the person who is alienated offers full account as an appeal to reason. It is a request for recognition of extenuating circumstances, unquestionable intentions, or unfortunate misunderstandings. This presents a disclaimer, offers a justifiable case for being excused, and requests recognition of innocence and release from consequences. Often this is perceived by one or both as an apology, but it is distinctly apologetic—in the defensive meaning of apologetics—not repentant in rapprochement. An account asks for reasonable understanding from the other by virtue of the explanation that either partially or totally denies authorship or responsibility. Covertly or unconsciously it is an attempt to deny responsibility, avoid answerability by pleading diminished capacity, mitigating circumstances, external causation, or some combination of all three.

There is a fine, but crucial, line between an apology and an account. An apology offers no excuses, an account is an excuse. An apology is an appeal to soul that points inward in sorrow or sadness at the injury done; an account is an appeal to the mind that points outward at circumstances and situational causes and asks the other to be reasonable. The former asks absolution from that which is unreasonable and unwarranted, and it recognizes that the asker may be patently undeserving; the latter asks the other to be reasonable by virtue of the explanation offered. One can give an account in reasonable forms without any authentic ownership, but to give an apology is to own one's part in the injury.

What is an apology? How does it differ from excuses, disclaimers, and justifications? "A full and sincere apology" acknowledges the fact of the wrongdoing, accepts ultimate responsibility, expresses sincere sorrow and regret, and promises not to repeat the offense. It is not undoing or mere repudiation of injurious words or deeds; it is a full recognition of the injury and its consequences. The singular achievement of apologetic speech lies in its capacity to effectively eradicate the consequences of the offense by evoking the unpredictable faculty of forgiveness.

An apology is a shared memento. In its most responsible, authentic, and hence vulnerable expression, it constitutes a form of self-punishment that cuts deeply because we are obliged to retell, relive, and seek forgiveness for sorrowful events that have rendered our claims to membership in a moral community suspect or defensible. The act is arduous and painful, the gesture reiterates the reality of the offense while superseding it, and the remorseful admission of wrongdoing is converted into a gift that is accepted and reciprocated by forgiveness. The world is miraculously transformed (Tavuchis 1991, 8).

An apology thus speaks to an act that cannot be undone but that cannot go unnoticed without compromising the current and future relationship of the parties, the legitimacy of the violated rule, and the wider social web in which the participants are enmeshed. It is a *relational* symbolic gesture occurring in a complex interpersonal field and moral order. It is a speech that ultimately entreats from the other forgiveness, redemption, and acceptance that seem to restore one's sense of reality and place in a moral order (Tavuchis 1991, 13–14).

An apology is social exchange. One "gives," "owes," "offers," "receives," "accepts" an apology since something tangible is being bartered. This fundamental pattern of sociation in apologetic discourse is dyadic—offender to offended. Thus there are four structural configurations:

1. Interpersonal apology from one individual to another, or *one to one.*

2. Apology from an individual to a collectivity, or *one to many.*
3. Apology from a collectivity to an individual, or *many to one.*
4. Apology from one collectivity to another, or *many to many.*

Misconduct or wrongdoing impacts on the one offended so that the victim and/or the community can, through the dynamics of the moral order and the social structures of the community, call for the offender to offer an apology. In such an oral statement of apology:

1. The offender acknowledges full responsibility.
2. The offender expresses sorrow and contrition for the harm done.
3. The offender seeks forgiveness from the offended party.
4. The offender implicitly or explicitly promises not to repeat the offense in the future.
5. The discursive loop is closed by the forgiveness of the offender, which symbolizes reconciliation and allows normal social relations to be resumed (Tavuchis 1991, 121).

An appeasement is any form of moving close to the other without dealing with the injury or alienation. One may seek to regain closeness or be readmitted to intimacy by passivity (groveling, acquiescence, placating, abject apologies) or inactive dependency (seduction, persuasion, manipulation) without any sincere attempt to work through the differences. All of these strategies avoid taking an "I-position" or defining a self in the relationship. By choosing to be a non-self, the person accommodates to the other, to circumstances, even to undeniable injustices, rather than risk taking a position and committing oneself to action.

In appeasement, the anxiety may be reduced by eliciting the other's nurturance or support. So the person may ask for escape from consequences or punishment for the inappropriate actions. Or the person may offer self-negation, humiliation, or self-flagellation to punish the self, invite further ventilation of anger by the other, and thus resume the fused relationship. There is no increase in maturity, no movement in differentiation of self through appeasement. If it fails, the person is highly likely to move either toward angry attack or passive attachment.

Thus we can say that there are three options in reconciliation (figure 2.4), only one of which works through the issues in authentic apology and affirmation of self and other. The other two alternatives avoid taking a clear I-position in self-definition. Of those two, one collapses in union, the other cuts off in separation; both maintain the old level of selfhood or give

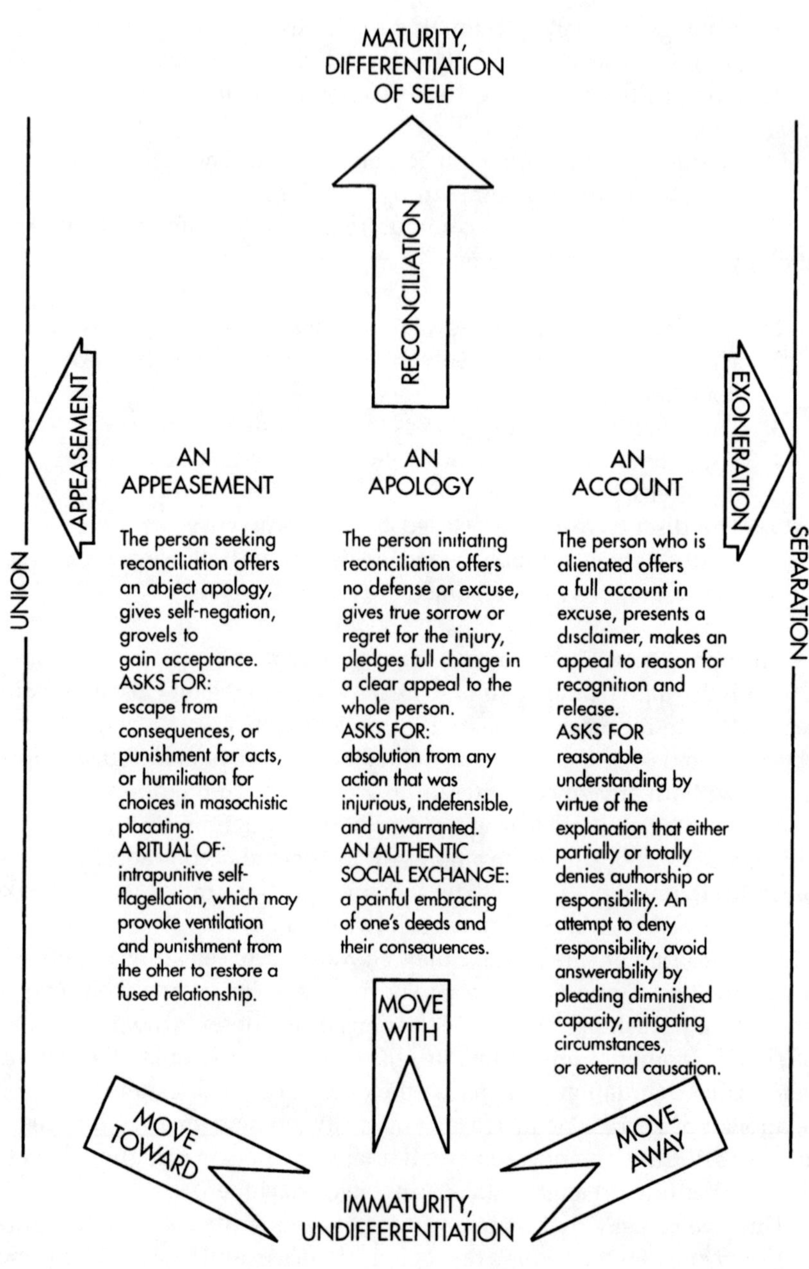

MATURITY, DIFFERENTIATION OF SELF
RECONCILIATION
APPEASEMENT
EXONERATION
UNION
SEPARATION
AN APPEASEMENT
The person seeking reconciliation offers an abject apology, gives self-negation, grovels to gain acceptance.
ASKS FOR:
escape from consequences, or punishment for acts, or humiliation for choices in masochistic placating.
A RITUAL OF·
intrapunitive self-flagellation, which may provoke ventilation and punishment from the other to restore a fused relationship.
AN APOLOGY
The person initiating reconciliation offers no defense or excuse, gives true sorrow or regret for the injury, pledges full change in a clear appeal to the whole person.
ASKS FOR:
absolution from any action that was injurious, indefensible, and unwarranted.
AN AUTHENTIC SOCIAL EXCHANGE:
a painful embracing of one's deeds and their consequences.
AN ACCOUNT
The person who is alienated offers a full account in excuse, presents a disclaimer, makes an appeal to reason for recognition and release.
ASKS FOR
reasonable understanding by virtue of the explanation that either partially or totally denies authorship or responsibility. An attempt to deny responsibility, avoid answerability by pleading diminished capacity, mitigating circumstances, or external causation.
MOVE TOWARD
MOVE WITH
MOVE AWAY
IMMATURITY, UNDIFFERENTIATION

Figure 2.4

Three Options in Reconciliation

up the self in regression. Low self-esteem reinforces, or is reenacted by, movement toward union or separation. Growth in selfhood, growth in relationship, growth in maturation—all happen along the center, where connectedness and clarity strengthen each other.

The Reconciling Center

The reconciliation process proceeds through a series of pull-ups. The list of steps given in figure 2.5 is multiple choice, although most persons touch on most of the steps listed in recovery from an injury. One begins by retelling the story, often repeatedly, until it is possible to separate oneself from the fusion in anger and reframe its meaning in a more freeing way. Now the telling is less a lament or a complaint and becomes more an urge to discuss the event, the issues, and the interests, and with increasing distance from the injury, to dismiss the less crucial of the demands. In this process, one is able to discharge a good deal of the emotional overload and begin to unhook emotionally.

The alternation from union in angry or injured attachment to reflective and separate agency continues. There is grief work to be done; then closure begins to emerge. One can feel the loss and gradually let go of the loss. Trust begins in germinal form, small but budding, and one risks a bit in relationship. With each risk, when it is honored by response and reciprocal risking, there is an increase in trust. The two, trust and risk, go hand in hand. Risk, in reality, is prior to trust. As long as one seeks to generate trust as the first step, one continues to evaluate the other's trustworthiness. "Can I trust you?" or "I can't trust you!" is a judgment on the other's duplicity or instability. The better question is, "How much am I willing to risk?" "What can I afford to lose?" When the onus is on one's own position and willingness to act, on one's venturing back into more open relationship, then one is free to choose, act, move toward the other. The question of trust, in contrast, places the problem at the other person's doorstep, delegates the responsibility to another, and then awaits the necessary guarantees.

As the risks increase and trust unfolds, an appreciation of the other's perspective, the other's point of view, the other's sincerity in apology, and the authenticity of the repentance finally grows to the point where a respect for the other as genuine is achieved and both recognize that forgiveness has occurred. They choose to forgo further conversation, further caution, further expectations for restitution or repayment, and the future is open once more.

These steps—involving differentiation of a self while clarifying connectedness—invite growth in personhood that is both affiliated and distinct,

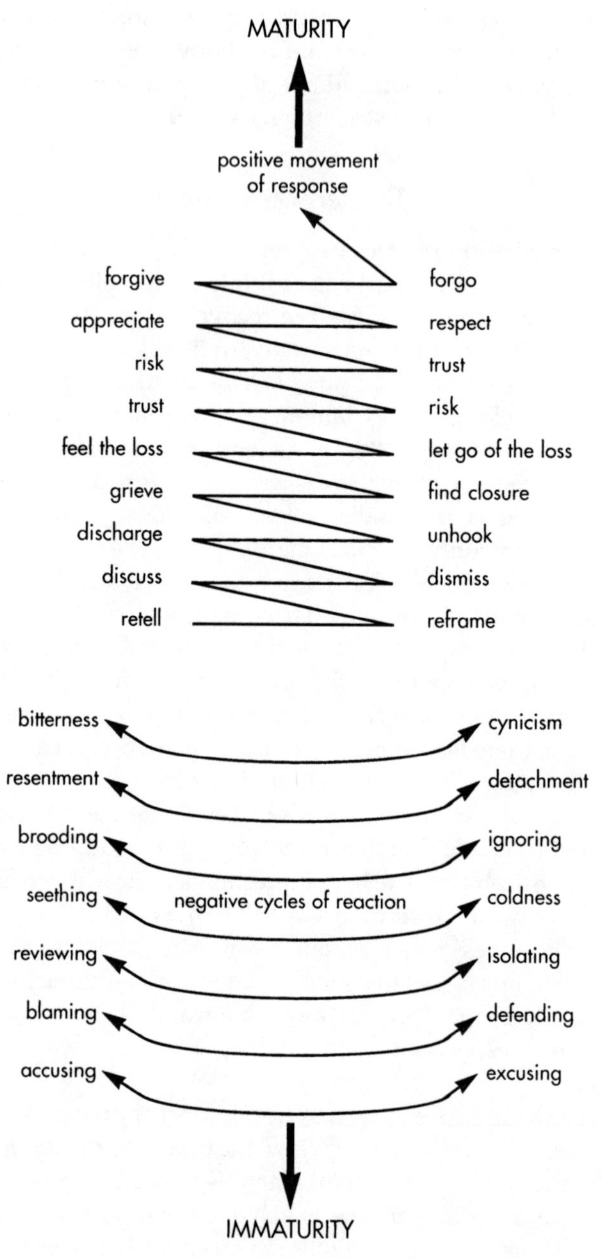

Figure 2.5

Moving toward Mature Reconciliation

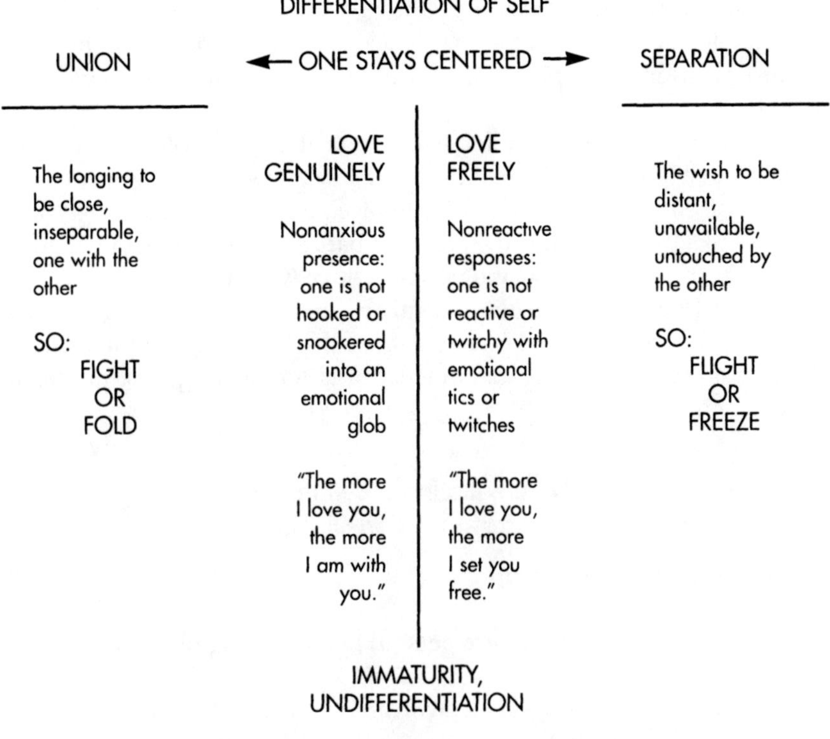
MATURITY,
DIFFERENTIATION OF SELF
UNION
ONE STAYS CENTERED
SEPARATION
The longing to be close, inseparable, one with the other
SO:
FIGHT
OR
FOLD
LOVE
GENUINELY
Nonanxious presence: one is not hooked or snookered into an emotional glob
"The more I love you, the more I am with you."
LOVE
FREELY
Nonreactive responses: one is not reactive or twitchy with emotional tics or twitches
"The more I love you, the more I set you free."
The wish to be distant, unavailable, untouched by the other
SO:
FLIGHT
OR
FREEZE
IMMATURITY,
UNDIFFERENTIATION

Figure 2.6
Love and Differentiation

connected and yet self-defined. In systems thought, sacrifice of either pole leads to loss of self and loss of relationship. Each pull-up in self-definition allows for more healthful connectedness; each clarification of connectedness increases the integrity of the self.

At the heart of this theory is the understanding of loving relationship. "Love is the tension between union and separation," wrote theologian Paul Tillich. "To love another is to move as close as possible without violating the other's dignity or freedom," argued Gestalt therapist Frederick Perls. It is this balance at the core of commitment, connectedness, and caring that defines a just, loving relationship (figure 2.6). One can be a nonanxious presence in closeness and trust while giving nonreactive responses in distinct clarity and honesty. One is not snookered into an emotional glob that flows amoeba-like through the other's boundaries. Nor is one defensively reactive, emotionally twitchy with anxious tics that interrupt the flow of give-and-take by freezing or fleeing into distance.

Love is the balance of union ("the more I love you, the more I am *with* you") and separation ("the more I love you, the more I set you free"). And the tension between the two poles, love, is composed of an equal-regard position, a keeping-faith position, an I-am-here-to-be-with-you position.

As love matures, concern for self and for the other become one at the center. Love of self and love of other are not two separate loves, but two aspects of one and the same attitude of equal regard. Equal regard, as Gene Outka has argued, is the essential nature of *agapē,* the love that expresses both self-valuation and neighbor-love (Outka 1973).

To clarify and confirm the central understandings of a systems approach to conciliation and reconciliation, the following multiple-choice test summarizes the theory and practice of differentiating a mature self in relationship.

Differentiating a Self in the Process of Reconciliation

Choose as many as appropriate.

1. The differentiated (mature person) in reconciling relationships

_____ a. stays in close contact with another without sharing the other's high anxiety.

_____ b. feels deeply with another person while not feeling controlled by, flooded with, or scared by the other's feelings.

_____ c. maintains his own sense of centeredness—neither fusing with the other in union (appeasement) nor cutting off in separation (giving an account), but staying both connected and distinct in a clear apology.

_____ d. separates herself from the anxiety field, from the fear process of the other, but not from the person or the relationship.

_____ e. gives up all attempts to get the other person to change; works solely at changes in his own response or position.

_____ f. discovers that her choices are not dependent on another's agreement, acceptance, or cooperation, but on simply taking her own clear position.

_____ g. declines another's provocation or irritation and does not join the other in reciprocal blaming, accusing, or attacking in anger.

_____ h. finds that he is more free when he neither explains a choice nor justifies an action by giving an account, but simply takes a clear position.

_____ i. finds that she is unhooked when she neither excuses a choice nor defends an action but simply affirms it openly and takes responsibility for its consequences.

_____ j. maintains a repertoire of neutral responses to defuse a volatile situation or ease an angry transaction with gentle humor or candor.

_____ k. discovers that he can see the humor in situations or relationships that were once seen as serious, all-absorbing dilemmas (the delicate boundary between tragedy and comedy becomes visible).

_____ l. does all of the above.

_____m. does none of the above. Maturity is ending dysfunctional relationships, writing off controlling persons, distancing from dominating people, getting out of trapped or manipulative relationships, becoming an autonomous, self-reliant individual with freedom from codependence.

2. Mature persons in reconciling relationships

_____ a. can provide a nonanxious presence in both stressful and nonstressful situations without getting either emotionally stuck (paralyzed) or emotionally twitchy (reactive).

_____ b. maintain calm in the face of hostile and antagonistic behavior so they can choose an appropriate response—be a responder, not a reactor.

_____ c. prefer to begin resolving any conflictual or stressful situation by defining themselves, their responsibility, their own part of a problem, rather than analyzing the other person's behavior or failure.

_____ d. see interpersonal problems as two-person dilemmas that lie between the two, at neither doorstep, and work only on their own behalf.

_____ e. can feel their most basic fears of being abandoned without clinging to the other (they remain centered).

_____ f. can feel their primary anxiety about being engulfed by another but without cutting off relationship (they stay balanced).

_____ g. do not become anxious when close to difficult people or afraid when distant from significant others, but deal creatively with both basic fears: fear of abandonment and fear of absorption.

_____ h. do not become over-responsible in pursuing, rescuing, controlling, or manipulating; do not become under-responsible

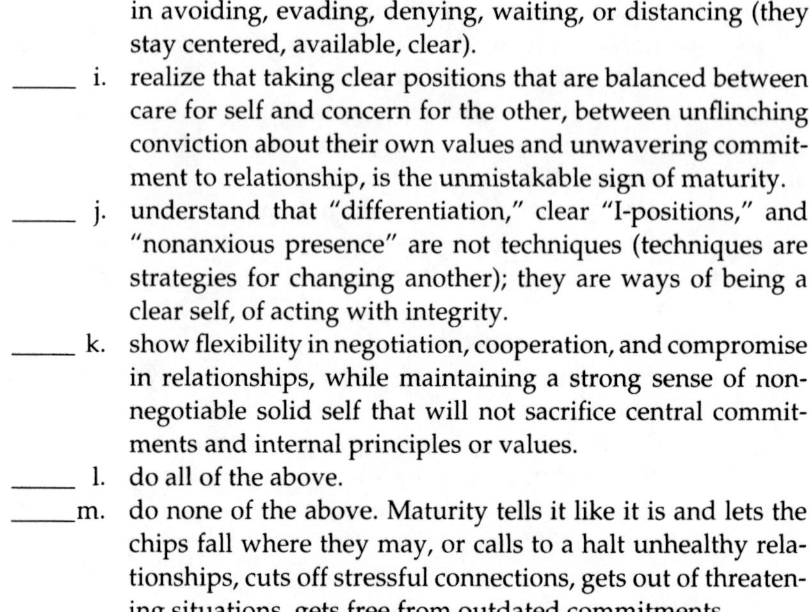

in avoiding, evading, denying, waiting, or distancing (they stay centered, available, clear).

_____ i. realize that taking clear positions that are balanced between care for self and concern for the other, between unflinching conviction about their own values and unwavering commitment to relationship, is the unmistakable sign of maturity.

_____ j. understand that "differentiation," clear "I-positions," and "nonanxious presence" are not techniques (techniques are strategies for changing another); they are ways of being a clear self, of acting with integrity.

_____ k. show flexibility in negotiation, cooperation, and compromise in relationships, while maintaining a strong sense of nonnegotiable solid self that will not sacrifice central commitments and internal principles or values.

_____ l. do all of the above.

_____m. do none of the above. Maturity tells it like it is and lets the chips fall where they may, or calls to a halt unhealthy relationships, cuts off stressful connections, gets out of threatening situations, gets free from outdated commitments.

"I Feel Dead Inside"—A Family Case Study

"I just didn't feel like going back to college. In fact, I didn't feel like doing much of anything. Still don't. I work at Pizza Hut just enough to stay solvent. Sleep a lot. And I don't go out. Don't care much about life."

Leo N. has dropped out of college at the end of his sophomore year. He comes to this appointment with the pastor primarily to escape continuing pressure from one of his roommates that he seek help.

"I'm crazy about half the time," he says suddenly. "I sit and stare at the wall. I think about dying. I get so low, I don't talk to anyone for days. I guess I'm depressed almost all the time."

A popular, successful class leader during his first year of college, Leo's whole world became invested in a relationship with Laurie during the first term of his sophomore year. Engaged by Christmas, his excitement with Laurie eclipsed everything else, absorbing all his thinking. By summer, she began to feel smothered, broke off the relationship suddenly, then discovered that she was pregnant. In spite of his intense protests, she went immediately for an abortion. "I haven't talked to her since," Leo says, "that's all over now. It's dead!"

An oldest son of a hardworking, driven pastor, Leo left home at seventeen, has little contact with either parent, but misses his mother. "I call her once in a while, but she makes me feel so guilty, I just can't listen to her complaining, and she exaggerates everything!"

Leo describes his father as an impatient, demanding, authoritarian, and incredibly strict man, "an abusive parent, I believe he'd be called. He never laid a hand on either of my brothers, or my little sister, but he was always on me. I guess I was always a problem. He often said I was just no good. He'd beat me at least twice a week over little things that happened at home or school or at church. He'd hit me around the head if there was any hassling in the car. Always me, never my brothers."

This cycle of violence and abuse came to a sudden end in the summer of Leo's sixteenth year. En route to the paternal grandparents' farm, a conflict broke out between the three boys in the back seat. The father began striking Leo in the face with one hand while trying to drive the car with the other and lost control of the car, running into the ditch and damaging the car slightly. Upon arrival at the grandparents' house, he took out his anger at the minor damages by beginning to beat Leo as soon as they got out of the car. For the first time, Leo struck back, hitting his father in the face, breaking his glasses and ruining his hearing aid. All violence ended between father and son from that moment. All contact ended, too, as the two lived in a mutual pact of ignoring each other's existence. At seventeen, Leo tore away from the family and moved into an apartment with several friends.

"It was an official divorce. We agreed to not see, speak, or write to each other again. I kept my part of the deal, but four months later my dad appeared at the door with an apology—well, more of an explanation—for all the beatings he had given me. I took the apology without inviting him in. He asked for my forgiveness. What could I say? That I needed to talk about it more? Hardly. We shook hands to part as friends. I see him maybe once a year. That's enough."

Leo's parents, Ronald and his faithful wife, Darlene, are both perceived as workaholics by their son. Married as college freshmen when eighteen and seventeen years old, respectively, Ronald and Darlene have sought to atone for their sexual indiscretion by pouring themselves into highly demanding work schedules. Her family's embarrassment and shame made the first years of their forced marriage an unhappy time for them both. Leo symbolized their less-than-perfect past. Darlene's parents and her sister and brother, who were also in the ministry, found subtle ways to remind them of their unforgivable bedding before wedding.

Ronald's flight from an abusive family (like his son, he made a total cutoff when he went to college) has never been bridged. Leo remembers the few painful visits as times of high anxiety for the whole family. Ronald's deafness was caused by blows on the ears from his father, whom he has "forgiven," but with no reconciliation (see figure 2.7).

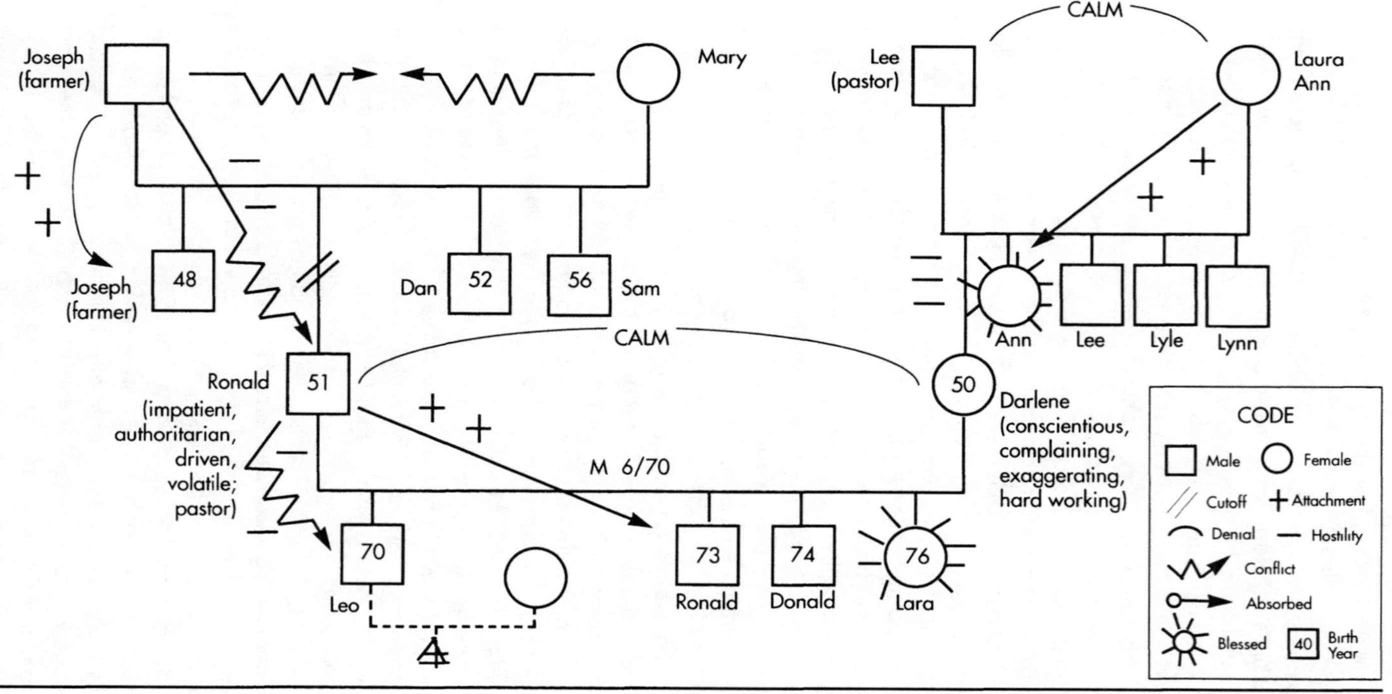

Figure 2.7
Family Genogram

Toward a New Paradigm of Forgiveness

1. Forgiveness that takes place within interlocking, intimate systems or interrelationships of invisible loyalties calls for a special clarity and connection, an "I-position" and a "Thou respect" that are stubbornly "centered."

2. An authentic apology, differing from either giving an account or offering appeasement, is a balanced position of responsibility and integrity which enables the one who apologizes to pull up to a clearer "I-position" of maturity.

3. Both love and justice, and reconciliation and reconstruction take place at the midpoint between union and separation, connectedness and individuation. Love is maximum closeness with minimum threat; it is contact without control; it is union that protects separateness.

3

The Origins of Reconnection

> The first time I visited Paris, I went to the monument of the deportation of the French who had died in German concentration camps I was horrified by the inscription over the main door
> "Let us forgive but never let us forget "
> All of a sudden I realized that the real virtue came in forgiving precisely while remembering. If I could forget, I would not have to forgive, it would not even be necessary.
>
> — Virgil Elizondo

> The stupid either forgive or forget,
> The naive forgive and forget;
> The wise forgive but do not forget.
>
> —Thomas Szasz

> Nobody ever forgets where she/he buried a hatchet
>
> — Kin Hubbard

In the ancient epic tale of forgiveness, Joseph is approached fearfully by his brothers—paranoid that he will revenge himself on them now that the patriarch, his father Jacob, is dead—with a plea based on the sacred last words of their father. "In his last words to us before he died, your father gave us this message for you: 'I ask you to forgive your brothers' crime and wickedness; I know they did you harm.' So now forgive our crime, we beg; for we are servants of your father's God" (Gen. 50:17, NEB).

In grief, after the death of their father, the brothers return to the paranoid stage of development, which has characterized their lives. The we-they splitting, the projection of rage on a scapegoat, the attempted murder of their brother, the sale of the boy into slavery, the blood revenge practices toward those who wronged them, now return in their fear of the younger brother who has become acting ruler of Egypt.

Profound forgiveness, acceptance of the injury, rescue of their families, care and support during a famine, special status and privilege in the land for seventeen years have all demonstrated Joseph's forgiveness. But the brothers still return to paranoid splitting and seek safety guarantees by invoking the sacred last words of the father and the power of the Holy, the father's tribal God.

Grief, sadness, and the mature ability to mourn and work at reconstructing relationships are signs of authentic maturity. Joseph, in contrast to his brothers, has achieved adulthood, and the unmistakable sign is his offering of forgiveness a second time. A clear recognition of both poles—evil and good—marks his words of healing. " 'Do not be afraid. Am I in the place of God? You meant to do me harm; but God meant to bring good out of it by preserving the lives of many people, as we see today. Do not be afraid. I will provide for you and your dependants.' Thus he comforted them and set their minds at rest" (Gen. 50:19–21, NEB).

The contrast raises a series of intriguing questions. What is the difference in childhood, family dynamics, and adult capacities between the brothers (sons of unloved Leah) and Joseph and Benjamin (the sons of the beloved Rachel)? The names given to Leah's sons are all vindictive, competitive shouts of triumph in lifelong competition with her sister's blessed wife status. How does this split affect their development? The father Jacob's open splitting between blessed and unblessed sons pits them in a life-and-death struggle. How does this affect their capacity to make authentic reparations? What does this archetypal narrative suggest of the dynamics of forgiving and being forgiven? Of reconciling and being reconciled?

Peace Within—Peace Between

Reconciliation, in the view of object relations theory, comes about as a result of peacemaking *within*—resolving intrapersonal relationships—leading to peacemaking *between* in personal harmony. The creative work of Melanie Klein offers us a positive alternative to the negating instinct theory of classic psychoanalysis. In Freudian theory, human beings, as atoms of self-interest driven by impulses and instincts, are able to live together civilly only by repressing these urges and desires. The individual's character traits are actually transformed instincts that have been reformed into socially tolerable behaviors. Their true nature is easily seen by observing what is denied, avoided, reversed, or displaced, so forgiveness is a thinly disguised form of anger denied, revenge reversed, retaliation avoided, or confrontation displaced. In the classical Freudianism of Otto Fenichel, the word *forgiveness* is used to designate a pathological defense against guilt feelings that are too painful to manage except by this compulsive mechanism. "The ego's need for punishment is, in general, subordinated to a need for forgiveness, punishment being accepted as a necessary means for getting rid of the pressure of the superego, . . . a need for absolution" (Fenichel 1945, 293).

But for Klein, relationships, not instincts, are the significant forces shaping human personality and behavior. The problems that arise in human relationships are the most crucial issues of development, not the repression of the instincts or the defensive reconstruction of our drives and desires. Her work with young children led her to draw connections between the infant's relating to its parents, its identification with parental attitudes, and the later character of the person. The child develops an internal world that influences perception and interaction with external reality.

Useful for our understanding of forgiveness and reconciliation is Klein's work on love and hate in relationship. In *Love, Guilt and Reparation* (1975 b), an early lecture on the infant's inner life, she observes that love and hate, with all the conflicts they engender, arise in early infancy and are active throughout the life process. The first object of love and hate—the mother—is desired as well as despised with all the intensity and totality of the urgency of infancy. The mother, and later the father, are incorporated into the internal world of the infant as "objects."

> The baby, having incorporated the parents, feels them to be live people inside its body in the concrete way in which deep unconscious phantasies are experienced—they are, in its mind, "internal" or "inner" objects, as I have termed them. Thus an inner world is being built up in the child's unconscious mind, corresponding to actual experiences and the impressions gained from people and the external world, and yet altered by its own phantasies and impulses. If it is a world of people predominantly at peace with each other and with the ego, inner harmony, security and integration ensue (Klein 1948, 312–13).

Inside the infant, the omnipresent, omniscient, and feared-as-omnipotent parental figures may supply profound security and safety. Or, if they are deeply at odds with each other and with the child's needs for safety and security, they may create an inner world at war. In either case, feelings of both love and hate emerge and are either resolved in harmony or accumulate, intensify, and lead to later splitting in deeper and more permanent rifts that block the normal progression into a grieving and healing resolution.

Feelings of love and gratitude arise directly in response to the love and affection of the mother. These spontaneous reflections also contain irritation and hatred.

> My psychoanalytic work has convinced me that when in the baby's mind conflicts between love and hate arise, and the fears of losing the loved one become active, a very important step is made in development. These feelings of guilt and distress now enter as a new element into the emotion of love. . . . [S]ide by side with the destructive impulses in the unconscious mind of the child and of the adult, there exists a profound urge to make sacrifices, in order to help and to put right loved people who in fantasy have been harmed or destroyed. In the depths of the mind, the urge to make

> people happy is linked up with a strong feeling of responsibility and concern for them, which manifests itself in genuine sympathy with other people and in the ability to understand them, as they are and as they feel (Klein et al. 1953, 65–66).

This deeply rooted—early formed—"urge to make happy" motivates identification with others, sacrificing some part of our own feelings and desires, and leads to the capacity for deep and strong feelings of love. This process of sacrifice for someone we love is essentially playing the earliest roles we observed—the part of the "good parent" toward another and the part of the good child toward the parent, which we wished to do in the past and now fulfill in the present. The "good parent role," as we felt that parents acted toward us or as we wanted them to act, remains within even the neglected child. We all have some—though to varying degrees—capacity to love, with the sacrifices it entails.

But hate, the desire to make another suffer, is there in our emotional origins as well. The grievances we hold against the parent who frustrated us and the feelings of hate and resentment that powered our desires for revenge all leave a residue of guilt and self-loathing. All this can be undone by becoming either the good parent or the good child in the present relationship and in fantasy, setting things right in reparation. We can work for justice and reclaim the missing virtues in retrospect.

> At the same time, in our unconscious fantasy, we make good the injuries which we did in fantasy, and for which we still unconsciously feel very guilty. This *making reparation* is, in my view, a fundamental element in love and in all human relationships (Klein et al. 1953, 68).

In making peace with another who has wronged us, or in making reparation where we have wronged another, these two parallel sets of dynamics unfold—reparations within the self, reparations between self and other. I become the just, yet forgiving, parent to myself and this enables me to be a "good parent" to the wrongdoer. At the same time I become the good child who sacrifices a part of my self-interest and am thereby able to receive the other's acceptance and reparation.

Stages of Infancy

Emotional development in early childhood, Klein observed, moves through two primary positions, the schizoid and the paranoid, to the depressive position in which one remains for life. It is in this third position that *reparation* becomes possible, although the inner damages caused by hate are incurred from the start of life.

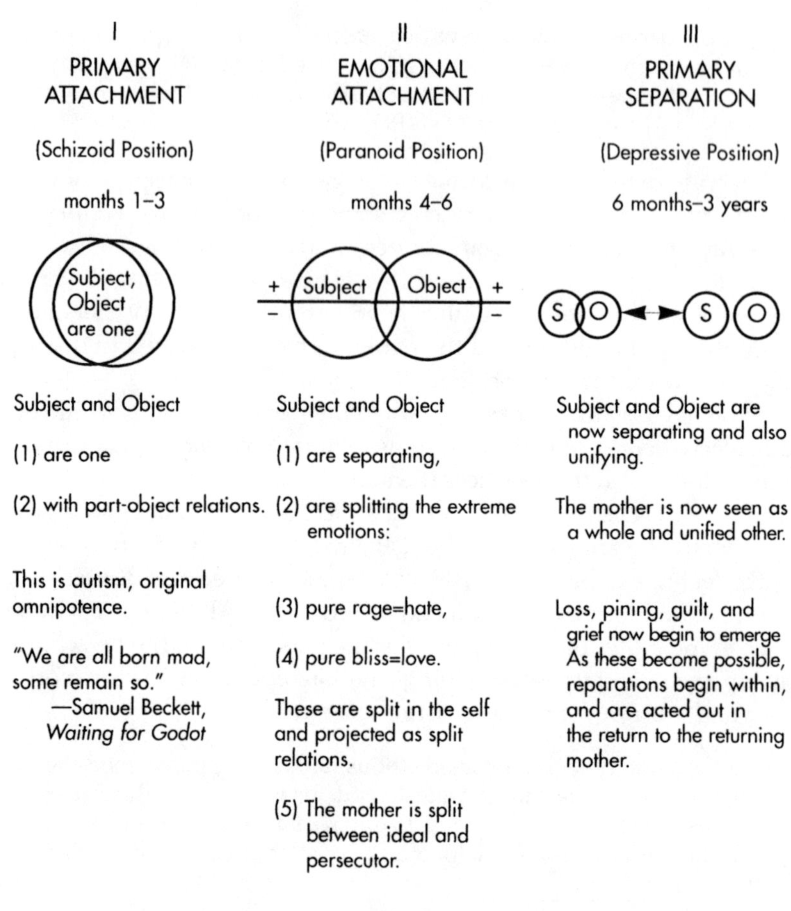

I
PRIMARY ATTACHMENT
(Schizoid Position)
months 1–3
Subject, Object are one
Subject and Object
(1) are one
(2) with part-object relations.
This is autism, original omnipotence.
"We are all born mad, some remain so."
—Samuel Beckett, *Waiting for Godot*
II
EMOTIONAL ATTACHMENT
(Paranoid Position)
months 4–6
+ Subject Object +
– –
Subject and Object
(1) are separating,
(2) are splitting the extreme emotions:
(3) pure rage=hate,
(4) pure bliss=love.
These are split in the self and projected as split relations.
(5) The mother is split between ideal and persecutor.
III
PRIMARY SEPARATION
(Depressive Position)
6 months–3 years
S O S O
Subject and Object are now separating and also unifying.
The mother is now seen as a whole and unified other.
Loss, pining, guilt, and grief now begin to emerge
As these become possible, reparations begin within, and are acted out in the return to the returning mother.

Figure 3.1
Attachments and Separation (Melanie Klein)

Klein views birth as part of a process, not an event. In Klein's sequence of positions (see figure 3.1), for the first three months the infant and mother are still one, subject and object are unitary, and the emotional life of the infant is attached to *part-objects.* These part-objects are sorted into gratifying, pleasurable experiences that come from good sources (the idealized good breast that satisfies with warm milk, for example) or into frustrating and painful experiences (the disliked bad breast, which is empty). The *part-objects,* experienced as continuous with the self, give the infant a sense of omnipotence. The power to influence pleasurable, gratifying experiences is essential to growth and the movement toward selfhood.

The paranoid position, which emerges in the second three months of life, begins as the pure bliss of love separates from the pure rage of hate. This splitting of the extreme emotions enables the infant to begin the separation between self and other. As love and hate are split in the self, they are also projected on the mother, who is increasingly loved as ideal and feared as persecutor. Subject and object are separating as the autistic period ends, and the ambivalent emotional attachment is characterized by splitting mechanisms that act as defenses against the persecutory anxieties arising from painful experiences—the bad objects.

The depressive position, reached around age six months, brings the child to psychological birth. "The psychological birth of the infant," as Margaret Mahler terms Klein's third position, is a breakthrough from perceiving part to perceiving whole, of recognizing the mother, or the significant caretaker, as a *whole object.* As the child separates from fusion to the mother, it also unifies within. The splitting mechanisms decrease. As the infant perceives the mother as a whole being, emotional growth is accelerated. If the mother has an autonomous life of her own, the infant, in comparison, becomes gradually aware of its own total dependence, its utter helplessness. The feelings of omnipotence are deflated. The discovery that the mother is a *whole object* dissipates the previous polarization into good and bad *part-objects.* Where the infant earlier feared that its hostile feelings toward the bad, depriving part-object were so potent that they had destroyed even the good, gratifying part-object, now both love and hate are focused on the one whole-object mother.

When love and hate are experienced together, a new set of feelings emerges for the first time: guilt, sadness, depression, and grief: guilt that one's hostile feelings have hurt the other, sadness at the loss, grief and depression in consequence. This emotional position—the depressive position—makes possible feelings of concern. (D. W. Winnicott calls this "the stage of concern" [Winnicott 1955, 89].) (See figure 3.2.)

The infant fears that loving feelings toward the caring mother may be overwhelmed by the hostile feelings toward the depriving mother, so concern emerges. From an attitude of taking, the child moves toward an attitude of giving, and passive infantile dependence is replaced by mature dependence. As the depressive position is being successfully negotiated, from six months to three years, the possibility of *reparation* is reached.

As the experiences of suffering, guilt, and depression are attached to a greater love for the whole person of the mother, the urge to make reparation expresses the life instinct, and is a reconciling force "which enters into all sublimations and remains . . . the great means by which depression is kept at bay and diminished" (Klein 1975a, 293). This urge to make

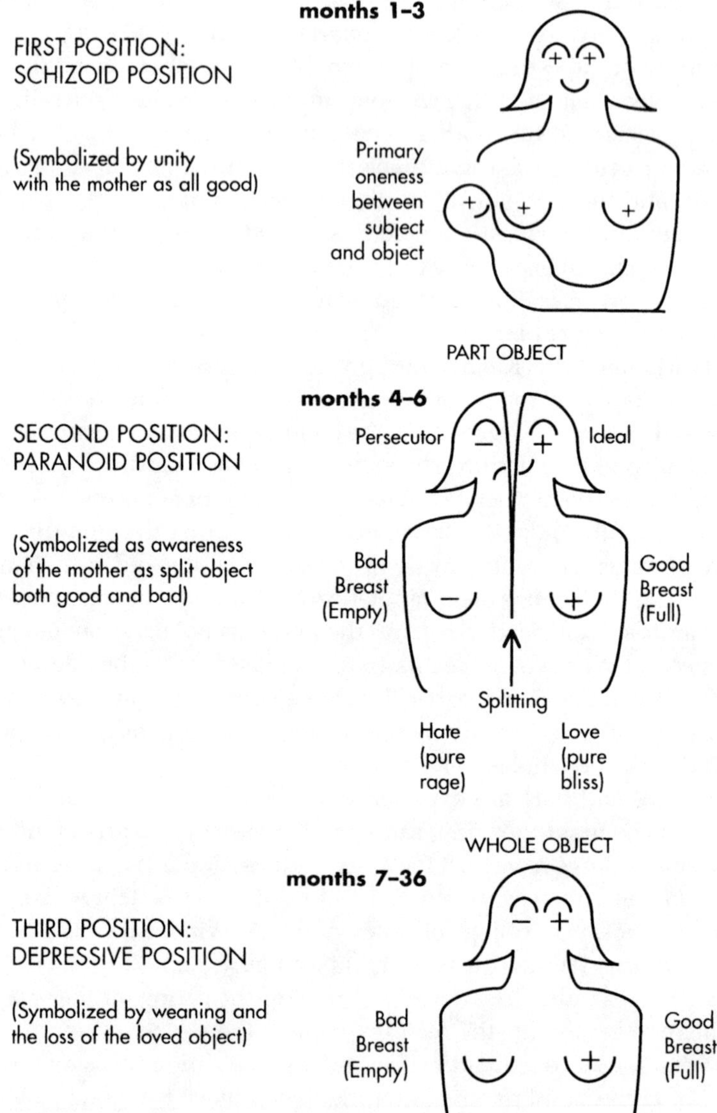
months 1–3
FIRST POSITION:
SCHIZOID POSITION
(Symbolized by unity
with the mother as all good)
Primary
oneness
between
subject
and object
PART OBJECT
months 4–6
SECOND POSITION:
PARANOID POSITION
Persecutor
Ideal
(Symbolized as awareness
of the mother as split object
both good and bad)
Bad
Breast
(Empty)
Good
Breast
(Full)
Splitting
Hate
(pure
rage)
Love
(pure
bliss)
WHOLE OBJECT
months 7–36
THIRD POSITION:
DEPRESSIVE POSITION
(Symbolized by weaning and
the loss of the loved object)
Bad
Breast
(Empty)
Good
Breast
(Full)
Hate and Love
Guilt and Grief
Reparations become possible.

Figure 3.2

Schizoid, Paranoid, and Depressive Positions

reparation, the capacity and longing for the restoration of the good object, both internal and external, is the foundation of the self's ability to sustain love and maintain relationships through differences and difficulties with others. "These tendencies to make reparation I have found in the analysis of small children to be the driving force in all constructive activities and for social development" (Klein 1975b, 293).

The drive toward reparation, motivated by the guilt associated with our ambivalent feelings of love and hate, resists the depression that would flood us if hostile and destructive impulses overwhelmed loving and connecting feelings. Reparation seeks restoration of the relationship and advances us toward greater integration, maturation, and solidarity with others. The motivation toward and the capacity for seeking forgiveness is one of the earliest mechanisms in infant development, with roots in the earliest emotions of love and hate, and in their resolution through the restoration of relationship. In becoming the "good child," one makes reparation. In internalizing "the mother" one takes a step toward learning the later capacity to forgive.

If the family context, and especially the mothering, offers a "facilitating environment" in which acceptance and forgiveness are constant, the child may move successfully through the depressive position. If the parent returns destructive responses to the child's destructive impulses, the two reinforce each other in depressive behavior. The child reacts to frustration by *retaliation.* If the parent lives by the *principle of retaliation,* the anxiety level of the relationship escalates. For the child, the anxiety is that he or she will be treated just as he or she would like to treat the objects that frustrate the child. The fear is that the environment is just as instinctually explosive as the child's own instinctual explosiveness. When the parenting offers acceptance even after destructive actions, forgiveness after bad behavior, the child internalizes a good parent into the internal museum of objects. The mother's forgiveness models a unifying resolution to splitting, a healing restoration to guilt and grieving which helps the child understand and redirect its own drives and impulses. As Klein concludes:

> If love has not been smothered under resentment, grievances and hatred, but has been firmly established in the mind, trust in other people and belief in one's own goodness are like a rock which withstands the blows of circumstance. Then when unhappiness arises, the person whose development has followed lines such as these is capable of preserving in the self those good parents, whose love is an unfailing help in unhappiness, and can find once more in the outer world people who stand for them (Klein 1962, 116).

Arrested (Manic) Reparations

True reparation, the healing mechanism we hope will emerge in the infant's development, may not be achieved. Arrested reparations—what Klein refers to as manic reparations—appear instead. True reparation leads to deeper integration and motivation; manic reparation is based on denial and blocks subsequent growth. True reparation is composed of psychic realities; manic reparation is created out of fantasies of control, contempt, and vindictive triumph.

Manic reparation rises from guilt feelings that are too painful to integrate into restoration of the relationship, "the underlying guilt which manic reparation seeks to alleviate is, in fact, not relieved, and the reparation brings no lasting satisfaction. The objects that are being repaired are unconsciously and sometimes consciously treated with hatred and contempt and are invariably felt as ungrateful, and, at least unconsciously, are dreaded as potential persecutors" (Segal 1973, 96).

True reparation, rising out of psychic realities between infant and mother, allows the experiencing of real pain and grief and a genuine desire to reshape the inner world of love, hate, and guilt into a new unity and to respond to the external reality in bonding ways. But in manic reparations one does not experience the guilt or the loss. Instead, the contempt for the other deepens, the omnipotent control strategies continue, and the fantasies of vindictive triumph block the subject from moving toward the object. In adult manic episodes, reparations regress to this triumphal defeat of the other with blithe apology and ironic asides glossing over relational injuries with superficial ease. The injured party is left confused by the overtures that both approach and avoid, conciliate and dominate, yield and attack, accept and reject.

Manic forgiveness—the other side of the equation—offers a pseudo-reconciliation in an ultimately destructive flight above the relationship. Among its many forms, two are worthy of special note. Histrionic forgiveness, which dramatizes the alienation and the reconciliation into mythic proportions, exaggerates the wrong done, elevating the generosity shown. Inadvertently it says "I have judged you and found you lacking in the very qualities that I possess. Henceforth our relationship will be defined by my generosity in the face of your unworthiness and guilt." Such superior, veritcal forgiveness freezes the relationship into chronic indebtedness. The one-up forgiver may hold the one-down offender hostage forever (Augsburger 1981, 10–18).

Reaction-formation forgiveness, which is a reversal of desires for retaliation, functions as a defense against vengeful aggression. "I could just kill you for what you have done to me" is reversed to "I will love you perfectly and pretend I don't feel aggrieved over your behavior." In analysis of such inverse acceptance, R.C.A. Hunter notes "certain telltale cues in the clinical picture. First, there is an obtrusive and onerous quality to the forgiving so that one feels the need for protection against such righteousness. Secondly, the forgetting aspect is missing; rather, the patient seems to nurture the memory of the past. Thirdly, there can be about the forgiver a quality of smug virtue that rapidly cloys and, in the compromise, the hostility is readily sensed" (Hunter 1978, 197).

Authentic forgiveness, in contrast, is marked by a reconciliation in which there is movement by both parties toward each other, cessation of continuing animosity over the injury, and a reopening of the future in trust as each accepts both the good and bad parts of the self and the other.

Adult Mourning

In adult life, the disappearance of the loved object (person, place, or thing) evokes internal representations of the loss of a parental or a sibling figure. This reawakens the conflicts of the depressive position. The external loss of the loved object (the other person) and the anger, rage, and hate at the person who left threatens the good internal object (the unified esteemed self). The fracturing of the relationship causes fragmenting of the self.

Primitive depressive fears (self-reproach and self-devaluation) appear, followed by even more primitive paranoid fears (blaming, persecutory fears, projected rage), as one is pressed back to the third and then second position. Manic defenses may erupt—defensive control, contempt, and vindictive triumph—as the omnipotent fantasies of the earliest position rise to defend the sorely threatened self.

Grief is blocked as the fragmented self carries out these desperate defensive strategies seeking to regain its center, its balance, its unification. Only as the self regains its autonomous internal object (a unified esteemed core) can it let go of the lost other in reality testing and accepting. This return from paranoid splitting and manic defenses to the depressive position allows the person to work at central anxieties—the terror of loss, chronic pining for the return of the other, guilt for the absence. As the depressive position is reactivated, a solid sense of centered self (the good internal object) maintains safety and security in the inner world. The lost loved object is now internalized as a prized, accepted part of the self, as the "good parent," good sibling, or good friend. We find a place for our grief, and its paralysis is overcome, security is regained, and a unified self emerges once more.

In abnormal mourning, the paranoid split is intensified, overpowering emotions erupt in projections of rage and blame, or manic defenses explode in control, contempt, and triumph. Control attitudes are a denial of dependence; contempt feelings relieve the loss and guilt by seeing the other as unworthy of caring; vindictive triumph fantasizes a vengeful defeat of the other. All three defenses express omnipotent illusions of a solution through power over the other. As the internal center is fragmented, the external object is viewed ambivalently at best, and malevolently at its lowest point. Mourning is protracted, grief is debilitating. The person must unify the splitting, re-own the projections, and move into true depressive grief, pining, and eventual letting go.

In normal mourning of injuries, losses, or alienations, splitting is common, and even more common in popular ideas of "forgiveness." When forgiveness is split off from reconciliation, then the forgiver deals primarily with resentment within but ignores the alienation between. Self is cut off from relationship. In genuine mourning the goal of the grief work is both healing within and healing between.

The focus in examining reconciliation may be placed on the forgiven, the one making reparations; on the forgiving, the one extending grace; or on the relationship between the parties and their process of giving and receiving forgiveness. Any discussion of one of the three is part process, and in its own way continues part-object relations rather than whole-object relationship; thus reparation and reconciliation are aspects of one dynamic process. Making self-unity, making amends, and making peace go together.

The ability to be a whole person comes from mature experiencing of all three aspects. One must be able to deal with guilt, failure, and depression within—the bad objects introjected in childhood must be accepted and redirected if one is to receive forgiveness. One must be capable of dealing with rage, injury, and resentment toward the offender—the good objects (loving parent) incorporated in childhood must be experienced and expressed to extend forgiveness. Both of these processes are needed in both parties of an alienation.

The Creation of the Enemy

The *enemy* is constructed from denied and detested aspects of the self—the unacceptable bad objects within—which are combined with the undesirable perceptions in others. We combine our own evil with the evil perceived in the enemy. "You shall hate your enemy as you hate (those abhorrent aspects of) yourself."

In fear we move backward through our depressive capacities and, as the ground opens, we split good and bad apart. We have returned to the paranoid layer and a projection process begins in our defense. This process, which we know as paranoia, is a complex of emotional, mental, and social mechanisms which begins with a splitting of the "good self" (the consciously chosen identity) from the "bad self" (the unowned, unacceptable parts of the self). The split-off portion (the shadow) threatens to appear and trouble our fragile good-self image. Then, to our relief, an enemy appears who truly embodies and owns all the cruelty, hatred, greed, hostility, duplicity, or sadism we feared and, in our unguarded moments, felt. As we see these traits in the face of the foe, projections though they are, they disappear in the self. Anxiety and guilt, aided by selective perception and recall, now diminish and disappear.

What is impossible for the person in the paranoid position is the experience of equality, commonality, or any hint of mutuality. The very notion of equality and reciprocity is abhorrent to the paranoid mind (such would end the splitting defense). In paranoia, one must be either angrily and sadistically superior or masochistically inferior to the other; one must dominate, judge, and condemn or feel threatened, attacked, and injured by the enemy. In the depressive stage, and throughout adulthood, persons can be equal to one another, share responsibility for good and evil, and move toward mutually satisfactory solutions to differences and difficulties. In the paranoid layer, the infantile world, there are no equals. The giant (the parent) has the power and is therefore morally responsible and in failure is despicable for not eliminating the pain and evil. Paranoia, an attractive refuge of children, of victims, of those early abused, allows an escape from guilt and responsibility by projecting all power on the abuser or victimizer. Blame produces blame in a bond of hate that creates an adversarial symbiosis. The degree to which one blames one's parents is the degree to which one is still stuck in the family of origin, is still a child.

Consensual paranoia, the social system of selecting a common enemy and projecting our group shadow (the dark side of a whole nation) on a chosen race or people is a major theme in human history. The group constructs a common social reality of fear and hatred from sophisticated political, economic, moral, philosophical, educational, and profoundly religious beliefs. This compound social myth, upon encounter with the enemy, fractures along the highly predictable cleavage between what is virtuous, moral, noble, and just and what is vice, immoral, ignoble, and unjust.

Two paranoid groups, like two paranoid persons, create a shared delusion, a mutually interlocking system (a paranoia à deux). The irony is, in the death of mutuality and equality, a new reciprocity springs up. It is a process of two or more adversaries dumping their psychological wastes, their unconscious pollutants into each other's backyards. What we despise and disown in ourselves we attribute to them and contribute to their toxic pool. Our vice needs and feeds their versa. Enemies *need* each other, *use* each other to contain and dispose of toxic accumulations, and unconsciously *create* each other to sustain their safety and security (the status quo) without the pain of recognizing their own shadow.

The rhetoric, familiar to us all, is in simple, clearly split, we-they form. "We are righteous, we are innocent, we tell the truth, we inform; they are evil, they are culpable, they lie, they use propaganda. We act forcefully only to defend or deter; they act aggressively to attack or invade." "We are law abiding, we honor our treaties, we uphold the rule of international law; they are lawless, they break their agreements, they are without conscience or humanity. We stand for justice and human rights; they brutalize, tyrannize, exploit and violate human dignity" (Keen 1986, 130–38).

In these splits are revealed the bad objects that must be disowned and projected if we are to maintain our purity, our inviolability, our superiority. We begin to know ourselves as a people, just as we come to know ourselves as persons, when we allow ourselves to see the slightest similarities to those we oppose. Gradually we may mature enough to observe the realities of our common humanity and to recognize the bad objects within as well as without. We enter maturity when we can say, "We have met the enemy and they are us."

Adult Reparations

Maturity emerges as idealization is assimilated into the self, which reconciles the omnipotent or super-potent internal objects into an internal community of more benign co-travelers. The ogres and angels of childhood become the models and mentors of adulthood. The inner museum is enriched by the learnings gained and the patterns embraced from those admired and the cautions claimed and the prohibitions accepted against those despised.

In the depressive position, the process of idealization undergoes transformation, and the ideal objects (goods become gods) and the hated objects (evil objects become demons) have been internalized as perceived giants, both heroes and villains. As the self unifies and adjusts to reality, idealizations break down and the world—within and without—becomes more safe. One becomes free as the awareness grows that no one—neither self nor other—matches the ideal; no one is as perfect as we demand of them, nor is anyone quite as monstrous as we fear. They are human, nothing more; ordinary, not alien to or superior to my existence. Nothing in any other is truly foreign to me. As I come to see myself as ordinary, others as ordinary, and our life as a common human experience, realization, not idealization or demonization, guides my perceptions.

The capacity to forgive another's offenses is directly related to the ability to deal with one's inner offender. As a person learns to deal with the bad objects within, bad objects in others become less troublesome. The ability to deal with the internal is requisite to dealing with the external.

The mechanism of relationships, for Klein, is the reverse of Freud's sequence of identification leading to introjection and then producing projections. Klein saw introjection of the primal figures, the internalized parents, creating both good and bad internal objects before identification begins. Identification with the parent first, and then in wider circles, proceeds in a series of complex processes motivated by various anxieties (persecutory or depressive) as well as by longings, mergers, and desires. This sequence remains throughout life, as our ability to identify with others is tempered or trapped by our introjected objects. Unacceptable bad objects within are projected onto another who offends us and are seen as unforgivable. Having insufficient good objects within reduces one's capacity for empathy, understanding, and acceptance. (See figure 3.3.)

Repentance can be understood as a realistic encounter with one's own bad objects and/or authentic facing and dealing with the bad objects of another. In repenting, I acknowledge and redirect my own bad objects from destructive to constructive ends. In acknowledging others' repentance, I hear their admission of the presence of bad objects and join with them in standing against the destructive and for the constructive. Philosopher Joram Haber describes this process in parallel language.

> As I see it, the only acceptable reason to forgive a wrongdoer is that the wrongdoer has repented the wrong she did—has had a change of heart (metanoia) with respect to her wrongful action. By repenting, the wrongdoer repudiates the wrong that she did and vows not to repeat such wrongdoing again. This being so, we are then able to join her in resenting the very act from which she now stands separated, without compromising our self-respect. In the absence of repentance, forgiveness amounts to little more than condonation of wrongdoing (Haber 1991, 90).

Repentance is composed of two elements: regret or remorse over a past misdeed and the promise to refrain from future misdeeds. The regret must be perceived as genuine, and the promise sincere. The regret may be (1) only intellectual, the admission of a miscalculation or of misjudging the facts; (2) largely moral, the recognition that one has done wrong without owning that one had wronged someone in particular; or (3) other-oriented, recognizing where and when the wrongdoing has injured someone in particular (Golding 1984, 126–29). Repentance is regret and redirection, sorrow and change, attitude and action. It is accepting the bad within and turning the evil toward virtue.

Repentance is neither a comfortable nor a common behavior. Some see it as a morally worthless exercise in self-deception and intrapunitive

INTROJECTION

1. We introject both good (+) and bad (-) objects in infancy.

2. Identification is the product of introjection.

(-) Negative identifications of unforgiving rage

(+) Positive identifications in forgiving love

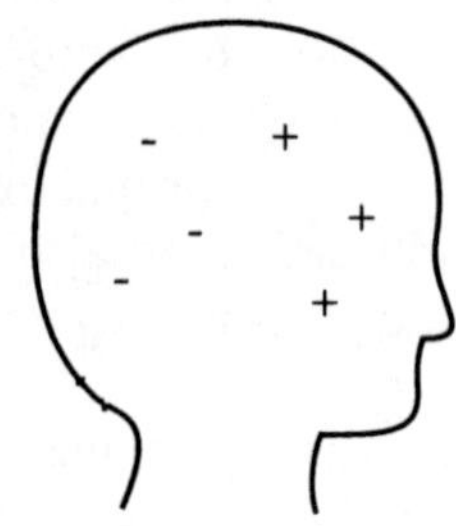

REJECTION

1. Unacceptable bad objects within . . . are projected onto the offender, who is seen as unforgivable.

2. Having insufficient good objects within . . . reduces the capacity for empathy, acceptance, understanding, sacrifice, and generosity.

The bad objects we have internalized can only be allowed into consciousness if it is felt safe to acknowledge them This requires

(1) A context that is accepting of the person in spite of the badness

(2) A context in which there is recognition of the presence of sufficiently good internal objects.

(3) A context that is forgiving:

a) It allows internal bad objects to become conscious.

b) It accepts their presence as a part of humanness.

c) It deals with objects by directing them to more constructive uses—identification in compassion.

Figure 3.3
External and Internal Forgiveness

abuse that deserves a bad reputation. When criticized as a backward-looking emotion, repentance is seen as a deceptive process of setting ourselves against a past reality and absurdly attempting to erase it from history. We repent our misdeeds, it is said, by confusing a negative memory image of the deed with the deed itself, feel remorse from the image, and punish the deed with the angry image. This bad conscience abuses the bad memory and punishes the bad self.

Klein offers a different understanding of the process. It is not self-deception; it is self-acknowledgment. It is not intrapunitive abuse; it is the recognition of bad internalized objects that can be disidentified, disarmed, and internally transformed. It is not a backward-looking process of opposition to a past reality; it is an inward-looking process of clarification of present realities. It does not seek to erase painful behavior from history; it changes the historical agent. It is not the result of splitting between two internal images, a negative memory image of wrongdoing/wrongdoer and an angry image who punishes deed and doer. This is manic reparation utilizing paranoid splitting. True reparation from a depressive position grieves the deed, without further injuring the doer, and changes the course of deeds by strengthening the doer.

Authentic repentance speaks from the self and for the self in exploration of the objectionable objects. It does not masquerade as pseudo-sympathy that is actually covert judgment. If a friend or lover says, "I'm very sorry that you are hurt," the offer is one of sympathy, not repentance or regret. If the other says, "What I did was wrong, I am sorry, you have every right to be hurt," the movement to repentance is clear. The first places the burden of change entirely on the one who is already injured; the second takes it upon the self. The first sees the other as projected bad object; the second deals with one's own inner museum.

Bad internal objects can be permitted to enter consciousness only if one feels safe in acknowledging them, and this requires a context that is hospitable to sharing both the good and the bad about oneself. In a context that is accepting of the person in spite of the badness, forgiveness is experienced. Forgiveness accepts the presence of bad objects as an inevitable part of humanness, and it deals with them by redirecting them from destructive/alienating uses toward constructive and bonding uses in compassionate identification with and understanding of others. Pastoral theologian David Atkinson writes:

> The capacity to forgive others is developed in an external environment which is forgiving and accepting. It is very important in Christian pastoral care that such an "external environment" is available to the consciousness of the believer from the fact that "God justifies the ungodly." It is part of our task as . . . congregations, to provide a "facilitating environment" in which we can help one another to understand and experience the forgiveness of God (Atkinson 1982, 21).

The pastoral counselor is a therapist functioning within a community—a context that can embody grace. When the community offers rejection and condemnation, it nurtures the internalization of harsh internal objects in its family units and its members. When the community is gracious in its response to frailty, clear in its confrontation of evil, and effective in maintaining its boundaries, it invites and supports the internalization of good objects. The forgiving community affirms its members as good objects and invites its members to experience and incorporate its reconciling processes within persons and to practice them between persons.

Grieving, Regrieving, and Forgetting

The third position in Klein's analysis of human development, the depressive position, requires the achievement of the capacity to mourn a loss, to grieve an injury, and to work through to healing. This important work—griefwork—is a lifelong task. With its cycles, spirals, or successive stages (it takes as many forms as there are grieving persons), griefwork is closely parallel to the many processes of forgiving. We might well speak of forgiving as forgrieving. In forgrieving we gradually forgo the anger at injury, the rage of betrayal, the resentment at duplicity, but without the aid of denial. Forgrieving refuses the shortcut to resolution that is offered by forgetting (the primary mechanism of denial) and intentionally remembers, returns to the loss, relives the event, retells the story as often as necessary until peace has been made at a level that permits the opening of the future.

Griefwork is a process of multiple journeys into memory. In grieving, one leaves the "here and now" and returns to the "there and then" because the emotional world has stopped its forward movement in frozen attachment to the ice-cold reality of loss. The many journeys backward—telling and retelling parts of the story—slowly thaws what has been frozen and at last melts the ice attachment. In griefwork, the speech is predominantly past tense, the stance is backward, until the bond with the loss breaks. The sudden appearance of future-tense verbs is familiar to grief counselors as the sign of turning outward, turning forward, returning to life.

Forgrieving, in parallel process, requires this revisiting of the past, reworking of the injury, and rebuilding of the loss through reframing and reinterpreting its meanings (see figure 3.4).

This process of forgrieving occurs at different depths for different persons. Some, through a long-accustomed and often spiritually phrased denial, may make an immediate resolution and a friendly reconnection; others work through an individual unilateral forgiveness that places them on the moral high ground as the forgiving one; still others find they must face the loss with deep pain, anger, resentment, rage, and walk through the hell gates of suffering called Gethsemane. They emerge only after the offended and offender have met at some appropriate level—or what level is possible—and constructive relating is attempted or perhaps restored.

For those who enter the Gethsemane of grief, and find that, for whatever reason, the offender is inaccessible (possible reasons are many—death,

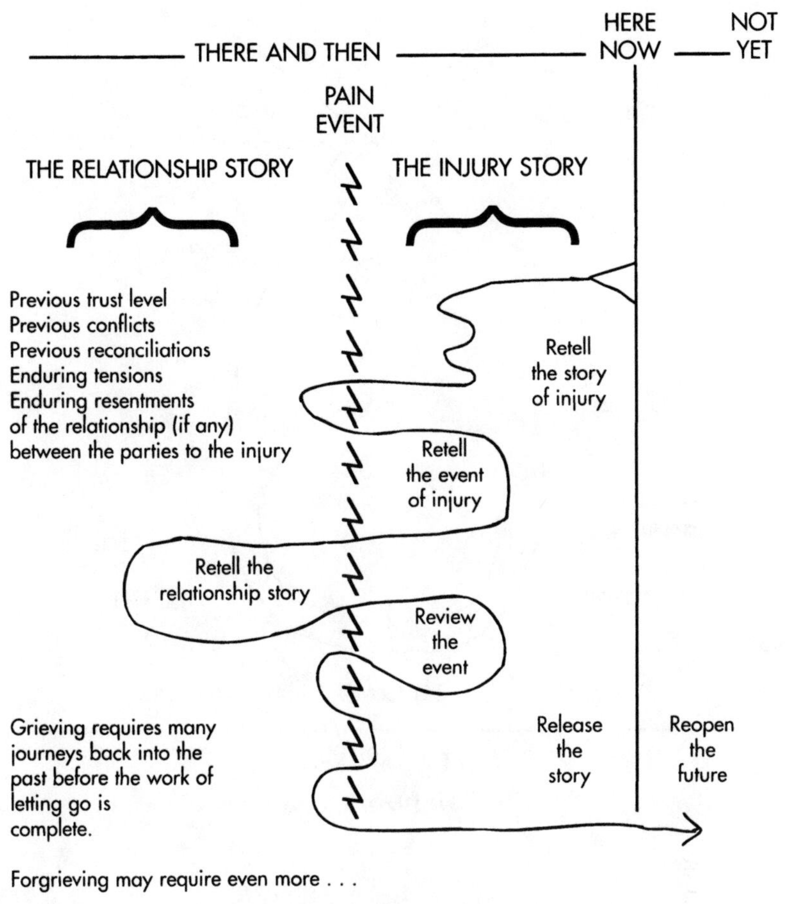

Figure 3.4
Grieving and Forgrieving

paranoid withdrawal, sociopathic unconcern, phobic flight, or ascension into some haven of righteous superiority), the option is to grieve fully, unilaterally, to an individual release. Grief, undistorted, follows its own line of development from the shock of "Oh no!" through the pain, anger, blaming, guilt, rage, brooding, withdrawal, and resentment to the depths, the crisis, of realities. This enables one to let go in resignation and reach out in acceptance, risk, and trust, until one emerges from the cyclical process to say, "Ah ha!" in realization of its meaning for the future. This movement is no unimpeded somersault through immersion in suffering; rather, it is a slow spiral of movement that doubles back upon itself, returning to earlier

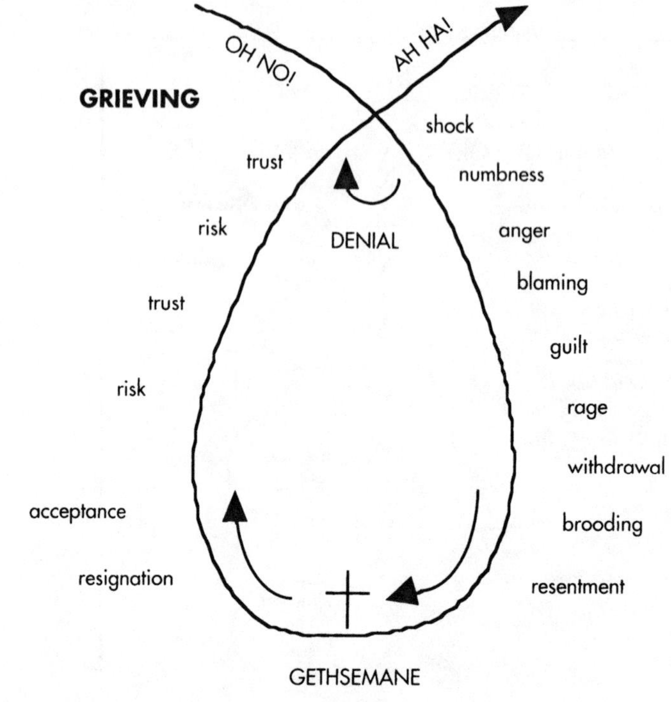

Figure 3.5
The Griefwork Loop

emotional confusion until, in Gethsemane, the ambivalencies of the soul at last join hands. "O my God, if it be possible, let this pass from me. Nevertheless, not as I will but as you will." The irreconcilable reconciles, the unacceptable nears acceptance, the unbearable is at last borne.

A diagram of griefwork (figure 3.5) shows this journey into the depths. It also shows the quick turnaround, the instant about-face, of denial. Why pursue the pain when one can leap from the "Oh no!" to the "Ah ha!" in advance? In twelve-step language, why struggle with all twelve steps of change when one can leap from step one, admitting powerlessness, to step twelve, helping others, and avoid the hard work that lies between?

Forgiving follows a cycle similar to that of grief (see figure 3.6). From the "Oh no" of injury to the "Ah ha" of insight, the offended person also descends into the depths of pain. Betrayal, injury, and loss must be faced before healing can occur. The descent into profound emotion—anger, resentment, and rage—provokes withdrawal. Rarely does the offended re-

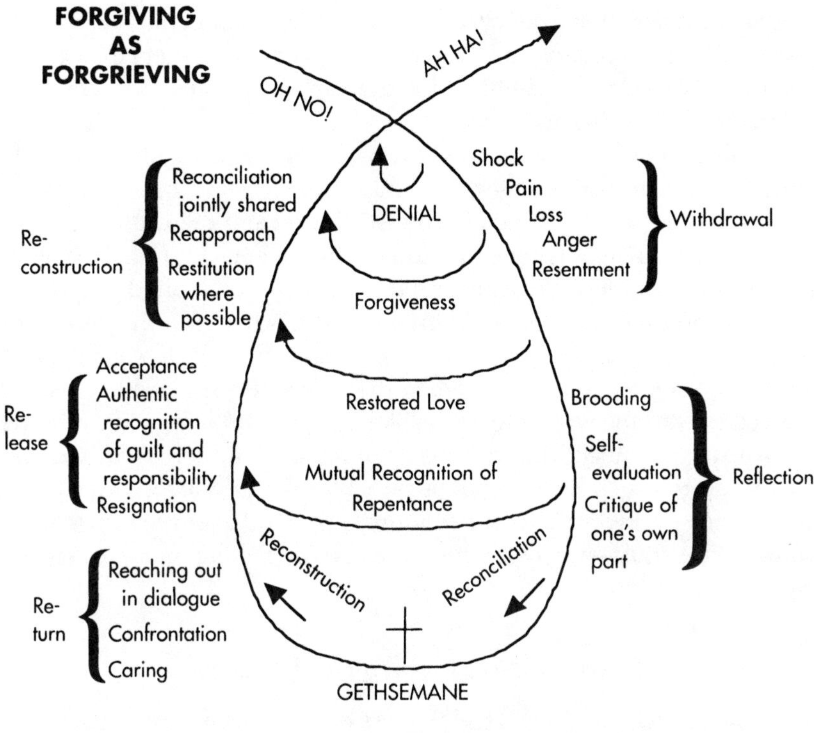

Figure 3.6
Forgiving as Forgrieving

main in contact with the offender or the offense during this stage. The intensity of the pain must be experienced and, in withdrawal, explored. A time of withdrawal, for days or for months, allows the person time, space, distance, and perspective to see the situation more fully, clearly, dispassionately. Brooding, which blossoms into self-evaluation, can lead to a critique of one's own part in the pain and to recognition of how one has passively permitted or actively participated in the alienation or injury. Slowly one claims ownership for one's own portion, and comes to terms with the reality of the other's choices. Anger and grief, rage and resignation meet in the Gethsemane of protest and the surrender of lament and release. The return to contact, to dialogue, to confrontation with caring moves one toward release and eventual acceptance. All this describes the journey into the depths of the hurt. Not many persons walk this lonely path of suffering through to a new possibility (see figure 3.6).

One may, as in the grief cycle, take the shortcut of denial. Or one may spiritualize the avoidance process in a "forgiveness" of piety that seals off the wound and claims insight and understanding by sheer force of will or a decision to "forgive and forget."

The deeper steps—restoring of love, the mutual recognition of repentance by one or both parties, and the reconstruction of some level of trust—all call for the ending of self-justification and the choosing of conversation with person(s) one previously saw as beneath human relationship. It is painful to restore perceptions of love, but wrongdoing is not a valid reason for ending love. When the hurt lies between the parties, not simply at one doorstep, it is excruciatingly hard to move toward the other with some step of repentance when the ratios of responsibility seem so skewed toward the wrongdoer; it is like dying and waiting to be reborn to reconstruct, reconnect, and resume open relationship across the chasm of an offense, yet such resurrection is possible. The journey into the depths is a journey backward into our common story and a journey inward into our separate souls—the two dimensions of forgrieving injury, or regrieving loss.

Toward a New Paradigm of Forgiveness

1. The capacity to grieve, feel the loss of relationship, and make reparations to those we have injured is learned early, and rooted deeply in childhood development. It is essential to our humanness and progressive in maturation.
2. The movement from the paranoid position (when hate, rage, blaming, and judgment are used to cope with frustration) to the depressive position (when grieving and regret lead to reparations and reconciliation) is the crucial passage of childhood and the ongoing challenge of adulthood. In stress, we all regress. But regression only to the depressive level, not to the paranoid level, is evidence of maturing.
3. Adult reparations and adult mourning are possible when the objects within (both good and bad internalized identifications) are accepted; then others who act evilly (external bad objects) can be seen with empathy and compassion.

4

The Roots of Rage and Resentment

Forgiveness is our surprised recognition of another's resemblance to ourselves

Forgiveness is not something we do,
It is something we discover.

—John Patton

In an age when forgiving oneself
  is the primary virtue,
Forgiving another
  is an act of unfaithfulness
  to one's beloved

In the great American novel *Moby-Dick,* Ahab, the mad captain of the whaling vessel, the *Pequod,* offers us a vision of hatred and revenge in their most passionate forms. Ahab has long pursued throughout the vast southern ocean a white whale of incomparable ferocity, size, and cunning. The monster has not only baffled and outwitted him but has destroyed his boats and stores and at last renders a fearful mutilation, tearing off with its terrifying jaws the old captain's leg. Ahab, totally consumed by a burning urge for revenge, at last encounters the whale Moby-Dick. The fierce combats end on the third day's chase with the death of the old captain, all his crew, and the sinking of the *Pequod.* Only one survivor, the narrator Ishmael, lives to tell the tale of consuming hatred.

Ahab's wound, the lost leg, has driven him to a monomaniacal desire to revenge himself on the whale.

> It is not probable that this monomania in him took its instant rise at the precise time of his bodily dismemberment. Then, in darting at the monster, knife in hand, he had but given loose to a sudden, passionate, corporal animosity; and when he received the stroke that tore him, he probably felt the agonizing bodily laceration, but nothing more. Yet, when by this collision forced to turn home, and for long months of days and weeks, Ahab and anguish lay stretched together in one hammock; round in mid-winter that dreary Patagonian Cape; then it was, that his torn body and

> gashed soul bled into one another; and so interfusing, made him mad (Melville 1922, 230).

When at last his raving ceased "and his mates thanked God that the direful madness was now gone, Ahab, in his hidden self, raved on. Human madness is oftentimes a cunning and most feline thing. When you think it fled, it may have but become transfigured into some still subtler form" (231). So Ahab's full lunacy "did not subside, it deepeningly contracted," Melville writes. "The mad secret of his unabated rage bolted up and keyed in him. . . . He was intent on an audacious, immitigable, and supernatural revenge." And the crew of the *Pequod,* "by some infernal fatality" were swept up in his monomaniacal revenge. "The subterranean miner that works in us all, how can one tell whither leads his shaft by the ever shifting, muffled sound of his pick?" (233).

Ahab, the tragic tormented hero, consumed by his rage, allows "his torn body and gashed soul" to bleed into one another. Conscious and unconscious interpenetrate to create not wholeness but madness.

When Starbuck, the mate, says, "Vengeance on a dumb brute that simply smote thee from blindest instinct? Madness! To be enraged with a dumb thing seems blasphemous," Ahab replies: "I see in him outrageous strength with inscrutable malice sinewing it. That inscrutable thing is chiefly what I hate. . . . I will wreak that hate upon him. Talk not to me of blasphemy, man; I'd strike the sun if it insulted me" (Melville 1922, 204).

The genius of Melville's characters, rich, multiform and multilayered, is woven together by multiple themes, and the central strand is primal archaic rage. Heinz Kohut, whose work we shall explore in this chapter, has commented: "Captain Ahab is in the grip of interminable narcissistic rage. Moby-Dick is the greatest rendition of the revenge motif, . . . of the insatiable search for revenge after a narcissistic injury" (Kohut 1974, 362).

What is it about certain injuries to the self that makes recovery so slow and painful? Why is it that specific insults to the self strike so deeply that a profound rage is stirred in the depths and refuses to be assuaged by apology or healed by time? When is it that these vulnerabilities to rejection or devaluation form deep within our psyches? How shall we understand the need for revenge that can grip the soul, stifle the heart, and silence all impulses toward reconciliation or forgiveness?

Kohut and Narcissistic Development

Heinz Kohut, in his analysis of the self, offers us another paradigm to sharpen our perspective on how healing of the deeper injuries of the self takes place or finds no place within us. He begins his explorations with several basic understandings. First, the norm for the human being is not independence but *empathic relationship.* The infant needs the empathic response of others in the first few months of life so that the budding self is adequately formed and structured. This need for empathy is never outgrown. The adult needs similar empathy throughout life to be emotionally nourished. Understanding and being understood are the undergirding on which we stand as emerging, developing, maturing selves. Self needs other. A mature self is not only a subject, it remains an object, an object of important subjects who give empathy and understanding.

The idea of total autonomy is not the goal of growth, the measure of maturity, or the process of therapy, Kohut argues in *How Does Analysis Cure?* "The healthy self always needs the sustaining response of self-objects from the first to the last breath" (Kohut 1984, 69). These self-objects include, in Kohut's view, the earliest objects (the parents), the many co-travelers through life (empathic others), and the final refuge (God).

Second, to become a human being, a person internalizes significant others. This hungry search for the other is profoundly expressive of our relational nature. If the person is not successful in finding and incorporating significant others in a healthy way, pathology results. The self needs to incorporate subjects—empathic, understanding subjects—who offer the recognition, validation, and affirmation necessary in forming one's core. These subjects become the recipients of transference—they become "self-objects" within the child. If the person experiences the subjects in the surrounding world as unavailable, nonempathic, and withholding understanding, the hungry self develops voracious narcissistic needs. When the rejection is extreme, the compensation for it by the empty self is also extreme. The unfulfilled needs leave gaps in the formation of the self, missing pieces in the self-structure.

Third, the person has two primary needs: mirroring by the empathic person and idealizing of the significant other. Mirroring is associated with the need for recognition and response—recognition by the significant other and response with joy to that reflection. Kohut refers to this as gleam, the sparkle in the eye of the empathic valuing person which mirrors the child's exhibitionistic display. As the child learns to elicit gleam, to draw out the admiration and excitement of the parent, it realizes its power to evoke gleam as well as basks in the warmth and approval. The mother first participates in the child's narcissistic play to offer gleam, then gradually increases selectivity to channel these impulses into realistic directions (Kohut 1978, 489). Idealizing is based on our human need to feel a part of a power greater than ourselves, to admire and to idolize it as beautiful, great, good, and potent. Both mirroring and idealization are grandiose in their early stages and later become realistic in dimension.

The child's original narcissistic bliss is inevitably disturbed by parental shortcomings so the child assigns these primal self-evaluative feelings to (1) a grandiose and exhibitionistic image (the narcissistic self); and (2) an idealized parent image—an imaginary, totally loving, all-powerful parent. Both of these archaic figures are gradually integrated into the adult self. The grandiosity is tamed and transformed into adult ambitions and purposes; the idealized parent becomes guiding values. If these two needs/processes do not go well, the grandiose self, with its exaggerated expectations from the idealized persons, its pretensions to entitlements, its inflated ideas of its own importance, abilities, and power, begins to come apart. When others do not respond with the expected mirroring, approval, and admiration for the "boundless exhibitionism of the grandiose self" then shame results.

Kohut offers two views of the self: on the one hand, as the center of its own psychological universe; on the other, as part of the total mental apparatus. In the first sense, the self has its own functions—that is, the regulation of self-esteem through actualizing ambitions and ideals in reality. The self has its own development—aided by the mother's mirroring and the father's idealizing function—and its own pathology in the failures of these two functions.

The mother's failure in mirroring arises from her lack of empathy for the child's grandiose exhibitionistic self. She is unable to understand or respond due to her own narcissism or depression or a psychotic state. It may be a specific emotional withdrawal because this specific child frustrates or interrupts the projections she is placing on the infant as an object essential in maintaining her own intrapsychic equilibrium. So her empathy may be flat or faulty or grossly amiss in its interpretations. The father's failure is a failure to connect with the child's emerging capacity to idealize, to encourage purposefulness and the creation of ambitions, dreams, and hopes that will risk moving out of the safe mothering matrix toward some goal. So the child has no effective mirror, no attractive goal.

Fourth, narcissism—the self over-concerned with itself—is the self's attempt to substitute self-indulgent self-care for the appropriate care by a significant other which is absent or woefully inadequate. The self-centered behavior of the narcissist arises from too little self-esteem and self-valuation, not from too much. It is the impoverished self that hungrily grasps for attention and affirmation (no matter how smoothly presented or artfully expressed).

Alongside the physical developmental cycle, or the cognitive stages of development, or the phases of moral or social development, there is a narcissistic developmental line of growth. From its earliest primitive moves to capture the gleam of the mother's eye to the most mature adaptive forms of self-valuation, the narcissistic developmental process flows from early dependency to adult interdependence. The infant needs for approval and affirmation mature into the adult needs for mutual recognition and valuation that consistently reflect the realities of life, role, and relationships.

Severely arrested development and stunted growth in self-esteem and narcissistic integrity leave the child with an internal chaos of archaic infantile emotional needs and with a grandiose view of the self and a merciless pursuit of its ideal image. These tyrants within become the pretentious structures that conceal the frightened shameful little self hiding behind a grandiose facade.

A normal, healthy self-structure develops within the child when its needs are not instantly and fully met and the frustration is sufficient to create inner conflict. This unsatisfactory state presses the child to introject something of the significant other to create internal balance. So the mother and/or father contribute to the formation of the superego and the ego ideal. Good parenting, like good therapy, offers optimum, not minimum frustration. The counselee must be frustrated enough to internalize the needed part from the self-other, but not frustrated so severely that the person retreats or denies relatedness. The self grows and develops balanced structures when an empathic relationship allows it to experience frustration and the shame and rage it evokes without either denying it or distancing itself from its pain.

If rejection is not severe and unrelenting, the self can endure the sanctions and maintain the relationship while coming to a realistic evaluation of self and self-other. When the rejection is severe and continuing, the grandiose reaction of "I don't need anyone else" continues the egocentric structure of early childhood grandiosity, and the idealized self is a continuation of a projected self-other (no internalization of a reality figure). Injuries to these archaic self-structures are exaggerated in significance, overdrawn in their impact, and receive an overreactive rage.

The person may split horizontally, through repression that cuts off awareness and drives the archaic grandiose self into the unconscious, or the person may split vertically in denial of the grandiose pretensions (see figure 4.1). In maturing, the ego becomes aware of the repressed and previously unconscious grandiosity and recognizes the grandiose narcissistic rage that erupts in substitute forms (the horizontal splitting is diminished); or the ego learns to understand and accept the disavowed and denied grandiose self and its propensity toward rage so that the narcissistic rage is gradually transformed into mature aggression.

There are two key consequences of the lack of integration of the grandiose self and the idealized parent imago. In the first, the adult person's functioning and personality are impoverished because the self is deprived

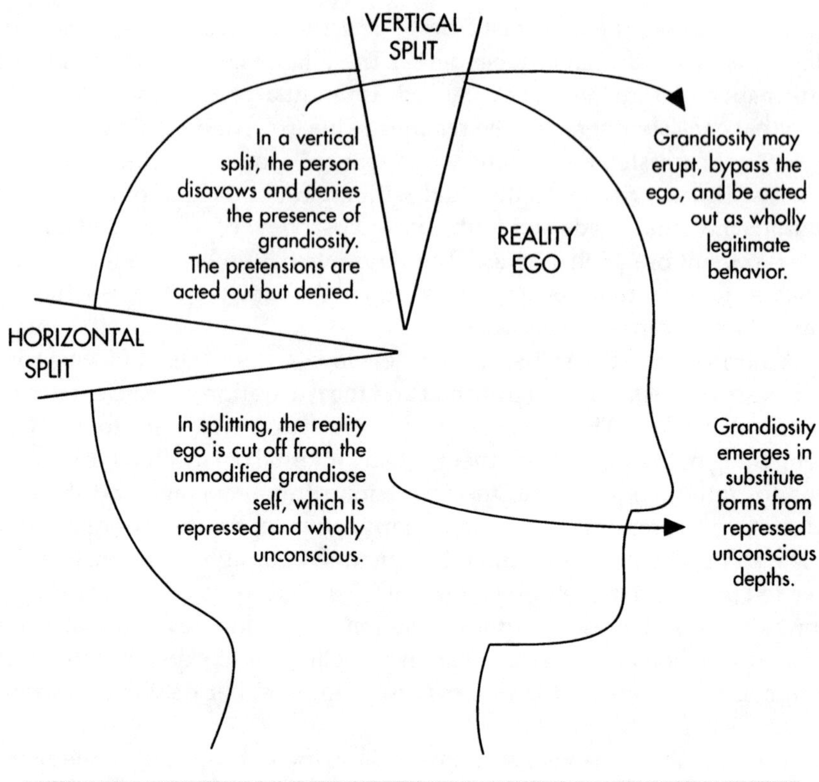

VERTICAL SPLIT
In a vertical split, the person disavows and denies the presence of grandiosity. The pretensions are acted out but denied.
Grandiosity may erupt, bypass the ego, and be acted out as wholly legitimate behavior.
REALITY EGO
HORIZONTAL SPLIT
In splitting, the reality ego is cut off from the unmodified grandiose self, which is repressed and wholly unconscious.
Grandiosity emerges in substitute forms from repressed unconscious depths.

Figure 4.1
Vertical and Horizontal Splitting

of energy that is invested in and sapped by the archaic structures. In the second, the adult personality and its functioning are hampered by the eruption or the intrusion of the archaic claims of the archaic structures. These old structures that refuse integration are either repressed (by horizontal splitting between awareness and unawareness) or disavowed (by vertical splitting in denial, disowning, or self-rejection) but they quickly appear in threat situations or in the safe emergency of therapy.

The horizontal split that conceals the grandiose self with its bizarre demands may drive one relentlessly into braggadocio, lying, name dropping, posturing, or pretensions that live up to the expectations of the grandiose self. The person may act out in dangerous or self-destructive ways that obey the convictions of omnipotence or grandiosity. The inflation of the self impairs all love relationships. Only as the person becomes more firm in the sense of self can there be an expansion of empathy and affection for the love object. As the person becomes more secure in identity and acceptability he or she is able to sustain intimacy with integrity. As splitting is reduced or rejoined, the capacities for empathy increase.

The Essential Empathy

Empathy, in Kohut's unique definition , is the modality of healing; it is a corrective emotional experience that offers care and cure. It is curative, not simply communicative. It offers both affirmation and confirmation; it affirms the other in nurturance and confirms the other in guidance by modeling what a mature, caring human being can be and become. The goal of empathy is not to remove the person's problems, but to go beneath them and strengthen the person, to support the growth of a more functional self, to facilitate the movement toward maturation. It is not simply a love cure, but is a caring understanding that offers the insight that heals, given in the empathy that cures.

Empathy is a disciplined intuitive understanding of another's experience that offers two crucial things: a clear and accurate understanding of another, and an available and assimilable model of the self-understanding person. The empathic experience is the interaction with both another's empathy and the other's empathic model of selfhood. In therapy, the therapist offers a model of the caring human person in a profound and authentic experience of relationship. In this empathic encounter of humanness, the narcissistic person makes contact with realistic, useful, mature experience of and information about selfhood, another self, and the self. All three of these are assimilated into the narcissistic matrix. The experience is both emotional and rational, both corrective and normative, both nurturant and transformative. It affirms and informs. It gives affirmation and confirmation to the hungry and needy narcissistic self.

Empathy is "the mode by which one gathers psychological data about other people and, when they say what they think and feel, imagines their inner experience even though it is not open to direct observation" (Kohut 1978, 450). This exhaustive empathic comprehension, which focuses intensively on the other's experience with an evenly suspended attention over an extended period of time, seeks to achieve a cognitive and affective resonance between two selves. It is not a direct process of inspection and information gathering; rather, it is a cautious and considered judgment that what is felt, seen, and thought by the counselor corresponds by and large with what the counselee feels, sees, thinks, and experiences both consciously and unconsciously.

Empathy is an early acquisition that is crucial to the capacity to forgive. The ability to feel with another is rooted in early infant periods of development. On the development axis of narcissism, which each person must complete, the mature transformation of one's early narcissism into a socially beneficial empathy provides the base for forgiveness. Empathy creates an emotional foundation that develops into a cognitive capacity to take the perspective of another, to assume a truly social position. A lack of empathy, characteristic of an arrested narcissistic personality disorder, renders forgiveness of injuries extremely difficult.

Genuine forgiveness requires an internal capacity for empathy with parts of oneself that are less than perfect, and an external empathy that accepts one's commonality with the imperfections of others. The result of empathic forgiving in community is the establishment of an empathic milieu. Such a context is necessary for authentic human existence; it is necessary for healthy society, a prerequisite in working for world peace (Kohut 1978, 707).

For Kohut, the importance of empathy in human life is in its threefold gift: one, the recognition of the self in the other; two, the expansion of the self to include the other; three, the accepting, confirming, and understanding human echo evoked by the self. The first, seeing the self of the other, is the indispensable tool of observation, insight, and understanding; the second, expanding the self to include the other, creates a powerful psychological bond between individuals; the third, accepting and confirming, is psychologically nutrient at all stages of human life (Kohut 1978, 705). All three of these serve to diminish rage, to increase bonding, to nurture growth. These are the essential components of forgiveness: to see the other as a distinct self; to expand the self to include the other as human, as a co-traveler, as a fellow sufferer; and to affirm, confirm, and understand our human coexistence in community.

Narcissistic Injury, Narcissistic Rage

When injury strikes the self, the injury to the core of the person, to the essential formula of selfhood—image, value, self-respect—is a deep narcissistic wound.

Everyone tends to react to narcissistic injuries with embarrassment and anger, but intense shame and violent rage well up in those who are gripped by an indispensable need for absolute control over an archaic inner environment. For them, self-esteem is only possible when an approving, mirroring, admiring self-object is unconditionally available within them or there is an ever-present opportunity for a merger with an idealized self-object. No shame, no imperfection, no failure dare be admitted within; pure rage, pure contempt, pure vindication through a vindictive

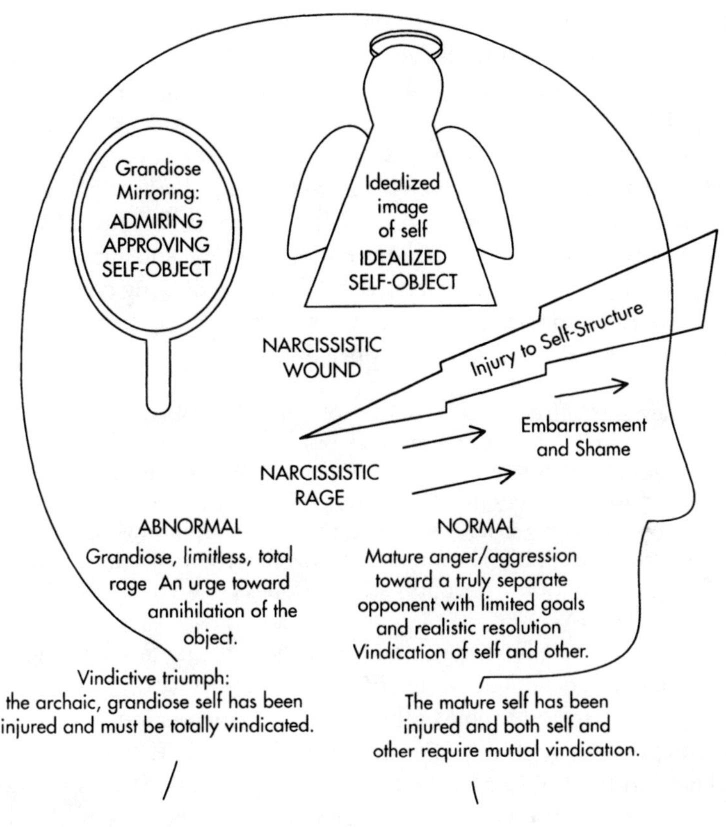

Figure 4.2
Narcissistic Wound and Rage

triumph is required. All of these forces are needed to retain the grandiose mirror on the wall of the soul ("Mirror, mirror, on the wall, who is fairest of them all?") and a beautiful ideal in the shrine of the soul (see figure 4.2).

When injured, rage is "mobilized by the archaic grandiose self" and "is deployed within the framework of an archaic perception of reality," Kohut argues. So an injury or a setback is not seen with mature anger and aggression toward a real, distinct, separate opponent. Mature anger has a clear and specific target; it is not limitless. It requires that the opponent be blotted out, the evidence of the shame be wiped out, so that the grandiose mirroring is confirmed, the fusion with the ideal self complete and satisfying. "The enemy, however, who calls forth the archaic rage of the narcissistically vulnerable is seen by him [her] not as an autonomous source of impulsions, but as a flaw in a narcissistically perceived reality . . . a recalcitrant part of an expanded self over which he [she] expects to exercise full control and whose mere independence or otherness is an offense" (Kohut 1974, 385–86).

This narcissistic rage is simply one color—black revenge—on a whole spectrum of rage experiences. There are red impulsive anger, purple collected resentments, and white deadly hatred, to name a few of the continuum of aggression with its "common metaphysical substance." Narcissistic rage can be identified as such from its self-threatening character, which issues in a need for revenge, for redressing the wrong or undoing the injury by any possible means as an unrelenting compulsion.

> When the selfobject fails to live up to absolute obedience expectations, narcissistic rage appears, characterized by no empathy whatsoever for the offender. The ego functions only as a tool and rationalizer for the attainment of revenge. Chronic narcissistic rage is even more dangerous, as secondary process thinking gets pulled into the archaic aggression and the ego attributes all failure to the malevolence of the uncooperative selfobject (Chessick 1985, 137).

Narcissistic rage, whether an acute angry outburst or an unrelenting resentment with chronic attitudes of unforgiving hostility, follows the experience of disappointment in the self-object (the person who is invested with the person's archaic dependency projections). This reveals a crucial weakness in the nuclear self, which can only sustain itself by a relationship to external self-objects for soothing or idealization. "You did not mirror my importance, brilliance, performance," the anger shouts, or "You have fallen short of my ideals, betrayed my demands, revealed your humanity and fallibility."

The loss of the self-object is a blow to the nuclear self, which then erupts in rage. The capacity for empathy and the ability to desire forgiveness are totally unavailable to the person.

Rage and Shame

Shame is a central process in human selfhood. It is necessary to social and moral development as well as to the narcissistic development of the self. Shame is central to the self-recognition, self-structuring, and self-regulating processes of the mature personality. It guides us in rightly relating self to self-other and then to those who are truly seen as other. It is a central part in all repair of relationships—in reparation, repentance, and reconciliation. Or an injury may expose the self to its own immature totalistic shame processes, which reveal the grandiose demands on the self and its exaggerated shame before an unassimilated ideal and harsh unrealistic inner structures. Shame is a normal, healthful, necessary inner control function that prompts us to discern, choose, and care about what is good; shame can be abnormal, unhealthy, and dysfunctional when it is overcharged, underdeveloped, out of control, or beyond rational limits.

The "shame-prone," Kohut observes, are those who suffered devastating experiences of shame during the self-formative period of life. They respond to potentially shame-provoking threat situations by seeking to inflict or imagining they are inflicting those narcissistic injuries they are terrified of suffering in themselves. The other is not a person, the villain is an error, a blip on the screen of realities which the enraged person must vaporize in a world that must be under total control in order to balance one's expanded grandiose set. The player has expanded to create a world that, as in a computer game, can zap and erase the offensive particles at will. There is a total lack of empathy, an unmodifiable wish to blot out the offense against the grandiose self, an unforgiving fury that is out of all proportion to the minor irritant (Kohut 1974, 387).

This defense against shame combines rage, power, and righteousness: *rage* in the intense barrage of demands coupled with the energy of frustration; *power* in its fantasies of omnipotence; and *righteousness* with its claims of total ownership of the moral high ground.

> Defending strategies such as contempt, blaming, rage or perfectionism are acquired principally in an attempt to cope with externally based sources of shame . . . [as a] means of defending oneself in, and thereby adapting oneself to, outer reality. . . . Alternatively, certain defenses may later become directed inward and aimed at the very self of the defending individual. For instance, rage, contempt and blame can be so turned against the self (Kaufman 1985, 86–87).

Kaufman's analysis of shame before others (in the area of the external world) or shame before the inner ideal turned contemptuous, angry, and blaming, reveals how its malignancy blocks reparations. The no-holds-barred defense of a fragile self does not allow for vulnerability, for risking a rapprochement, for repentance and the admission of failure. Instead, rigid defenses protect the core self and make empathy with the other's pain or understanding of their offer of reconciliation virtually impossible. Rigid defenses distort relationships with others and failure follows failure in communication and trust formation. Reconciliation is ruled out.

> The kind of failure which is most critical here involves some severing of the interpersonal bridge such that trusting once more those we depended upon has become blocked. Failure in a relationship

> can be transcended when the one depended upon can honestly own his part in activating shame, his imperfect humanness, *and* can enable the other to *feel* genuinely understood. In this way trust, and hence the relationship, become eventually restored. Through such restoring of this vital, interpersonal bridge, which provides the needed experience of identification, shame is indeed transcended (Kaufman 1985, 87).

Rage and Righteousness

An unmistakable sign of shame-prone defenses is the need to be right, so right that one possesses unassailable righteousness. Grandiose claims to one's goodness coupled with identifications with idealized self-objects can create a righteous avenging or angelic pretending self who needs to be perfect or faultless with neither spot nor blemish. The claim to moral superiority, impunity, or wounded innocence can be so profoundly satisfying to the self that any rapprochement is utterly unattractive. Forgiveness is difficult for anyone who has claimed the high moral ground. The feeling of "good me" alleviates the shame of "bad me," and certainty of one's own righteousness vis-à-vis the other's evil makes one safe and unassailable.

One may claim the righteous role by *blaming* others, circumstances, or events. The degree to which one places the blame internally or externally is crucial. Righteous blame turned outward gives one the satisfaction of being judge and jury; turned inward, it offers condemnation.

One may take the righteous stance of *perfection* as a strategy for rising above shame, to claim the expansive solution to any doubts about one's self-worth or superior standing.

One may assume a righteous position out of *innocence* and simplicity. The childlike purity, which in the artist or poet is revelatory and profound, in the adult-child is saintly naïveté.

One may leap to a righteous vantage point in *rage*. Intense anger—the grandiosity of omnipotence—and the idealized view of self (the ideal parental image with divine pretensions) join in a holy wrath, a virtuous vengeance, or a deeply religious revenge. Righteous *religiosity* can provide a rationale and ritual for working out anger with unquestionable justifications.

Rage, religiosity, perfectionism, innocence, or blaming, or multiple combinations of these strategies, can forestall any recognition of the realities that have blocked or broken the interpersonal bridge.

Healing for the narcissistically arrested is not an immediate, short-term intervention process. It is an extended journey of growth in the core self which demands empathy, much modeling, and patience with the person's own pace. Although there is a natural human striving to become an adequately structured and functioning self, Kohut argues, when this striving is frustrated to the point that the person must turn for help, it is a deep insult to the psyche. No one, ultimately, wants to receive help; it is far more blessed to give help than to receive it. The treatment process offends anyone's pride, but especially the narcissistically wounded. It contradicts the fantasy of independence and triggers rage at feeling dependent as well as shame at being found out.

Therapy, according to Kohut, progresses as we explore the person's concern with these conflicts within the self, the sense of being injured, shamed, and therefore vulnerable. As the person relaxes the over control (no need to achieve the idealized self), reduces the pretensions and posturing (no need to perpetuate the grandiosity), and reconstructs a reality orientation that accepts the self as less than godlike and others as more than demonic, shame is diminished. The goal is to assist the person in talking about and experiencing this shame within the caring context of an empathic relationship. Gradually a more realistic and related self is substituted for the grandiose self that was created to hide or deny the shame. As an adequately structured self functions with freedom and balance, the person can accept the self, release the rage at the old projected self-other, and come to accept the other as truly other. Acceptance and forgiveness go hand in hand; in fact, they are two aspects of the same reality.

Fury and Forgiveness

Forgiveness, for one overwhelmed by narcissistic fury, is not a direct possibility. It is not achieved by any appeal to the will to impose impulse control, to the conscience to evoke moral restraints, or to the ego to release demands. Forgiveness is an indirect process resulting from a change in the matrix of narcissism that drives the anger. Healing comes not from removing the defense but by moving close to the defender. As the therapist enters into an empathic depth with the defensive person, a strengthening of the self occurs which allows the grandiose pretensions and ambitions to diminish, and the model of the therapist's "maturely modulated aggressions will be employed in the service of a securely established self and in the service of cherished values. The relinquishment of narcissistic claims—the precondition for the subsidence of narcissistic rage—is, however, not absolute. . . . Narcissism need not be destroyed, but it can be transformed" (Kohut 1974, 388).

The key insight Kohut offers us is that narcissism "neither should—nor indeed could—be relinquished." Narcissistic rage is a sign that the developmental process is arrested, and the narcissistic matrix from which the rage arises needs transformation. Deep change is facilitated by empathy and patient understanding in an emotionally secure and significant relationship where the flaws of past relationships can be healed and the impoverished self nourished.

Rage rises from deep injuries to the self. One does not resolve it by ventilation or escape it by the various forms of suppression. Ritual does not fix it; religious belief may assist in its movement toward healing or it may complicate and distort the process further.

In his very helpful reflections on Kohut and forgiveness John Patton comments on the tendency of religions to expect the announcement of God's forgiveness to enable human forgiveness.

> If we are forgiven, then we should be forgiving. This may be true—and in many ways I believe it is—but human beings have significant capacities for avoiding that truth. They simply are not what they ought to be, nor do they do what they should in spite of impressive religious announcements and expectations. Undoubtedly the announcement of forgiveness is important, but the schedule upon which that announcement is apprehended by the forgiven one remains highly unpredictable. Kohut's view of narcissistic rage is another reminder for us to take human recalcitrance seriously. (Patton 1985, 72).

The actual reasons for giving forgiveness are many, and most are tactical, practical, personal, but not moral.

We may forgive for old times' sake, out of loyalty to past friendship, for what the other once was, out of sentimentality.

We may forgive to regain past security in relationship—to restore marital harmony, to spare the children, to save face in the family system.

We may forgive to reform the wrongdoer—in paternalistic, messianic, or benevolent arrogance, which often evokes resentment.

We may forgive to achieve closure and decrease the likelihood that unresolved anger will infect future loving relationships.

We may forgive to seek forgetfulness, the amnesia of acceptance that silences resentments and ends ruminations.

We may forgive to avoid the subtle control of our emotions that comes from past injuries, painful memories of individuals and their actions that intrude into our thoughts and feelings.

But forgiveness may not be the morally responsible way to respond to a particularly unjust injury. It may be better to resent responsibly than to forgive irresponsibly, to resent in love of principle, of self, of other, and of moral community rather than forgive in negation of one or all of these. Resentment can flood and dominate, or we may learn to resent cleanly.

We may deal with excess resentment and come to feel it in a focused, accurate, limited manner.

We may learn to resent moral injustice in a morally just way—feel it in the right way, at the right time, and directed at the right object.

We may affirm the moral integrity of principled resentment even when forgiveness offers practical consequences that appear utilitarian, attractive, desirable, and cost effective.

We may continue to feel resentment from the principle that persons possess rights that deserve respect, that wrongdoing is not to be condoned even though there are utilities to be gained from forgetfulness.

Rage-based or Reality-based Resentment

Forgiveness, according to Bishop Joseph Butler in his *Fifteen Sermons* (1726), is the forswearing of resentment, the resolute overcoming of the anger and hatred that are naturally directed toward a person who has done an unjustified and non-excused moral injury (Butler 1726, VIII and IX). In two sermons, "Upon Resentment" and "Upon Forgiveness of Injuries," Butler grounds the capacity for enmity, bitterness, and hatred in creation, not in the sinfulness of humanity. Bitterness and hatred are bad only when they are not in proportion to the injustice of the injury done against one, or when one seeks to take revenge. "The indignation raised by cruelty and injustice, and the desire of having it punished . . . is by no means malice. No, it is resentment against vice and wickedness; it is one of the common bonds by which society is held together; a fellow-feeling which each individual has in behalf of the whole species, as well as of oneself" (Butler 1896, 141). To love one's enemies, he says, is to encounter them with "a due natural sense of the injury, and no more" (160). This distinction between legitimate and illegitimate anger over an injustice recognizes that anger at another's act need not hinder one in forgiving another. To grant forgiveness when resentment still persists is not uncommon or at all surprising.

Resentment is an important dynamic in the soul. Its demands for justice and equity are part of the process in reconciliation, and they offer both functional and dysfunctional contributions to forgiving. "Resentment (in its range from righteous anger to righteous hatred) functions primarily as a defense, not of *all* moral values and norms, but rather of certain *values of the self*," writes philosopher Jeffrie Murphy (Murphy and Hampton 1988, 16). The passion of resentment is a defense of *self-respect*, and a person with no resentment of a moral injury is almost necessarily one lacking in self-respect, in clear perceptions of self-worth. In a limited sense, resentment is a good thing, not as a final end, but as a balance to the impulse to seek restoration at all costs—even the cost of one's very human dignity.

> If I count morally as much as anyone else (as surely I do), a failure to resent moral injuries done to me is a failure to care about the moral value incarnate in my own person (that I am, in Kantian language, an end in myself) and thus a failure to care about the very rules of morality.
>
> If it is proper to feel *indignation* when I see third parties morally wronged, must it not be equally proper to feel *resentment* when I experience the moral wrong done to myself? Morality is not simply something to be believed in; it is something to be *cared* about. This caring includes concern about those persons (including myself) who are the proper objects of moral attention (Murphy and Hampton 1988, 18).

> Showing resentment conveys to a wrongdoer that we respect ourselves, others, and morality in general and that, for this reason, it is morally valuable as a response to injury and may help foster a sense of *community* when it works to inspire moral reform (Haber 1991, 82).

For Joram Haber, resentment can be a form of moral protest that ultimately expresses respect for the wrongdoer. By voicing our objection, we show that the wrongdoer is being taken seriously. Overlooking is irresponsible, silence is morally indefensible. Theologian James McClendon describes resentment as "God's good gift, protecting us in an injurious world from greater harms and inciting us to secure a justice we might otherwise be too placid or too compassionate to enforce" (McClendon 1986, 225).

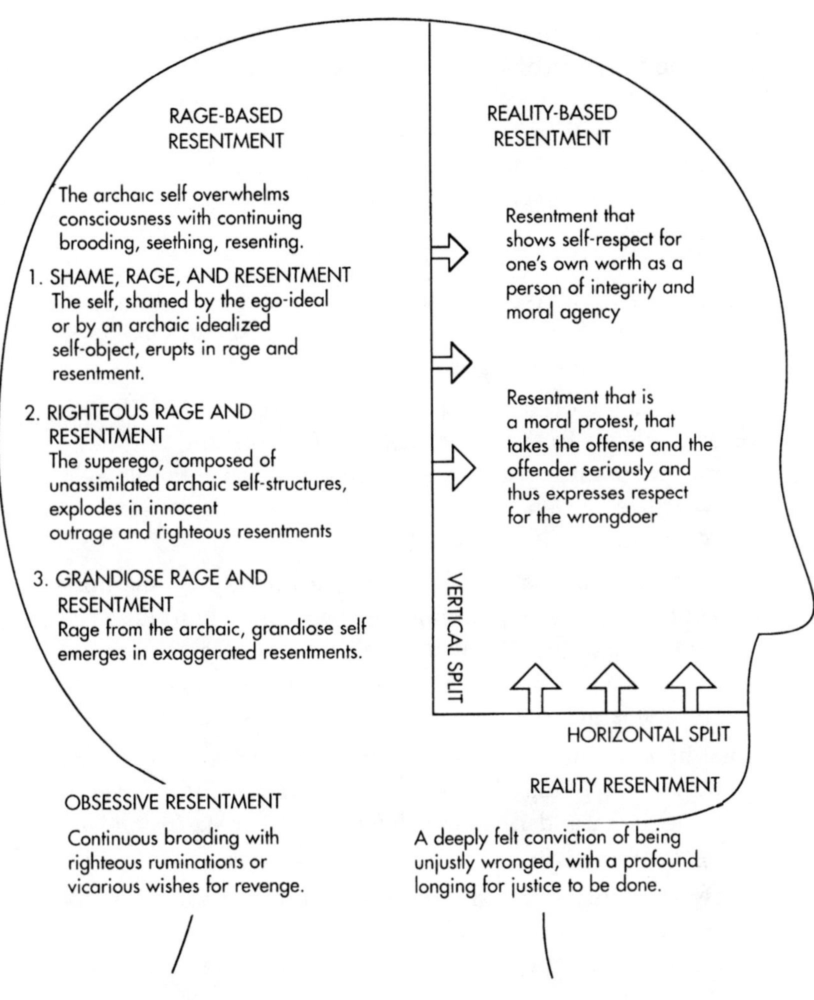

Figure 4.3

Rage-based and Reality-based Resentment

The dark and destructive side of resentment has often been described in morbid words that decry its ability to eat away at self and relationships while fantasizing harm done to another (see figure 4.3). "Resentment is among the most obsessive and enduring of emotions, poisoning the whole of subjectivity with its venom, often achieving moodlike scope while still maintaining its keen and vicious focus on each of the myriad of petty offenses it senses against itself" (Solomon 1976, 350).

The developmental journey from such archaic undifferentiated rage and resentment to a mature demand for justice is central to the narcissistic line of development that moves from archaic self valuations to mature empathic respect for self and other.

From our journey into Kohut's thought on the development of the self, we gained elements for constructing our revised paradigm of forgiveness and reconciliation:

A deepened understanding of the emotional inability of persons with deep deprivation in infancy and childhood to experience and express *empathy.*

A perspective on the intense eruptions of rage that follow any wound to the self-structure of the person without a maturely differentiated self—injury to an infantile self-structure hidden in an adult triggers infantile rage and resentment.

A sensitivity to the temptation toward splitting—the horizontal splitting of pressing the unmodified grandiose self beneath the floor of awareness or the vertical splitting of drawing a curtain that denies or disowns grandiosity even when it is present in the person's self-presentation.

Insight into the power of shame—the immature shame that overwhelms the person with archaic infantile self-structures—and its many defenses that make reconciliation unthinkable.

Understanding of the grandiose self and its claims to innocence, righteousness, and perfection, and the barriers these erect to admission of failure and to repentance and rapprochement.

Awareness that building the interpersonal bridge requires adult skills that are not learned by an immature self. Therefore, the work begins with self-structures, with development of mature narcissistic capacities and abilities.

A new appreciation of resentment as a good gift of prizing one's own worth and affirming the worth of others.

The Violation of the Child

We cannot leave the discussion of Kohut's thought without correlating it with that of another social theorist with parallel conclusions. Philosopher and psychoanalyst Alice Miller has become the most influential voice on the roots of violence in the child and in the family system. She asks "whether it will ever be possible for us to grasp the effect of the loneliness and desertion to which we were exposed as children, and hence, intrapsychically, as adults" (Miller 1981, 5).

Children are ideal candidates for exploitation by virtue of their complete dependence (emotional and material) on the adults in their lives. "The love a child has for his or her parents ensures that their conscious or unconscious acts of mental cruelty will go undetected. . . . [Children's] tolerance for their parents knows no bounds" (Miller 1983, 4). Children may be exploited, abused, and manipulated by adults and accept it without critical awareness of the injustices being perpetrated. Unable to react to the controlling adult, they internalize the behavior, its impact, and the adult image as well. In contrast:

> Adults are free to hurl reproaches at God, at fate, at the authorities or at society if they are deceived, ignored, punished unjustly, confronted with excessive demands, or lied to. Children are not allowed to reproach their gods—their parents and teachers. By no means are they allowed to express their frustrations. Instead, they must repress or deny their emotional reactions which build up inside until adulthood, when they are finally discharged, but not on the object that caused them (Miller 1983, 254).

Adults who were humiliated as children unconsciously reproduce that humiliation. Corporal punishment is a dramatic reenactment of an adult struggling to regain the power once lost as a child. The subjection of the child is the basic building block of socialization into the wider sociopolitical structures of domination. The "silent drama" of the child unfolds in the following acts:

1. Being hurt/dominated as a young child without anyone knowing the humiliation
2. Being unable to react to or to process the resultant anger
3. Internalizing the sense of betrayal by rationalizing or idealizing the parent's "good intentions"
4. Repressing the painful memory until it is forgotten
5. As an adult, discharging the unconscious store of anger onto either self or others

"A vicious circle of contempt for those who are smaller and weaker" results and becomes institutionalized in the patterns of domination that are repeated from generation to generation. The patterns of domination that are psychically and socially enforced (introjected psychically, projected socially) create depression within and oppression between persons.

In consequence, adults passively accept the practices of oppression, then actively defend and promote them as necessary. In the service of these practices they are as dominated as they were in childhood (Miller 1983, 66). As an example, Miller points to the "heroic willingness of adolescents to fight the wars of old men" in which they are permitted "to avenge their earlier debasement" and to "divert this hatred from their parents if they are given a clear cut enemy whom they are permitted to hate freely and with impunity" (1983, 170). A Swiss who remembers the impact of Hitler on her generation, Miller writes: "When a man comes along and talks like one's own father and acts like him, even adults will forget their democratic rights or will not make use of them. They will submit to this man, will acclaim him, and put their trust in him . . . without even being aware of their enslavement" (1983, 75).

Miller's contention that child rearing is the fountain of social domination and political violence may in some measure suffer from the reductionism that seems to finally crown virtually every social theory. But her insight into the interconnectedness of parent-child, family, and social systems is a stark challenge to the abuses of patriarchalism. "It is part of the tragic nature of the repetition compulsion that someone who hopes eventually to find a better world than the one he or she experienced as a child in fact keeps creating instead the same undesired state of affairs" (1983, 241). A new social order cannot be constructed unless we confront the sources of our oppression and until we challenge the unconscious springs of our violence.

For both Kohut and Miller, violation in childhood creates profound emotional inability to experience the bridge of empathy. The woundedness creates intense eruption of infantile rage, overwhelming shame, alienation through splitting within and estrangement between, and the creation of villains and demons who fully deserve our exaggerated impulses to aggression.

The interpersonal bridge requires deep pilings, bedrock foundations, and secure suspension cables. We strengthen our bridges, to extend the metaphor, by driving our pilings deeper through the chaotic unconscious to its creative central core, the creative unconscious, by touching the bedrock of our souls that longs for trusting and enduring connections with others, and thus suspend our bridges of empathy, caring, and nonviolence to meet the other.

Offender-Offended Grid

Empathy, as Kohut has taught us, enables the offended to enter the world of the offender and perceive it with increasing accuracy. Maturity, as Kohut envisions it, empowers the offended to enter dialogue with the offender and

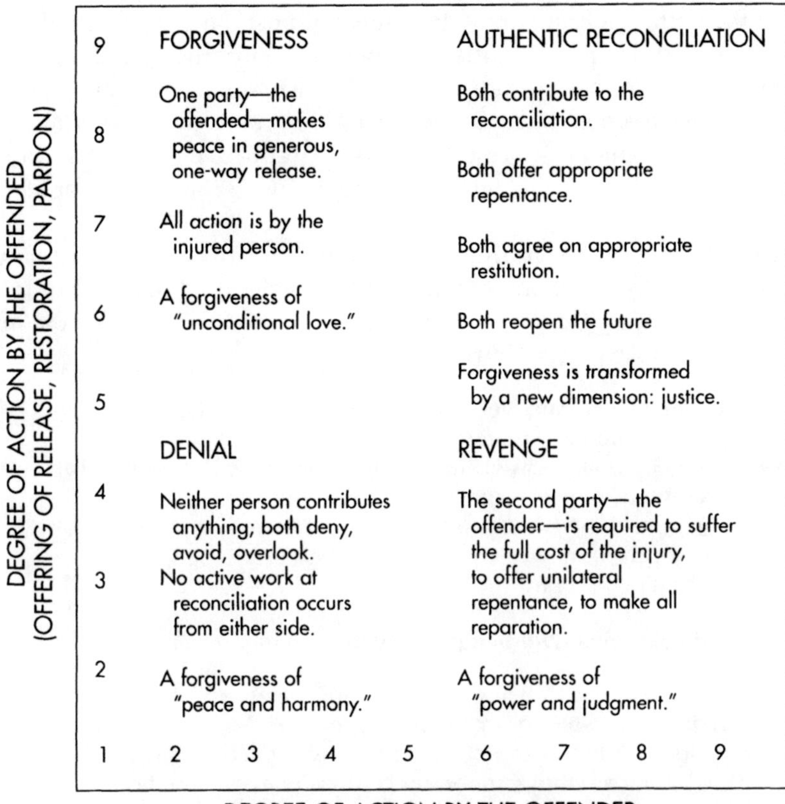
9 FORGIVENESS
AUTHENTIC RECONCILIATION
One party—the offended—makes peace in generous, one-way release.
8
All action is by the injured person.
7
A forgiveness of "unconditional love."
6
Both contribute to the reconciliation.
Both offer appropriate repentance.
Both agree on appropriate restitution.
Both reopen the future
Forgiveness is transformed by a new dimension: justice.
5
DENIAL
REVENGE
4
Neither person contributes anything; both deny, avoid, overlook.
No active work at reconciliation occurs from either side.
3
The second party— the offender—is required to suffer the full cost of the injury, to offer unilateral repentance, to make all reparation.
2
A forgiveness of "peace and harmony."
A forgiveness of "power and judgment."
1 2 3 4 5 6 7 8 9
DEGREE OF ACTION BY THE OFFENDED (OFFERING OF RELEASE, RESTORATION, PARDON)
DEGREE OF ACTION BY THE OFFENDER (DEMANDS FOR REPAYMENT, RESTITUTION, PUNISHMENT)

Figure 4.4
Offender-Offended Grid

invite movement toward reconciliation. Forgiveness is always of an offender, by the offended, for an offense. This definition opens several intriguing questions. Can one forgive an offender and still abhor or resent an offense? Or can one forgive an offense while still resenting the offender? What degree of action is necessary by the offender? By the offended?

The offender-offended interaction can be helpfully visualized on a two-by-two grid (see figure 4.4). The horizontal axis measures the degree of action required of the "offender" if reconciliation is to occur (demands for repayment, restitution, punishment, etc.). The vertical axis designates the degree of action required of the "offended" (offering of release, restoration, pardon, acceptance). This offers four main responses to injury arising from the different interactions between the two.

In the bottom left quadrant, beginning at position 1/1, is denial. Neither the offender nor the offended person contributes anything. Both deny, avoid, overlook, withdraw. No active work at reconciliation occurs from either direction. Such denial serves important functions of defense against further injury. It preserves distance, reduces emotional flooding, excludes overwhelming reality, and enables one to cope, but all at a high cost.

Denial has many self-protective forms, from the silent unacknowledged refusal to talk about it to the stubbornly declared refusal. Maria, in Robertson Davies' *The Lyre of Orpheus,* explains to her counselor the infidelity to her husband, Arthur:

> "I haven't been frank yet. There hasn't been a good time."
> "You could have made a good time."
> "A good time to crawl and weep and probably be forgiven. I absolutely refuse to be forgiven."
> "You've done what you've done, and there is a price for that. Being forgiven may be a part of that price."
> "Then I won't pay."

Later Maria explains why being forgiven is an insult to her:

> "It would come to being forgiven, and being one-down on the marriage score-board for the rest of my life. And I simply won't put up with that. I'm not going to spend years of saying, 'yes, dear,' about anything important because I have a debt I can't discharge. . . . I'm not going to have Arthur sighing and rolling his eyes and being marvelously big about the whole damned thing" (Davies 1988, 244).

In the bottom right quadrant of the grid, the 9/1 position, is revenge. Here the second party, the offender, is required to suffer the full cost of the injury, to experience commensurate pain or loss, to offer unilateral repentance, and make all reparation demanded by the offended. Feelings of revenge are an essential human emotion with deep roots in childhood discoveries of fairness and the adult sense of justice. Aggressive revenge arises from a matrix of narcissistic needs for value, respect, well-being, and justice, which are thrown into imbalance when the injury to the self has been deep, and as such are necessary and legitimate forces in the personality. These feelings result from a combination of repressed grief and frozen separation anxiety (I cannot let go of the pain and grieve; I will not let go of the other and give up my demand for undoing the wrong or repaying the injury; if I let go, all is lost; I have abandoned my own power and I will feel abandoned). When the feelings become self-reinforcing and cyclical, they constitute chronic vindictiveness. So revenge stops the processing of pain and postpones any resolution by not giving up the other and holding on to the injury. Vengeance is a reaction against an injury that maintains the consequences of the misdeed. In revenge, one is bound to the original injury, caught in the chain reaction that continues the repetition of the injury.

In a more subtle and pervasive way, forgiveness is equated with power. For those who have traditionally equated love and control this eclipsing of the two is instinctive and inevitable. The act of wrongdoing places the offender in a one-down position. The wrong suffered lifts the offended into a morally one-up position.

> The view that associates power and forgiveness is a rather widespread assumption. . . . [A] significant part of the problem with human forgiveness is its having been understood as a power which persons may possess. This fact, coupled with the destructive ways in which we are tempted to use our power, suggests that it is important to find a way to understand human forgiveness that is less associated with our defensiveness and sin (Patton 1985, 89–90).

The claiming of, use of, or passive acceptance of attributed power distorts forgiveness into the quadrant of revenge. It becomes an action of power and judgment. Acceptance may be withheld to punish or offered to penalize.

At the top left of the grid, the 1/9 position, is unilateral forgiveness. One party, this time the offended, makes peace in a generous one-way release. All action toward reconciliation is done by the injured person. The need to affiliate, the high value placed on harmony, the social interest that draws us toward maintaining and restoring relationship motivates the person to return to the offender and the offense and seek reunion. Unilateral forgiveness, though generous, sacrificial, and self-effacing on the surface of relationship, may pair with the injured narcissism in an unconscious revenge of covert retaliation. The virtue of forgiveness, consciously affirmed and acted out in superior, vertical cancellation of all expectations, serves to place the other in an inferior, indebted, one-down position that satisfies repressed needs for revenge. "I not only forgive you, I'll not let you forget who did the forgiving."

The supreme example of such forgiveness is Karenin's choice to cover his wife's adultery with Christian grace in Tolstoy's *Anna Karenina.* Her response to his powerful letter which defines the requisite repentance and conformity is

> "He's in the right!" she muttered. "Of course, he's always in the right; he's Christian, he's magnanimous! Yes, the mean, odious creature! And no one understands it except me, and no one ever will; and I can't explain it. People say he's so religious, so high-principled, so upright, so clever; but they don't see what I've seen . . . ! How was it I didn't guess what he would do? He'll do what's

consistent with his mean nature. He'll keep himself in the right, while he sees to it that I, poor lost woman, sink still farther, am still more disgraced . . ." (Tolstoy [1873] 1954, 314).

In the upper right quadrant of the grid, the 9/9 position, the persons join in seeking reconciliation. Genuine reconciliation pursues mutuality in the face of injury in a collaborative way—both the offender and the offended contribute to the outcome. Both offer appropriate repentance (to the degree that each has felt and expressed alienating rage or scorn); both agree on appropriate restitution; and both reopen the possibility of future relationship.

This reconciliation expresses authentic forgiveness—a forgiveness that is more than an act that takes place when hurt or revenge are spent. Rather, this reconciliation is the introduction of a new element: grace. Reconciliation requires compassionate love as well as pragmatic justice. Justice in reconciliation is not a goal we can seize, it is a journey we travel as far as it is open to us, a process we pursue to its present availability. We accept what is possible for two persons, not what is absolute or ideal. The search for integrity with solidarity is never easy; it drives us to work through to a mutually satisfactory solution with a joint investment in the process and the outcome. Forgiving and being forgiven require a measure of goodwill and graciousness on both sides. It requires the restoring of perceptions of love in spite of the wrongdoing and an acceptance of the other's repentance as genuine even in the face of enduring injury or irreplaceable loss. Some measure of transformation takes place. Forgiveness acts in the unexpected way. Neither participant is conditioned by the act that provoked it; both are freed from its consequences.

Motivations for Reconciliation

"Forgiveness is another way of saying, 'I'm human. I make mistakes. I want to be granted that privilege, and so I grant you that privilege,'" writes Philip Yancey, describing forgiveness as a natural act of exchange which is ultimately "an unnatural act" (Yancey 1991, 37).

We may need to forgive because we discover that we are also in need of forgiveness. We act, in the course of our lives, in ways that are injurious to ourselves, in ways that are injurious to others. We have double needs for forgiveness. Thus we should be willing to extend the same forgiveness to those who have injured us. Forgiveness springs from humility—humility with profound honesty. However, virtuous as such honesty and humility may be, there are situations of wrongdoing in which the moral history of the one offended is not at issue. Why should the sexually abused person, violated by her father when she was age six to twelve, forgive the perpetrator out of recognition of her own need for forgiveness? Regardless of whether she stands in need of forgiveness, such a reason is not valid in every forgiveness situation. Forgiveness, writes Bishop Stephen Neill,

> recognizes the wrongdoer as a person. Wrong has been done, about this there is no pretense. But this is not the whole truth about the wrongdoer. He or she is still of infinite value as a person, since every person is unique and irreplaceable by any other. Since the wrongdoer has so greatly injured his/her self by doing wrong, there is special need of help, and help that can be rendered only by the one to whom the wrong was done. Only the hair of the dog that has bitten can heal. Forgiveness can spring only from a self-forgetfulness that is more concerned about another's well being than about its own, and that longs for the renewal of fellowship even when fellowship has been flouted and destroyed by the willful aggression of another (Neill 1959, 210–11).

Naming the wrongdoer as wrongdoer can be an act of righteous self-defensiveness which requires blame to maintain its skewed equilibrium. But forgiveness requires a return to the center, where one sees and accepts one's own imperfections, failures, and wrongdoing, either in the relationship in question or in other situations of failure. Reinhold Niebuhr comments on this need for self-awareness: "Forgiving love is a possibility only for those who know that they are not good, who feel themselves in need of divine mercy, who live in a dimension deeper and higher than that of moral idealism, feel themselves as well as their fellow humans convicted of sin by a holy God and know that the differences between us all are insignificant" (Niebuhr 1941, 237).

The offended and offender need each other, if reconciliation is to occur (see figure 4.5). The *offender* needs the offended for her or his healing. (In repentance, in restitution, and in restoration comes healing.) The *offended* needs the offender for his or her healing. (In reclaiming the humanity of the other, in validating the injury, and in purifying the anger comes healing.) Short of this, we seek to find the two poles interiorly, within the self divided by the injury and its associated rages. We divide within and "forgive ourselves" to regain unity, then seek to forgive the other while remaining isolated. This attempt to resolve the brokenness without the other who has broken away or broken in leaves the central relationship untouched. As a result, the offended searches out, consciously or unconsciously, surrogates who can heal or substitute targets who can suffer. These agents are at best of only partial satisfaction, so the offended continues with unfinished injury, fragmented and unhealed.

We cannot heal ourselves; healing is either actualized, mediated, or surrogated within community. We are healed by the other; we heal each

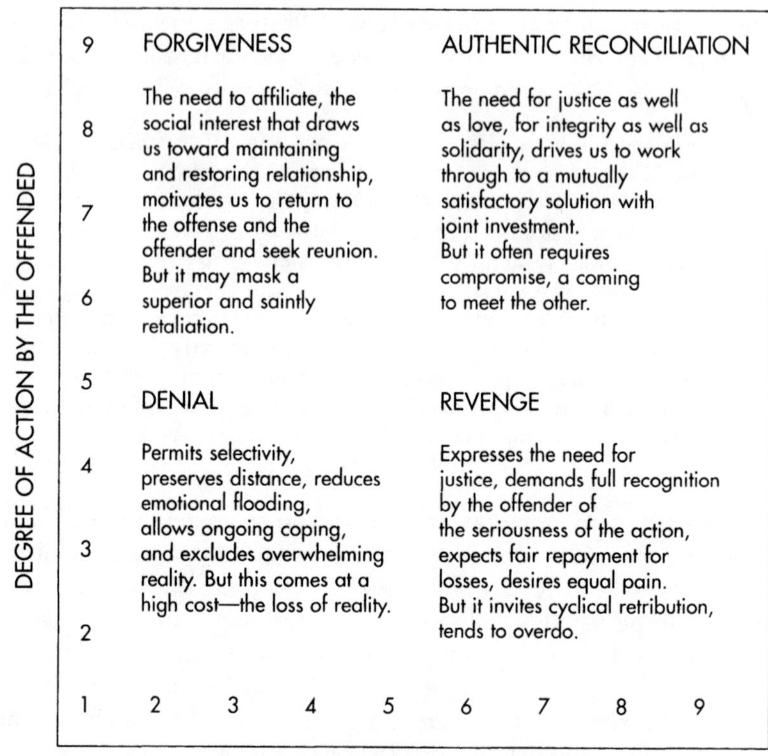

Figure 4.5
Motivations for Reconciliation

other. The offended's need for the offender, and vice versa, can be partially fulfilled by substitutes. Where fear or flight intervene, where meeting becomes impossible, where community fails us, we settle for a proxy, not the perpetrator, to be the necessary other. But this alternate pathway heals in part, not in the whole, and it achieves acceptant forgetfulness, not acceptant forgiveness.

What is here defined as the exception necessitated by unavailability—that is, meeting of offended and offender is impossible—has become institutionalized within our culture as a norm for the healing process. Nonetheless, when in an alienation or injury a surrogate process becomes necessary because the offended and the offender cannot or will not meet, the surrogate can give actuality, authenticity, and availability on behalf of the forgiving community that supports and empowers the interaction.

The counselor—therapist, pastor, priest, sister, or brother—can act as a surrogate when necessary. As such, the counselor supports, assists, confronts, or reflects as the offender or the offended seeks to find forgiveness for the self or give it to the other. In so doing, the counselor as surrogate represents and takes the place of the other party's absence due to deviance, death, recalcitrance, etc. The counselor's right to act as a forgiving agent is granted by some moral community that recognizes her or him as a representative of integrity and accountability to the community's ethic (which includes the virtues of prudence, love, and justice, which stand on the ultimate ground of morality and being, on God who is Author and Legitimator of all value and virtue).

Once there were two brothers. The older was strong, intelligent, athletic, a brilliant student. Sent off to a private school, he quickly made a name for himself. As the popular and respected student leader from this South African school, his influence grew. The younger brother was neither good-looking nor intellectual. A hunchback, he was self-conscious and very private. But he had a great gift—he could sing like a nightingale, with a tenor voice of surpassing sweetness.

The younger brother arrived at the school in his brother's senior year when the older brother's success, influence, and grandiosity were unquestioned. The second week, the hazing of new students turned into a mob action. The student body cruelly mocked the younger brother, forced him to sing, then tore off his shirt and exposed his hump to the cheering crowd. He had become the screen for the projection of every boy's secret contemptible self. The older brother silently watched the shaming from the window of the laboratory. One word from him would have brought a stop to the brutality, but he turned his back. He betrayed his brother, as he had done in childhood.

The younger boy survived, but he was never the same. He dropped out of school and went home to the family farm. He no longer sang. The older brother entered the army, was awarded a commission as an officer, and distinguished himself on several fronts. One night, in Palestine, recovering from a wound, he dreamed he sat at the Last Supper. He knew himself as Judas. "I had a brother, but I betrayed him," he confessed. And Jesus turned and said, "Go to your brother and make your peace with him."

The journey home to South Africa was harrowing. At the door, he met his brother's tight-lipped wife and knew the bitterness of their life. He found the brother watering his parched orchard, and he told him of his dream, his betrayal, his repentance, his longing for forgiveness. They cried together, they held each other. The breach was, at last, healed. And as he walked back to the house, he heard in the distance, the sound of his brother's voice. He was singing again (adapted from Van der Post 1970, 120–38).

Toward a New Paradigm of Forgiveness

1. Forgiveness is the extension of empathy to become mercy, and the capacity to experience and express empathy is profoundly shaped by the experiences of deprivation or adequate parental "gleam" (affirmation) in infancy and childhood.
2. Forgiveness or each person's capacity for forgiving is shaped by the wounds to the self-structure, the splitting utilized to cope with threat, the overwhelming power of shame, and the defensive emergence of the grandiose self.
3. Forgiveness, as an interpersonal bridge, requires adult skills; achieving adulthood requires resolving the unresolved dilemmas of childhood, strengthening of self-structures, and developing mature narcissistic capacities and abilities.
4. Forgiveness limits but does not eliminate resentment; it directs it from obsessive resenting to realistic resenting; it becomes a profound passion for justice, social transformation, and ultimately reconciliation.

5

The Virtues of Forgiving, the Practice of Reconciling

> Unless we belong to a community where we are able to tell one another the truth through the practice of reconciliation and forgiveness, we are condemned to live in a world of violence and destruction
>
> —Stanley Hauerwas

A young woman is seen leaving the church of St. Francis in Assisi. The watcher is a passerby, a man who has lived a life of deceit, violence, and wickedness. He is totally captivated by her beauty and forsakes his busy life of crime to follow her, to shadow her for days. His inquiries reveal her name, her virtue, her devotion to St. Francis, her life of service to the poor given in charity and simplicity. His attempts at a meeting all fail. She gives him less than a glance.

Over coffee with a priest in the square before the church, he learns that she has sworn to love only a man with the calling, the devotion, and the innocent face of St. Francis—the face she sees on the statue, at morning prayers. The man is totally smitten by this single-minded creature. He devotes himself to the study of St. Francis, lives for a while with a community of Franciscans, and slowly comes to share the passion for service to others. But nothing can change the deep lines of depravity that mark his face from an ill-spent youth.

Then he hears of a maskmaker, a woman of great magic who creates new faces from the skin of unborn lambs and magically glues them to the face so they can never be removed. Yes, she can duplicate the statue of St. Francis, and the man receives a new face costing him all he owns. The evil visage disappears beneath a face of serenity.

At last he meets the object of his love. Soon she returns his devotion. They marry and commit their lives to serving the poor. Years of work and sacrifice and obedience follow.

One day, as they were giving aid to a group of gypsies, a woman who had been his partner in evil recognized his rich voice as he preached. Jealous of his new life and suspicious of his sincerity, she sprang forward in front of the audience, scraped up his neck with long fingernails, pierced the skin, and tore the mask from his face.

"Hypocrite, deceiver, liar!" she shouted. "See who this is, people. See his true face."

The man stood exposed, knowing all was lost, dying in humiliation, yet knowing that "it is in dying that we are born to eternal life."

But all who saw him showed no surprise, for in doing the works of St. Francis in loving obedience, his face had been transformed. It was even more lovely than the mask (attrib. to Max Beerbohm).

On April 6, 1992, Jonathan McDonald stole a Jeep Cherokee from the driveway of a Santa Monica home. It was just another car theft for seventeen-year-old McDonald, nearly his fiftieth. The Cherokee belonged to Anna Phelan, a screenwriter with a different sense of justice. When McDonald was arrested later that night, then tried for car theft and imprisoned, Phelan followed the case and went to visit him at the California Youth Authority.

"After meeting him," she said, "I knew this was a young man on the brink and open to any help he could get. He was extremely smart, funny, and just needed a support network under him." Thus began an unlikely friendship between the two.

"When she came to see me, I thought she had some kind of death wish out for me," McDonald said. "She said she wanted to help me, but I thought she was lying." But his distrust of the Anglo woman soon evaporated, and the network of friends she connected to him urged him to begin a life outside the world of crime, to use his gifts in education.

Well aware that there is no guarantee of Jonathan's success in building a new life, Phelan says, "I'll feel that everything was done to support him. A hand was reached out and he was not willing or not capable of taking it. But all of us in Jonathan's circle are better off for having given it a shot. To do nothing is inexcusable."

Recently Jonathan took his driver's license exam in the Jeep Cherokee he once stole. His job, at five dollars an hour, takes more effort than swiping cars to sell to chop shops for $1,000 a car. Yet he is finding his way to a new world of values.

"In nineteen years of work in corrections counseling, I've never heard of a case of a victim helping a perpetrator," says a supervisor at the California Youth Authority. It is a reversal of middle-class attitudes toward offenders, a courageous response that turns our expectations upside down. It is the creation of community where no human connections previously existed (Collins 1994b).

Beerbohm's story is a parable of profound character change. What begins with joining a new community leads to a radical shift in values and behavior, and then in appearance, resulting in a transformation of the core person and personality. The Phelan-McDonald story is real, not fantasy. Both offer visions of prophetic action in community leading to human cooperation and co-responsibility.

For many people in this postmodern age the metaphors are different. Instead of self-renewal through bonding with a community with standards of ethical behavior and empowerment by a new world of virtue, we stress the separation of an individuated self from external codes of behavior and the discovery of an autonomous cluster of values defined from within as "authentic."

The ideal self has undergone a major shift in modern and postmodern times. *Authenticity* has replaced *morality*. A *therapeutic sensibility* has taken precedence over a *moral sensibility*. The ideal of the former is to be true to one's own "needs," to be "authentic and congruent with one's real self," to be in touch with one's feelings. The ideal of the latter is an integrity that limits the fulfillment of one's private desires whenever pursuing them freely would infringe on other people's rights. Morality is both an assent to principles of justice and an internalization of those principles into a trait or virtue of justice. Internalization results in the creation of moral emotions and cognitions such as shame and guilt at one's wrongdoing.

> In the contemporary age, authenticity is viewed as the chief "virtue" to which one should aspire. In a very limited sense, authenticity resembles the old Greek doctrine of living according to one's nature, of "knowing thyself" and "becoming what you are." But for the Greeks, one was regarded essentially as a rational being who was susceptible to moral education. . . . Today, by contrast, . . . authenticity is now pursued in the absence of any ideal about what reason or rationality requires (Phillips 1987, 23–24).

In the new authenticity, one is encouraged to fulfill one's emotional requirements, to seek immediate gratification of impulses, to act rationally on the basis of needs, feelings, and desires. We are told to follow our own natures without being told what that nature is or can become. Frankness about one's own feelings, no matter how sincerely expressed or authentically lived, may include the crude, rude, immoral, or criminal. If human beings are to live together in community, we must subordinate authenticity to morality as the proper standard of human maturity and adequacy.

What motivation to reconciliation arises from authenticity? What possibilities for forgiveness emerge from the authentic person when the injury is deep, the alienation severe? Will it be more than the self-release of detachment?

Authenticity: The Therapeutic Sensibility

The contemporary sensibility, the *Zeitgeist,* is therapeutic, not religious. People hunger not for salvation as spiritual connection and direction but "for the feeling, the momentary illusion, of personal well-being, health, and psychic security" (Lasch 1979, 7). People choose out of preferences that are based on values, selected subjectively or individually by standards they assemble or construct themselves. Therapists help them achieve the modern equivalent of salvation: mental health through "authenticity." Moral judgments get reduced to issues of subjective personal taste; social behavior is guided by technique, relational skills, and conflict management, not by moral principle. Should-ism is replaced by is-ism.

Every culture has its own stock of "characters," types that provide a cultural and moral ideal and model and legitimate a certain mode of social existence. A complete set of traits, characteristics, quirks, and tics come to mind as one visualizes such characters: the English public school headmaster, the Puritan clergyman, the frontier scout, the country doctor, the Mother Superior, the small-town librarian.

Alasdair MacIntyre argues that in modern Western society there are three such "characters": the Manager, the Rich Aesthete, and the Therapist. The Manager represents the rational bureaucrat who is the company or organization personified. The Rich Aesthete represents "the rich and famous" who possess the means but are in search of satisfying or worthy ends. The Therapist is not concerned with values or ends but with technique, "with effectiveness in transforming neurotic symptoms into directed energy, maladjusted individuals into well-adjusted ones" (MacIntyre 1984, 28–29).

The "character" of the Therapist has embodied a cultural movement that has generalized psychological technique into a cultural program of change; "truth has been displaced as a value and replaced by psychological effectiveness. The idioms of therapy have invaded all too successfully such spheres as those of education and religion" (29).

The Manager represents the world of bureaucracy, the Aesthete and the Therapist the private world. These two modes of social life define our modern attitudes—the private realm in which the free choices of isolated individuals are sovereign, and the public world in which the bureaucracy is sovereign so that it may limit the free choices of isolated individuals (33). In the organizational realm, the ends are given and not available for rational scrutiny; in the personal realm debate and decision about values are central factors, but they have been privatized, internalized, individualized so that no community of opinion, common life of discussion, or shared world of discernment now exists. "The triumph of the therapeutic," as Philip Rieff named this worldview (Rieff 1966), has led us into a value-free world that generalizes the therapeutic process into a social process for all relationships.

Therapeutic values, experienced as a culturally sanctioned retreat for healing or creative change, are not adequate norms for an entire culture. But in American society, therapeutic values are becoming cultural values. Objectified moral goodness turns into subjective goodness; being good becomes feeling good.

Pastoral counselors must work (as Robert Bellah and associates have discussed in *Habits of the Heart*) within this therapeutic society. The therapeutic mentality is understood as a culture of self-absorption, of limitless growth. The growth has many levels—growth in the ability to tap into and savor one's present feelings; growth in one's own ability to choose, create, or experience a novel lifestyle; growth in tolerance for alternative lifestyles in one's relationships and one's society (Bellah 1986, 129, 131, 65, 48).

The therapeutic ethic is centered in nonjudgmental openness. Its central biblical text is "judge not that ye be not judged." When an angry student seized the microphone in a public demonstration arguing "we're dealing with morality here. Morality is a relative matter. You can't impose morality on other people," he was affirming a therapeutic morality with its own paradoxical moral imperative. "One ought not to impose one's moral oughts on others—one imposes the ought which insists one ought never impose oughts" (Mouw 1989, 133).

In a therapeutic ethic, marriage is grounded in communication and letting one's spouse be her or his own person; family is shaped by freedom from emotional constraints—relief from conflict, shame, or guilt. (Conflict occurs when one violates inherited standards of value; shame, when one is seen as the offender; guilt, as one recognizes the failure before these standards.) Shame is intolerable, guilt is unenlightened, and conflict is unnecessary in a therapeutic sensibility. When self-acceptance transcends all value conflicts, when acceptance of the other renders shame and guilt irrelevant, then no-fault relationships emerge from these central moral norms. Transcendent values present artificial barriers to individual growth and therefore must be challenged and preferably discarded. Individual preferences and feelings serve as the measure of value, no matter how fragile, alterable, or idiosyncratic.

Therapy cannot proceed without values, but it offers them implicitly. It does not exist without virtues, and it teaches them explicitly. Authenticity, autonomy, and altruism have become the three cardinal virtues. Conventional morality, rooted in a particular tradition, is seen as other-directedness, dependency, or immaturity. Or if grounded in a philosophic or theological framework, it is seen as "intellectualizing, conformity, or compulsivity."

There is a moral context to all acts of caregiving. No form of counseling or psychotherapy is politically, culturally, or morally neutral. The moral context is background to all counseling even though the foreground being processed is not focused on values. At times the demands of the moral context may be temporarily relaxed in inviting awareness of aggressive impulses or unacceptable feelings, but even when bracketed, both counselor and counselee know that there are realities that must ultimately be faced.

Although a therapist may avoid invoking the moral world except in cases of extreme violence, abuse, or damage to the self, the moral context is assumed, utilized, and relied on in the therapy. The pastoral counselor, as a minister, represents the moral world in a direct way, as one responsible for helping shape and support the universe of virtues and values. "The secular psychotherapies are not neutral scientific formulas for curing people. . . . No matter how scientific is the theory behind various secular psychotherapeutic disciplines, the actual practice of psychotherapy is always a practical human art" (Browning 1976, 12). All therapy happens within the broader spheres of cultural meaning and is either countercultural or culturally conforming. It is a value-laden operation. The very nature of psychotherapy is boundary setting, boundary clarifying, boundary broaching, boundary constructing. Every counseling encounter embodies values; every agreement of relationship is grounded in the character and virtues of the parties to the transaction.

In pastoral care and counseling, for example, values are central. When we care for a couple in marital pain, we draw from what we believe about the meaning of marriage and utilize a theology that helps us separate myth from truth. When we work with persons in sexual difficulties, we respond from our own ethics and theology of sexuality, gender, and intimacy. When we walk people through alienation, illness, aging, life review, and death, we practice a theology of interpersonal relations and life-with-others-in-responsible-community.

Caring as a positive emotional attitude is not enough. Authentic caring is bidding another to grow (Mayeroff 1971, 5). Growth is not growth for growth's sake (that is the nature of cancer), it is growth toward a goal, growth with meaning and destiny, and this is the stuff of theology and ethics. Caring requires character, or it is empty.

A purely therapeutic sensibility, with "therapeutic values" and ideal models for mature personhood reduces both personal and public morality to a matter of personal preference. So that which is seen as good is good because I value it, rather than valued because it is good; that which I defend is seen as right, rather than defended because it is right. This is emotivism, not ethical sensitivity.

> To a large degree people now think, talk and act as if emotivism were true, no matter what their avowed theoretical stand-point may be. Emotivism has become embodied in our culture. The Enlightenment project of providing a rational vindication of morality . . . decisively failed; and from henceforth the morality of our predecessor culture—and subsequently of our own—lacked any public, shared rationale or justification (MacIntyre 1981, 48).

Character, Vision, and Ethics

In the last decades of the twentieth century, many ethicists have recovered the notion—as old as Plato and Aristotle—that ethics must respond not simply to the decisions and dilemmas a person faces but especially to the character of the person facing these decisions and dilemmas. The moral self may be seen as a problem-solving agent (situationalist), or as a judge making decisions based on fairness and justice (decisionist), or as an intellect utilizing analytic reasoning (juridical), or as a person of character expressing convictions that are shared in solidarity with a particular community (visional ethics).

The major threat to all systems of ethics comes from emotivism—the view that the debate over principles, rules, and values only functions as a mask for expressions of personal preference. Emotivism reduces morality, as MacIntyre argues, to a subjective, preferential, and feeling-based process of individual autonomous juridical choice. His argument turns away from emotivism, decisionism, situationalism, or analytic reasoning to espouse an ethic of character. This visional ethic explores the nature of the actor, that is, the decision maker, the person, and the community that forms, supports, and stands alongside in decision. Character, meaning a distinguishing mark, denotes those qualities that distinguish the central essence of a person. In psychology, it refers to the basic behavioral pattern of the individual and its substructure, which gives a certain shape or bent to the personality but is not the whole of it. Character is the skeleton; personality, the muscles and fat; the emotions, the organs; the brain, the mind; the heart and circulation, the soul.

Aristotle, who defined character as a settled state of (1) seeking excellence or "virtue," (2) refusing deficiency or "vice," (3) exercising self-control, and (4) overcoming weakness, believed that character is developed by habituation more than by nature or teaching. Habituation relies on the emotional bonds within the family and the larger community; it involves cognitive and emotional training; it is the gift of a community's integrity and morally exemplary life together.

Character persists through time, but it is most often a system of traits shared with one's community of reference, family of origin, circle of spiritual co-travelers. It is an expression of solidarity with significant others rather than of individuality and autonomy. So character is the determining center of our self-agency, formed by community and expressed in our intentions and actions.

In diagnostics, the term *character disorder* refers to a long-term, developmentally based deficiency in *volition*, as distinguished from a deficiency in *emotion* or *cognition*. Today that term has been replaced by *personality disorder*, to include all three elements and to be less evaluative when referring to alcoholism or delinquency. Analytic thought linked character to the first three developmental stages—oral, anal, or phallic character—as derived from unresolved childhood conflicts. It was seen as primarily defensive since character armor moves the skeleton to the exterior, as in crustaceans. Character structure was viewed as relatively unalterable; it may be modified to some extent, to be more adaptive, but the basic pattern cannot be radically changed (Lapsley 1967, 52). *Character* as used by ethicists has a radically different meaning.

A theological ethics that emphasizes *character* seeks to provide the community with a vocabulary for moral responsibility and integrity, and a process to assist each other in character forming and reforming activities. Central concerns of such an ethic are the formation and expression of character in the practice of virtues (skills of the good life) or vices (failures in the good life or the pursuit of lesser or inappropriate goals) (Bondi 1986, 82). The ethical community connects, clarifies, and offers a moral vocabulary through its stories, which direct the many other stories in the individual's life and compete for the allegiance of the heart.

A return to an ethic of virtue places a renewed emphasis on the development and maintenance of character and community. The role of community in forming character is to provide stories of the good life that evoke *intentions,* model authentic and congruent *emotions,* inspire *affections* with their desire for union and participation, empower *volition* with confidence in the ability to choose and act, and support *perseverance* through the accidents of history. Accidents of history include events beyond our control; the givens of historical, biological, psychological, economic, and cultural circumstances including the past which is beyond change; and the network of special relationships of friendship, marriage, family, and professions which come to us as gifts (Bondi 1986, 83).

Virtue, Personhood, and Character

An ethic of virtue begins with the assumption that being is prior to doing, that what one does or does not do depends on being a "self" that is capable of taking responsibility for choices, acts, and consequences. More significant than what we do or do not do is how we do what we do or how we choose not to do what we reject.

Ownership

"To be a person of virtue, therefore, involves acquiring the linguistic, emotional, and rational skills that give us the strength to make our decisions and our life our own," writes Hauerwas (1981, 115), and this ownership is the key element in freedom. "Freedom is more like having power than having a choice. . . . [B]eing free does not imply a choice but the ability to claim that what was or was not done was one's own." An ethic of virtue, then, links freedom and self-possession with character and integrity. A person of virtue "possesses character" with such integrity that it is that person's *own* character.

Integrity

To be a person of virtue requires integrity—an integrative core of character—that allows one to act with a power of self-possession that neither yields nor reacts to the parameters of life that others impose. Virtue provides such power to constitute a self that functions in response to internal rewards. The axiom "Virtue is its own reward" reminds us that "we choose to be virtuous for no other reason than that to be so is the condition under which we would desire to survive. Only by so embodying the virtues have we the power to make our lives our own" (Hauerwas 1981, 125).

Reconciliation requires that at least one party act out of integrity, taking ownership of cognition, emotion, volition, and action and affirming a deep sense of worth of both parties and of the relationship.

Worth

To be a person of virtue involves acquiring a sense of worth so that one acts out of a center of self-other esteem. Such esteem is not built on performance, appearance, and compliance. It has deeper roots, roots in character, roots in the person's power to both conceive and live this personal and interpersonal reality of shared worth in the human community. Hauerwas's basic argument contrasts decisionism with an ethic of character. While he agrees that truly moral acts require self-involvement, it is on the nature of the self that is deciding that he differs (see figure 5.1). The

JURIDICAL	VISIONAL
What is the problem?	Who are the persons?
What is the right thing?	What is right or wrong in the relationship?
What are the options?	What is the ultimate good for all concerned?
What shall we decide?	How shall we then live?
What ought I to do?	What is the good/virtuous thing to do?
The moral self is a reasoning, analytic, problem-solving agent, who decides on the basis of the rules of fairness and the principles of justice defending the right of every person to equal consideration of his or her claims in every situation, using the highest level of moral reasoning possible for the persons involved.	The moral self is a responsible, visional person of character living in accountability to a significant moral community. The moral agent envisions the good, and in its light sees the particularity of person, the balance of relationships, the needs of and fair options for each person, the responsibilities and the rights, and acts with moral consistency, internal unity, and shared integrity, which we call "character."

Figure 5.1
Juridical and Visional Ethics

self that decides and acts, if it is moral, must be a self with moral ability; that is, it must be capable of decision and action. And such a self does not exist in isolation from but exists in solidarity with other humans. The moral choice maker and actor shares both language and central convictions with a community that surrounds and supports the person. A responsible choice maker or moral self is shaped by the continuities of selfhood we call character. So any idea of moral choice is meaningless apart from its community and tradition. You and I have formed and been formed—this is character in community—in distinct ways that make "free action" a logical possibility (Hauerwas 1975, 231–32).

Both character and community have length: that is, they possess a history, a narrative vision, and a sense of the ongoing story that opens with Jesus and his disciples and in which contemporary Christians participate. The stories that Christians remember and retell create community and form the character of its members. The story of Jesus, for example, is a story of one who taught the way but also radically lived the way—indeed, *is* the way. A community that continues his unending story participates in the social ethic of human solidarity in love, integrity, and justice that then forms the individual character. Christian ethics is distinct from all other systems in its vision of the inseparability of Jesus and the community that extends his work and presence, the inseparability of Jesus and the kingdom (kin-dom). Jesus is "the *autobasileia*—the Kingdom in person" (Hauerwas 1981, 45).

Since an ethic emerges from a particular human community, there is no universal, general, value-free starting point. Every ethic must be identified by an adjective, qualified by the name of its community (Christian, liberal secular, Muslim, Jewish). Such location presses the issue of truth in morality to the character of the community and the actor in question. Virtues are those excellencies of character, those skills of living, that enable personal, social, and moral health. Vices, in contrast, are those defects within that diminish personal integration, prevent social cooperation, and divert moral congruence.

Virtues such as hope, love, and trust are basic elemental human needs, with an organic base yet requiring skill development and training.

> To give virtue in this way an organic base would not counter the idea that virtues require training; rather moral development might be understood as building upon the organic foundations of life the skills required for its living, much as architecture assembles materials into habitable structures. Thus particular Christian virtues could be picked out by asking what sorts of development of *Homo Sapiens* could best fulfill the promise implied by the open *instincts* of our species, what traits could assure the meeting of those *needs* of the embodied self that Christians can identify in themselves and others, what skills might enhance our natural *delights* and respect our natural *horrors,* what qualities could best respect our germinal character as creatures liable to *shame, blame,* and *guilt,* and what might develop our capacity for moral *judgment* (McClendon 1986, 104).

A minimalist and basically naturalist perspective would suggest that virtues are those things that fulfill the free exercise of human instincts, that enable the meeting of individual needs, that maximize our delight, reduce our horror. Virtues offer a balance between our inner controls—anxiety, shame, and guilt—and the social controls of custom, law, and order. The therapist develops the requisite skills to assist the person in achieving a workable compromise with sufficient harmony within and between self and others.

Virtues do not exist as independently defined qualities; they are always located in context and community. The courage of Achilles is the reverse of the courage of Jesus. For Homer's hero, courage was violent, deceptive, and virtually invincible; for Jesus it was nonviolent, truthful, and vulnerable. One person's virtue was the other's vice. Any particular virtue is a part of a shared story, a community narrative that is sufficiently truthful to guide the virtuous person in shaping a character in coherence with its truth (Hauerwas 1981, 156). Virtues must be grounded in the shared practices and the consensually prized goods of a particular community and tradition (MacIntyre 1984, 263).

Virtues Emerge from Practices

The virtues of common life depend on the presence of common human social *practices,* practices that act out the narrative of our lives provided by our community. The communal story contains a wide range of possible stories from which we each construct a story by assembling the preferred practices. The communal story offers us a narrative understanding of life, its meaning and destiny. The more complex of these practices we commonly refer to as the practice of medicine, the practice of psychiatry, the practice of law, the practice of psychology, the practice of social work, the practice of ministry, the practice of architecture, to name the obvious. Each of these vocational practices contains within it many particular practices common to each other and to the entire community.

Alasdair MacIntyre defines *practice* with some precision:

> Any coherent and complex form of socially established cooperative human activity through which goods internal to that form of activity are realized in the course of trying to achieve those standards of excellence which are appropriate to, and partially definitive of, that form of activity, with the result that human powers to achieve excellence, and human conceptions of the ends and goods involved are systematically extended (1984, 175).

Architecture is a practice; carpentry and masonry are not; they are skills that find their place within a practice. Marriage is a practice; sex is not; it is either a function or an art. Football is a practice; tackling, refereeing, or cheering are skills of varying physical, mental, or emotional difficulty. Leading a congregation in liturgy, worship, and prayer is a practice; saying grace at dinner is not. Art is a practice since it is dependent on a particular tradition, such as painting, and on a community of fellow artists, a public that supports art and artists, the dedication of its practitioners, and a unique configuration of skills, the artistic virtues of color, balance, form, line, perspective, and use of light (McClendon 1986, 162–68).

Practices are housed in and sheltered by institutions. Universities house education, hospitals are hospitable to medicine, building departments with inspectors and codes support architecture. But institutions corrupt practices, MacIntyre warns: "The ideals and the creativity of the practice are always vulnerable to the acquisitiveness of the institution" (1984, 181). Institutions are characteristically concerned about external goods—about acquiring money and material goods. They are structured in terms of power and status and distribute money, power, and status as rewards, obviously external rewards.

A practice is directed and empowered by a configuration of virtues (although a practice may also be motivated by vices). MacIntyre suggests that several virtues are common to every practice. He offers justice, courage, and truthfulness. The general consensus is that these three, and perhaps also temperance, can be recognized as essential central or cardinal virtues that are universal. What is not clear is what truthfulness entails or justice truly means.

Truthfulness, justice, and courage are virtues necessary to any social structure, but these "central invariant virtues" are never adequate to constitute a "morality," since a morality requires ends as well, future beliefs about the true nature of the person and the true end of a life. In the absence of such a "scheme," MacIntyre concludes, the traditional virtues, when not pursued for themselves, in reality become vices (MacIntyre 1975, 103–5). Truth, for example, when separated from a context of responsibility, can brutalize; justice without loyalty and love can become mechanical; courage without wisdom is foolhardy bravery and derring-do.

To name these cardinal virtues universal must be a tentative designation since they must be set in vastly different stories from contrasting cultures. Various cultures frame these concepts in differing narratives that provide, at times, diametrically opposite meanings. We must proceed with caution in universalizing virtues whose definitions are less than identical.

> But what does all this (the discussion of practices) have to do with the concept of virtues? It turns out that we are now in a position to formulate a first, even if a partial and tentative definition of virtue. A *virtue is an acquired human quality the possession and exercise of which tends to enable us to achieve those goods which are internal to practices and the lack of which effectively prevents us from achieving any such goods* (MacIntyre 1984, 178).

Every practice—in the particular focus of this study, the practices of pastoral counseling, pastoral psychotherapy, mediation, or conciliation—requires a certain kind of relationship between those who participate in its work. Virtues are those goods which define our relationships with colleagues or clients, with all who participate in the particular practice. In the work of reconciling persons estranged from themselves or from others, the goods that we offer in consolation, confrontation, conciliation, and human connection are internally rewarding as virtues. Or they can be studied techniques of treatment that are used for the purpose of external rewards—payment, prestige through research and publication, advancement in status. In the latter case they become media of exchange.

Virtues, MacIntyre argues, offer internal rewards. Of the three central virtues—truthfulness, justice, and courage—truthfulness offers the internal good of trustworthiness in relationships, justice is the respect of other's merits or deserts according to uniform standards, and courage is the willingness to risk harm or danger to oneself out of genuine care for others. In the practice of psychotherapy, truthful, trustworthy, just, equal, mutual, courageous, risk-taking, caring relationships characterize the role and reality of therapeutic presence; they embody the successful outcome of therapy for the client. When they are chosen because of their internal rewards, because of the satisfaction, security, and significance they give to life, they have become not techniques or therapeutic strategies, but virtues.

Forgiveness: Empty without Ethics

Forgiveness has no content in a context devoid of virtues or values. At best, it is reduced to a value-free acceptance, or a nonconditional love. Love without conditions is either divine—the infinite love of God—or devoid of meaning. Human love is never unconditional, except in a flattened world of neutrality. Acceptance is a value-free word: it can be expressed in a pluralistic world where values are reduced to the lowest common denominator. It is the appropriate modality for forgiveness in a radically individualized culture. Love can be reduced to attachment, tolerance, emotional warmth, and positive regard that, being nonjudgmental, offers no criticism, critique, or correction.

Forgiveness requires an ethical context. Without norms, values, mores, structures, and moral categories, forgiveness is formless and meaningless. In a community with a minimal core of shared values and commitments, forgiveness is reduced to tolerance, indulgence, or denial. Without a shared understanding of the moral meaning of love, Don Browning notes, "we do not know whether love means giving another person a massage, sleeping with his wife, inviting him to a cocktail party, joining him for a potluck dinner or what. We need to know the indices of love—the marks of love" (Browning 1976, 79).

Forgiveness has been drained of its essential meanings as Western culture has become increasingly individualized and moral contexts have been reduced to the lowest common denominator. Forgiveness is reduced to a passive tolerance or a "judge not that ye be not judged" withdrawal from injuries or betrayals. Forgiveness becomes significant once more when moral values matter, when ethics are more than aesthetics, when character and virtue become central to the meaning of personhood.

As one moves across the spectrum from forbearance, to forgiveness, to reconciliation, to re-creation of relationship, the ethical aspects increase step by step. Where forbearance requires only tolerance and indulgence in a virtual suspension of ethical issues, forgiveness demands the facing of justice, love, mercy, and the uncomfortable behavior we call repentance. Reconciliation must struggle with deeper levels of all these and the complexities of restitution and restoration. The ethical content and context become central. The character of those forgiving and the virtues of mercy, love, and forgiveness become the central foci.

Forgiveness as a Virtue

In classical Greek philosophy—Socrates, Plato, Aristotle, the Stoics, and so on—a virtue (*aretē*) is that form of knowledge which makes the wise person truly good or virtuous. Wisdom provides the spiritual faculty that can control instincts and passions, subject them to reason, and order them toward the attainment of happiness. A virtue may be acquired, learned, and developed in practice. Forgiveness is seen not as a virtue, but as an attitude or disposition rising from the virtues of temperance, fortitude, justice, and prudence.

What for the Greeks were anthropocentric virtues achieved through cultivation of the intellect, became for the scholastic philosophers spiritual qualities received from God as the divine gift of grace. The virtues (*virtutes*) were not patiently learned and studiously or laboriously acquired, they were bestowed by God. Such were love, temperance, justice, courage, and prudence, and forgiveness was not among them.

The Christian virtue of forgiveness—forgiveness as a true virtue—becomes clear as it is seen in its full New Testament declension as the spiritual, emotional, volitional content of the practice of reconciliation. Not just a disposition to be forgiving, or an intention to offer or seek forgiveness, authentic forgiveness is that cluster of motivations which seeks to regain the brother or the sister in reconciliation.

Reconciliation, in its broadest meaning, is the central task of a series of practices—pastoral care, counseling and psychotherapy, mediation, social work, psychology, psychiatry, law, diplomacy. In contemporary usage, the word *reconciliation* has become a designation of the desired end state; conciliation is the process. Conciliation is the work—one of the primary goals of all the practices named above. Reconciliation is the hoped-for outcome. Each of the practices has its own language to express this tension. In the practice of mediation we are hard on process, soft on people, open on outcomes. In the practice of psychotherapy we value accurate empathy, genuineness, and disinterested nonpossessive warmth. In pastoral theology, we affirm conciliation as our work, reconciliation as God's work. The movement to reconnect, to reconcile, to restore relationship can be modeled, but not motivated, from without. We can remove the obstacles, reframe the circumstances, renew the communication, but we cannot rebuild the relationship.

The choice to forgive arises from within—from the character of the person. The willingness to forgive is a distinguishing mark of deep social interest in the character (Adler), of the union of wound and healing in the archetype of restoration (Jung), of authentic reparations (Klein), of empathic self-object relations in mature narcissistic development (Kohut), to begin a short list of theorists. The courage to forgive is an excellency of character, a virtue that enables one to act in restoration of personal relationships, to risk in reconstruction of social networks, to commit oneself to live in moral integrity.

To understand forgiveness as a virtue, it may be helpful to examine a parallel virtue, a very particular goodness but one largely unnoticed in lists of virtues. I am indebted to James McClendon for his suggestion of *presence* as a model virtue for consideration. *Presence* is the quality of *being there* for and with another. It is being oneself for someone else. Its reverse would be not absence but mental withdrawal, emotional detachment, relational estrangement in empty coexistence. Its parody is the actor's simulation of "authentic contact" or the salesman's intense intrusion or the politician's guarantee of concern for each constituent (McClendon 1986, 106).

Theologically, God's presence is celebrated with bread and wine, symbolized by baptism's outpouring, claimed at every gathering of believers. The presence of God is guaranteed by covenant, seen in the incarnation, experienced in the coming of the Spirit, anticipated at the end of all things. The believer is called to be present with others in steadfast and stubborn commitments of loyalty, in compassionate and caring actions of help in situations of injury or loss, in courageous and sacrificial interventions of confrontation in contexts of injustice or oppression. "I have to be there to be true to myself, I cannot be uninvolved if I prize my own integrity," we explain. It is Martin Luther King Jr. walking in marches with oppressed people; it is Mother Teresa choosing to live in Calcutta slums; it is undramatic but demanding pastoral availability or everyday Christian concern for friend or neighbor in need or pain.

This *presence* becomes a virtue as it expresses the narrative of a community that acts in the tradition of incarnation, of embodiment of neighbor-love, of willing service to human need. This virtue is a particular requisite for the pastoral counselor who discovers that presence provides the floor of all healing encounter. It becomes a virtue as it is lived for the sake of rewards internal to the relationship and internal to the persons present to each other. We may speak of forgiveness as a parallel virtue. *Forgiveness* is the quality of *being with* another in spite of injury done or alienation mutually experienced. Its reverse would be resentment, bitterness, and hatred within; alienation, distance, or avoidance between. Its parody is superficial acceptance, denial, or fatuous tolerance.

Theologically, God's forgiveness is offered to us both as a personal reality of our being accepted and as a social reality of our being included in forgiving community and becoming agents of forgiveness to others in community. All forgiveness, human or divine, operates from the same model. Both center in the mutual recognition that repentance is genuine and that right relationships—just and loving—have been restored or achieved. It is not simply the freeing of oneself from being held hostage by bitterness, grief, or anger, although forgiveness does give the gift of freedom. Nor is it the resolution of exhausted emotions, the fatigue of tired memory, or the finishing of discharged emotions, although forgiveness does require a time of withdrawal, reflection, remembering, and gradual release. It is, instead, a clear, present transaction that finishes past situations of failure, forgoes future mistrust and suspicion of betrayal, and forgives in an act of acceptance grounded in whatever repentance is possible for either or both.

This forgiveness becomes a virtue as it embodies and extends the narrative of a forgiving community that acts in the tradition of the cross, of the shared table of forgiveness, of the common life of forgiving-forgiven people. This virtue is the central empowerment of the pastoral counselor or caregiver who knows that all healing slowly grows from the forgiving centers of life—the center within, the center between self and other, the center above and beyond us both. It becomes a virtue as it is expressive of internal rewards (although many acts of "forgiveness" may be done for external rewards of advantage, arrogance, superiority, control, manipulation, or abuse).

Virtuous Stories

In *After Virtue,* Alasdair MacIntyre sets forth *story* as the central feature of the human experience. "I can only answer the question 'What am I to do?' if I can answer the prior question 'Of what story . . . do I find myself a part?' " (1981, 201). One's individual life story is framed in a larger communal story which gives definition to our identities as persons. One's communal narrative, or history, records significant persons, events, and actions in the past and points toward character, occurrences, and options for the future. Stories give us *vision.* Vision is a future foreseen in which "certain possibilities beckon us forward and others repel us, some seem already foreclosed and others perhaps inevitable. . . . If the narrative of our [individual life] is to continue intelligibly . . . it is always both the case that there are constraints on how the story can continue *and* that within those constraints there are indefinitely many ways it can continue" (MacIntyre 1981, 200–201).

Each community's story invites its members to claim a role as a participant in a narrative quest, which they embody, and which pursues a future goal or end. So the story offers guidance, safeguards, warnings, and prohibitions. It contains its own listings of goods to be sought and evils to be avoided, its own recognition of what constitutes failure or success, regress or progress.

Within our community narratives, MacIntyre observes, there are certain *recurring kinds of performances* we call *practices;* there are certain *habitual ways of performing these practices;* these are *virtues.* Virtuous stories sustain us in the relevant kind of quest for the good by enabling us to overcome the harms, dangers, temptations, and distractions that we encounter, and will furnish us with increasing self-knowledge and increasing knowledge of the good (1981, 204). In pledging our lives to a particular community and its story, we choose the meaning of our existence! To which story, in what community, in which values ought we to invest our lives?

We dwell, within a culture, in a shared set of myths, argued Rollo May. Myth is our primary way of making sense in a senseless world. Myths are narrative patterns that give significance to our existence. Myths are the narrative stories that hold our society together. There are multiple layers of myths in each society, but there are a few central myths that possess the power to link together large pieces of social behavior. The core myth of our time, May argued, is the myth of Narcissus. Narcissus fell into unrequited love with his own reflection in a pool, and sadly pined away until he died.

The narcissist is utterly self-absorbed, self-centered, and self-indulgent, so full of self that the person is emotionally, morally, empathically empty. The narcissist is lonely (ruggedly individualistic), shallow (fixatedly superficial), self-defined, and self-obsessed (self-good is the highest value; what feels right is right; personal gratification is the goal of adjustment). The culture that fosters narcissism, Christopher Lasch concluded, is insecure, desperately dependent on the approval of others, frantically pursuing intense emotional experiences to feel something within the inner void, overwhelmed by suppressed rage, and alienated from the larger values that offer meaning to life and support in the face of suffering, aging, or death (1979).

It is clear that each virtue—love, justice, honesty, courage, forgiveness—requires a community to give it content as well as context. Such a community does not exist in the general social system, MacIntyre argues; it must be created. It is indispensable to our moral existence, to the formation of character, to the existence of virtues.

> What matters at this stage is the construction of local forms of community within which civility and the intellectual and moral life can be sustained through the new dark ages which are already upon us. And if the tradition of the virtues was able to survive the horrors of the last dark ages, we are not entirely without grounds for hope. This time the barbarians are not waiting beyond the frontiers; they have already been governing us for quite some time. And it is our lack of consciousness of this that constitutes part of our predicament (MacIntyre 1984, 263).

The Healing Narrative

Forgiveness is grounded in a healing narrative. It is rooted, obviously, in the story of the two parties involved and beneath this in the common story they share with each other in community. We each need a connective story to provide a moral context for our efforts at reconciliation. The criteria for an adequate story (see Hauerwas 1977, 21, 80) that offers a moral framework to the community and is authentically truthful include at least the following:

> A true story should have the power to release us from destructiveness;
>
> It should provide a way of seeing through our current distortions;
>
> It should have room to keep us from having to resort to violence;
>
> It should have a sense for the tragic, for how meaning transcends power;
>
> It must be one that helps me to go on.

Both the offended and the offender are able to change a tragic story of injury and victimization into a story of forgiveness and reconciliation when it is seen, not as the central story of one's existence or of the universe (as one feels in shame, anger, and pain), but as a subplot in a larger story.

The human story of forgiving the sister or brother is a fragment of the divine story. "All sorrows can be borne if you put them into a story," Danish author Isak Dinesen wrote. We turn our pain into narrative so we can bear it; we turn our ecstasy into narrative so we can prolong it. But no matter how compelling, how transforming, how satisfying the denouement of one's story, it is never enough. One's personal story is inadequate, told as an individual tale of a solitary self. It is in need of another story, of others' stories, to complete it. The healing narrative looses the old bonds of one's binding story and assists in binding up one's wounds in a caring and comforting way. The healing narrative looses one from the bonds of old obligations, fears, and entrapment; it offers new possibilities that are binding settlements, binding pledges of trustworthiness. It is truly a binding and a loosing (Matt. 18:18–20).

> Every "binding" requires a "loosing," as we cannot and should not be bound to everything in our past. It may even be true that some of us inherit a history so destructive we may rightly wonder how we could ever be bound to it. Yet my freedom from such a history cannot come by having "no history" but by acquiring a narrative that helps me have a stance toward my past without resentment (Hauerwas 1981, 276).

The therapeutic process requires a review of the person's story which reveals how he or she is bound and where he or she has been loosed. It proceeds by supporting persons as they are (1) unbinding what has been bound for them by family and community, which must be loosed and bound in new ways; (2) rebinding what has been bound in stable, enduring, creative ways and might easily be discarded in a time of change; (3) unbinding and being enabled to live without bounds or binds in a new story of liberation.

When bound by resentment, as Hauerwas notes, one continues to bind the self to destructive events since the self-story defines its own being as a creature of injustice. To be truly free is to learn to live by a new story without resentment. This is possible as one learns "that our life, including the destructive past, is nothing less than a gift" (Hauerwas 1981, 276). A gift story replaces the old guilt story; a grace story now includes the injuries and losses, lifting them out of a truncated resentment story and setting them in an open-ended story of forgiveness.

The person's story must be set into a larger story, James McClendon has argued, and it finds its true meaning in not just the family story but the community narrative that makes some sense of our personal and familial pattern of events, dramas, and plots. "*Our* story is inadequate as well: the story of each and all is itself hungry for a greater story that overcomes our persistent self-deceit, redeems our common life, and provides a way for us to be a people among all earth's peoples, without subtracting from the significance of other's peoplehood, their own stories, their lives" (McClendon 1986, 356). We need a story that

> is more compelling than any contemporary therapeutic sensibility and ideal therapeutic model, no matter how "authentic" the sensibility or model may be in itself.
>
> embodies character, offers vision, and inspires ethics.
>
> expresses the virtues of justice, courage, and faithfulness, and even more, of love, mercy, and forgiveness.
>
> will empower our practices to inspire us to live for internal rewards, not the external rewards of status, money, position, power, and their friend, greed.

We need a story greater, larger, longer than our own little narratives, a story that is capable of offering us content for our moral lives and context for our ethical decisions. Such a story must be greater than any social, communal, or national narrative. It is a faith story, an eternal narrative of the meaning of our existence. Only such a story can reconcile us to ourselves, to each other, and to God, who is author of all reconciliation.

In the early eighties, in Southern California, a young woman was abducted, brutally raped, and murdered. The murderer was arrested, tried, convicted, and sentenced to life in prison, but this judicial process brought no consolation to the mother. Goldie Mae Bristol was outraged, depressed, sleepless. Unable to shake the anger and the feeling of impotence to change a tragic situation, she quit her job and with her family moved to a new community to start again. Then moved again, and then again. Nothing changed except the deepening of the bitterness.

One day a new acquaintance persuaded Goldie to attend her church. Goldie's response was indifferent, but the friend persisted and gradually something started Goldie's journey of change and the beginning of healing. The warmth of the church community, the support of a prayer group, and then the beginnings of personal Bible study slowly, over three or four years, reframed her memories of her daughter and her ruminations about the murder.

Goldie made several surprising discoveries: the recollections of her happy days with her daughter began to offer peace rather than remorse; forgotten memories returned to awaken gratitude and renewed delight in her daughter's life; the feelings toward the murderer began to soften and the monster began to take on human dimensions. In astonishment, she heard herself use words about forgiving what had been eternally unforgivable. She began to talk about this with friends, in small groups, and in church services.

Goldie's transformation, once begun, accelerated. She accepted invitations to speak to parents of murdered children, and then to several groups of prisoners. Through the chaplain of a nearby state penitentiary she was invited to share her experience in a prison chapel service. She gripped the pulpit on the platform of the prison auditorium and began to tell her story to the thirty men in prison garb. The account of years of torment, of slow and inexplicable recovery, of the hard-won victory of a forgiving heart came out with deep emotion. "I am here to tell you that one person on the outside has forgiven the man who crushed the life out of her cherished daughter. That person forgives you, and in the name of Christ wants you to feel loved and prized as a human being. Whatever you have done, I forgive you. God forgives you, and wants you to return to a respected and useful place in society."

Her transparency was shattering. In the silence that followed her address, a man stood and said, "Mrs. Bristol, my name is Michael Dennis Keyes, and I am the man you have forgiven." She gasped, totally unprepared for this surprise. Tears filled her eyes and slowly she opened her arms. Michael Dennis Keyes came to the platform, choking with emotion, and they embraced.

Her journey of offering forgiveness had come to an end. His journey of finding forgiveness was just begun (Collins 1991, 1).

From a paradigm of unilateral forgiveness, a parent's act of forgiving a daughter's murderer suggests the presence of great love, compassion, and understanding of human frailty. It models letting go, releasing the other, restoring something for the other that may lead to healing. But from a paradigm of mutuality and forgiveness which takes repentance and justice as central elements in reconciliation, the parent's forgiveness can be seen as unfeeling, unloving, and disrespectful of the daughter's worth. Without knowing the conditions under which Goldie comes to final closure (for example, did the wrongdoer offer sincere repentance? Did he offer to make some act of amends?), we cannot judge the virtuousness of this transaction, but we must feel perplexed about its character. As Friedrich Nietzsche wrote, "Forgiveness may, in certain circumstances, be harmful and wrong, a vice instead of a virtue."

Certainly the first of such vices is the choice to simply forget the offense. This is apathy; it is yielding to memory fatigue. Forgetting implies that the action is so insignificant it is lost or discarded from memory. Forgiving indicates that there is an injury, and the injured is aware of the injury. The memory is central to the process of resolution and restoration. Forgiveness is a moral action in response to memory of an injury. It is not forgetting, not condoning, not pardoning. All three of these fall short of authentic forgiving. Forgetting drops the act down the memory hole; condoning accepts it within the memory collection, while denying its significance. Pardoning recognizes its significance but cancels the consequences (no recollection, no significance, no consequences). Forgiveness deals with all three.

She forgave her attacker even as he was raping her. The eighty-six-year-old Adventist Sabbath school teacher was standing outside her National City, California, church, waiting with a box of supplies destined for Bangladesh, when a man seized her from behind. He dragged her out of sight of the street, then crudely picked her up and carried her to a secluded area.

She began praying aloud: "Forgive him, Father, forgive him. I know you love him as much as you love me." The prayer in no way stopped the man from raping the woman. She lost consciousness, then awoke to find him wrapping tape around her neck, trying to strangle her.

This time she prayed in behalf of herself: "Dear God, send your holy angels to save me." She remembers hearing the voices of children from the church school approaching. The attacker fled; the children discovered her and ran for help.

"I forgave him from the beginning," she says with the certainty of a lifetime of practicing her faith." For her, forgiveness is more about healing yourself than demanding any reparation from the other person. "It actually probably does more for me than the other person," she says. For her, it is about discovering wholeness for oneself. A lifelong Seventh Day Adventist, a former missionary who is the daughter, widow, and grandmother of pastors, she says, "you forgive whether the other ever asks for forgiveness or not" (Dolbee 1994).

Jim Wade was accused—falsely, as time would show—of raping his eight-year-old daughter. Authorities removed her from their San Diego home in 1989. One year later, Wade was arrested and charged. Finally in November of 1991, he was cleared after investigators at last tested the semen that had been overlooked on the daughter's night clothes and found it did not match his.

But in the intervening two and one-half years the family had been severely injured; Wade was publicly maligned. How can he make peace with everyone involved in the tragedy?

Back in his hometown in Missouri where he has retired to begin his life again, Wade insists that forgiveness is a two-way street. He thinks he has done his part—"letting go of something and carrying on with your own life and not sitting around and worrying about it." But the people who wronged him, county and city investigators among them, need to do their part. When asked what he would do if his accusers called and apologized, he replied, "I'd probably forgive them."

But for now, Wade has not forgiven them. "I don't think they learned anything. I think they're hurting people even now as we talk." To press for some sign of recognition and justice, he sued and settled the process against various agencies for $3.7 million. "It wasn't about money," says Wade. "I think that was the only handle we had on them. I don't think there was anything else we could do to get some sort of attention drawn to the problem they created" (Dolbee 1994).

During the 1915 massacre of more than a million Armenians by the Turks, a military unit attacked a village, killing all the adults and taking the young women as hostages. An officer raided a home, shot the parents, gave the daughters to his soldiers, but kept the beautiful oldest daughter for himself. After months of captivity, servitude, and sexual abuse, she escaped and slowly rebuilt her life, ultimately completing training as a nurse.

One night while on duty in a Turkish hospital, she recognized the face of a desperately ill patient in intensive care. It was her captor and abuser, the murderer of her parents, the Turkish officer. He was comatose and required constant care if he was to survive. A long and difficult convalescence followed, with the man too ill to be aware of his surroundings.

One day, as he was returning to health, the doctor said to him, "You are a very fortunate man. Had it not been for the devotion of this nurse, you would never have made it, you would certainly be dead."

The officer looked long at the nurse. "I've wanted for days to ask you, we have met before, have we not?"

"Yes," she replied, "we have met before."

"Why didn't you kill me when you had the opportunity? Or why didn't you just let me die?"

"Because," the nurse replied, "I am a follower of one who taught, 'love your enemies'" (Wainright 1980, 434).

Toward a New Paradigm of Forgiveness

1. Forgiveness, to be at all meaningful, requires an ethical context. Without norms, values, mores, and moral categories, forgiveness is

formless and meaningless. In a permissive context, it is reduced to tolerance or indulgence.

2. Forgiveness is the virtue that enables the practice of reconciliation. It becomes a true virtue as it embodies and extends the narrative of a community that draws persons together, bridges breaches, and invites reconciliation.

3. We need to embrace our communities or create new communities that prize and retell communal stories, and strengthen their connection to larger stories that unite us, reconciling us with each other across all boundaries.

6

The Curse and Blessing of Scapegoats

> Whenever A annoys or injures B on the pretense of saving or improving C, A is a scoundrel (Mencken's Law)
>
> —H L Mencken

> One of them, Caiaphas, the high priest that year, said, "You don't seem to have grasped the situation at all, you fail to see that it is better for one man to die for the people, than for the whole nation to be destroyed."
>
> —John 11·49–50, JB

> The notion that we can transfer our guilt and sufferings to some other being who will bear them for us is familiar (to the most primitive understanding) Because it is possible to shift a load of wood, stones or what not from our own back to the back of another, [one] fancies that it is equally possible to shift the burden of pains and sorrows to another, who will suffer them in one's stead.
>
> —Sir James Frazer

A lion, a leopard, a hyena, and a donkey met at the watering hole one hot afternoon and began to talk of how bad conditions were. There was no rain, the water hole was dangerously low, and food of all kinds was scarce.

"How can this thing have happened?" they said over and over.

"Some one of us must have sinned," said the hyena.

"Yes," they all agreed. "Certainly a great sin else God would not be punishing us so sorely."

"Perhaps we should confess our sins and repent," the leopard offered.

To this all shook their heads in agreement, and the lion began: "Oh, I have committed an awful sin. Once I found a young bull near the village—obviously he was their domestic property—and I stole him and ate him." The animals looked at the lion understandingly. They all feared him for his strength, so they shook their heads.

"No, no," they protested. "That is no sin, it is only your natural right, your nature as a hunter."

Then the leopard said, "Ah, I have committed a dreadful sin. When I was in the valley I found a goat that had strayed from the herd and I caught him and ate him while the shepherd boy watched."

The other animals looked at the leopard, whose hunting talents they all greatly admired and whose speed they feared, and protested: "No, no, that is not sin, it was your right."

Then the hyena spoke: "Oh, I have committed a terrible sin. Once I stole into the village by night and snatched a hen from her roost, carried her away, and ate her."

"No, no!" the animals cried together, "that is no sin!"

Then the donkey spoke: "Once when my master was driving me along the road he met a friend and stopped to talk. While they talked, I went to the edge of the road and nibbled the grass along the edge of the man's yard."

The other animals looked at the donkey's long face. No one feared him or the retaliation of his friends. There was nothing about him that any of them admired. There was the silence of reflection, then they all shook their heads sadly and said: "*That* is a sin. That is stealing, indeed a terrible sin. You are the cause of all our misery."

And so the lion, the leopard, and the hyena turned upon the thieving donkey and devoured him (Courlander and Leslau, 1950).

A terrifying tempest blows across the Mediterranean Sea. A small ship is foundering in the mountainous waves. The mariners are desperately bailing water, tossing their cargo overboard to lighten the ship, and saying their ritual prayers to their various gods, but all in vain. The wooden craft wallows helplessly in the waves.

In the midst of this desperation, the captain discovers one passenger fast asleep in a dry corner of the hold. "Up, you fool," he cries. "Don't you know the danger we are in?" On deck the sailors are casting lots to discover whose great evil has brought this tragedy down on their heads. The sleeper, Jonah, is thrust into the circle. The lot falls on him.

"Who are you and what have you done?" they ask.

"I'm fleeing from the God of all Gods, who sent me to carry out a task I couldn't stomach. I was to go to Nineveh to warn the people that their city would be destroyed unless they repented of their ways. If Nineveh burns, no one could be happier than me, so I boarded this ship for the far end of the sea."

The sailors are horrified, but still hesitant to obey Jonah's orders that they sacrifice him to the sea. But at last, when all their attempts to stay afloat are failing, they pitch him overboard, and the sea is immediately calm.

The story, one of the purest forms of the scapegoat ritual in ancient writings, does not end in the death of Jonah: the Jewish tradition was already rejecting the concept of appeasing or influencing God by use of the scapegoat. The second act of the drama unfolds with surprising twists. But this introduction reveals the pattern of religious ritual in virtually all cultures. The ship is community; the tempest the sacrificial crisis; the jettisoned cargo the cultural system; the diverse prayers the breakdown of the religious order; the lot is the revelation of the divine will through chance. The resolution is the sacrifice of the scapegoat.

Girard and Sacred Violence

A startling yet stimulating new theory of religion was proposed by René Girard in *Violence and the Sacred* (1977). His theory is rooted in the hard reality of human violence and the rituals employed to contain it. Violence is endemic. Religion offers the only answer; Girard says: killing can be ritualized and rationalized as "sacrifice." Religion offers a violent solution: controlled rituals of sacrifice to replace the terror of uncontrolled killing.

"Sacrifice is the most crucial and fundamental of rites [and . . . also the most commonplace" (1977, 300). The phenomenon of sacrifice stands at the center of the whole human experience. All systems that structure human society have been generated from its vortex—languages, moral codes, taboos, etiquette, rites, kinship, exchange of goods, hierarchy, civil institutions. The rituals of sacrifice lie at the core of the myths that shape each culture, and these rituals are enigmas to be pondered. In the most diverse forms of human culture, a ritual killing is central to the essential story of each culture's religion.

Ritual reenacts a prior event. It represents or substitutes for that event. The ritual of sacrifice reenacts a killing, reinterprets that act of killing, and so ritualizes a past killing to sublimate the urge for ongoing violence. Girard suggests that the "prior event" is a collective murder, an act of mob violence that all ritual killings rationalize, mythologize, and ritualize. "Sacrifice" is a complex term that condenses this cultural phenomenon of a collective killing of a human victim, a culture's mythic rationalization of this story, and its ritualization into religious practice. A collective murder stands at the beginning of culture, Girard posits, and the drama of religion in virtually all cultures arises from the same plot.

Humans are aggressive. They have no braking mechanism for intraspecific conflict. Rivalries, once begun, lead to manslaughter. Murder the sole answer to murder. Revenge and reciprocal retaliation spiral ceaselessly. To end it, a "final" killing is necessary. This is accomplished by "the mechanism of the surrogate victim." One person, from within the group, is identified as victim. The surrogate must represent the guilty (party, parties, or the group itself). The surrogate must be vulnerable, nonresistant, without champions to continue retaliation and revenge. The group becomes unanimous in assigning blame. When unanimity is achieved, the victim is condemned, killed, or ostracized. The violence ends. Aggression is redirected. The group becomes collaborative and cooperative.

Girard models his work on Freud, but he stands on Freud's shoulders. His theory of mimetic desire was achieved in his struggle to understand Freud's theory of Oedipal conflict. Where Freud's theory is locked into the primary triangle—rivalry with the same-sex parent for the affection of the opposite-sex parent—Girard places the dynamic between any model-rival and any object valued by the model. The process is not unconscious but one of mythic mentality (participation in the collective unconscious, not the personal unconscious). Instead of desire for the object leading to rivalry and then being resolved in mimicry, it is the other way around. Mimesis of the admired model leads to desire for the object, which creates rivalry. The Oedipal triangle is transformed from familial to social relationship. The parent-child mimicry turned into rivalry becomes model-disciple competition. The order of events is radically inverted. Only societies that discovered some means of containing violence and its endless retaliation survived. Society is the outcome of successful management of violence.

Universally, violence has been contained by the scapegoat mechanism. Studies across cultures past as well as present confirm the omnipresence of these phenomena. Whether Girard is right in positing this primal collective murder event as the starting point of culture and the generative power of religions will be an issue for research and debate for years to come. Clearly he has stimulated new perspectives for many disciplines—anthropology, literature, theology, history, biblical studies, sociology, and psychology, for example.

A fully satisfactory theory of the origin of the scapegoat mechanism awaits ongoing research into our violent origins, and Girard's theory is one among several deserving close examination (see Walter Burkert, *Homo Necans* [1983] and Jonathan Smith, *Imagining Religion* [1982]). What is indisputable is the nearly universal presence of the scapegoat phenomenon in the histories of culture and religion.

Having read and compared the myths, tragedies, and great novels of the Western tradition, Girard finds at the center of it all these common elements: mimetic desire, the sacrificial crisis, sacrifice, and the surrogate-victim mechanism. The uniting of these elements, he concludes, creates the generative matrix of culture and social existence. The Greek tragedies, Shakespeare, and major novelists are primary sources for the discovery of the myth that sustains us in an ongoing "sacrificial crisis" that is prolonged in Western culture, and manifests itself with overt violence at every level of social process. Violence, overt and recognized as well as covert and denied, is at the center of virtually every culture.

If the violence is to end, it must be faced, the mechanisms must be exposed, and the truth about our inherent destructiveness must be disclosed. Who dares expose it? Who will disclose the truth? Whence comes the courage to face it? All this, Girard suggests, is present in the literary foundation of the Judeo-Christian tradition, since both the Hebrew scriptures and the New Testament make a radical transformation of the surrogate-victim mechanism by exposing its central injustice.

Sacrifice and the sacrificial crisis are present in all cultures that surround the Bible and are also present within it. But the biblical stories stand in contrast. They do not conceal the violence, press it into the unconscious, and proceed to reconstitute the surrogate-victim mechanism in the creation of myths of redemptive violence. Instead they reveal the guilt, they identify the responsibility of the violent, they uphold the innocence of the victim. The plot is not reversed, but the characterization is the inverse. The meaning is transformed. There is another pathway to resolution: the truth can be told, reality may be faced, the mythic solution with a guilty victim may be exposed as delusional. Instead of projecting our violence onto a surrogate victim, sacralizing the sacrifice as a necessary action, one can proclaim the victim as innocent rather than ceremonially guilty and so expose and shame the mythic falsehood. Or one might yield to evil as an "innocent victim" and offer oneself as did Jesus. One need not demand "full rights" and perpetuate the endless cycles of retaliation, recrimination, and revenge.

The Scapegoat Mechanism

The scapegoat mechanism comprises a cluster of elements that create mimetic conflict—the mirrored rage of violence between adversaries:

1. *Mimetic desire attracts.* We become human beings by learning what is desirable from others and imitating them. We learn to desire what they desire (mimesis); we come to value what someone we admire values; we want what is wanted by those whose approval we want.
2. *Mimetic rivalry results.* We cannot have all we want. It is a world of limited resources, and competition is inevitable, conflict unavoidable. The rivalry, Girard argues, creates a double

bind. The admired model invites us to "Be like me: value the object I value." When the imitator reaches to take it, rivalry erupts and the model says, "Do not be like me, the prize is mine." The third command of the double bind is "You will never have a share unless you win it by violence."

3. *Crisis escalates.* Boundaries are threatened, violated, destroyed. The differences that insulated and buffered the rivals dissolve in crisis. The distinctions that maintain the social order collapse. Girard has named this "a crisis of distinctions." As distinctions fail, the social system is in emergency and in danger of total collapse. But the collapse can be avoided, even averted, if a scapegoat can be found.
4. *The victim is chosen.* The scapegoat is chosen to bear the rage and pain and receive the festering violence. A necessary fiction is constructed to finger the victim as the cause of the crisis. The fiction of the scapegoat's guilt must be sustained regardless of the truth of the matter. The sacrifice is made and the hostilities cease. The termination of hostility is all the proof that is needed to verify that the actual cause of the conflict has been identified and therefore the execution or ostracism was fully justified. Violence drains from the group and mutual cooperation becomes possible again, reconciliation may follow, and then the victim is seen as sacred.
5. *The victim is sacralized.* The victim, made necessary by the group's violence and their fear of communal collapse, is now rendered sacred as their salvation. Simultaneously regarded as accursed and life giving, the victim is bestowed special honors or even elevated to divinity. The violence has been averted; one person dies for the entire community; ritual and religion are generated and integrated into the group's life.
6. *Ritual is established.* The sacrificial mechanism, once ritualized and sacralized, is repeated in strictly controlled religious rituals, then in legislative codes, and finally in the popular myths, stories, and songs of the culture. Internal aggressions in the people and external aggression in the group are now diverted and expended ritually. The social fabric is preserved; the pain of the body politic is vented on one body.

Religion is organized violence in the service of community, sacrifice of a victim to preserve social harmony and tranquillity. The sacrificial mechanism itself is concealed under layers of myth, ritual, mores, and prohibitions. Its origins are denied (we do not permit our violence to be known, especially by ourselves); its true nature is concealed (the myth of necessity, the aura of divine ordination, the amnesia about its origins mask its malevolence and justify its cost to the victims).

Violence hides itself beneath the layers of bureaucracy, behind the screen of language. The ugly specter of anti-Semitism is an undeniable example. The holocaust with its religious rhetoric concealed the heinous nature of genocide so successfully that millions of Christians could not see the obvious. Doctrines of manifest destiny, racial superiority, and the inhumanity of the "savage" have supported genocide in the Americas, Australia, Africa, and Asia. The ethnic cleansing of a European state with a Christian theological rationale at the end of the twentieth century reveals the scapegoat mechanism's permissive and persuasive power.

Violence in Biblical History

At the beginning of faith history, Abraham believed that he must kill his son Isaac as a human sacrifice. He set out to the holy place to offer his son. Søren Kierkegaard wrote, in analysis of Abraham's dilemma: "The ethical expression for what Abraham did is, that he would murder Isaac; the religious expression is, that he would sacrifice Isaac" (Kierkegaard 1954, 41). At the moment of murder, Abraham froze, arrested by an angel; he repented, and substituted an animal for the original victim, his son. The ritual of sacrifice remains a constant throughout the Hebrew scriptures.

Violence is the central theme of the Hebrew Bible, notes Raymond Schwager. There are six hundred passages of explicit violence, one thousand verses where God's own violent actions of punishment are described, a hundred passages where an express command is given by God to kill people, and several enigmatic accounts in which God kills or tries to kill for no apparent reason (for example, Ex. 4:24–26). "No other human activity or experience is mentioned as often, be it the world of work or trade, of family and sexuality or that of knowledge and the experience of nature. For the biblical authors, the most impressive and distressing experience seems to have been that human beings war with and kill one another" (Schwager 1987, 47).

The Hebrew Bible, according to Girard, recounts a long and laborious exodus out of the world of violence and sacred projections, an exodus plagued by many reversals and much falling short of its goal in the Pentateuch, Prophets, and Writings. The mechanisms of violence and projection on the scapegoat remain partly hidden; the old sacred notions continue in force and are never quite exposed in their true meaning throughout the process of revelation (Schwager 1987, 47).

There is, however, a counterforce to the myths, rituals, and religions that sacralize violence, Girard argues, a force that tends toward the exposure of the immortal lie of sacred violence, a revelation of the true nature of evil, and this is the Christian gospel (1986, 100). Its roots lie in the Hebrew scriptures, where for the first time in human history God is seen as identified with the victims of violence. All other religious myths are written from the point of view of the victimizers (see the Exodus account; Isaiah 53; Micah 4:2–4; Isa. 19:19–25; Psalm 5). "In the Hebrew Bible," Girard argues,

> there is clearly a dynamic that moves in the direction of the rehabilitation of the victims, but it is not a cut-and-dried thing. Rather, it is a process under way, a text in travail; it is not a chronologically progressive process, but a struggle that advances and retreats. I see the Gospels as the climactic achievement of that trend, and therefore as the essential text in the cultural upheaval of the modern world (Burkert, Girard, and Smith 1987, 141).

The New Testament, as well as the Hebrew scriptures, is a whole collection of books written from the point of view of the victims, of the abused and oppressed. God is on the side of the oppressed, not the oppressors. God is not the authorization for demanding sacrifice—God is on the side of those sacrificed. God opposes the violence that is central to society. The chain of murder calling for murder is interrupted. Capital punishment in mimetic repetition of the original is no longer justified by the stories of God's acts and interventions.

In the arrest, trial, sentencing, and execution of Jesus the scapegoating mechanism is totally exposed, fully revealed for all who will see. The Gospels explode the scapegoat myth, but the early Christians could not sustain this revolutionary insight and soon began to combine it with the old scapegoat theologies. (1) The Gospels and Acts tell of God exposing and exploding our scapegoat myths. The powers of this world have totally violated justice; they have acted corruptly in blaming and killing an innocent victim. His death is not justifiable; it is not necessary for the peace of the society, the security of the state, or the sanctity of the religious order. Their rationale is a lie. The myth of redemptive violence—that one man die to protect and substitute for the safety of the whole—is shattered. The powers are exposed. (2) The apostles vacillate; the vision becomes confused. Instead of maintaining the revelation that God has entered and ended the scapegoat mechanism, they return to the mechanism. God sends the son to be the scapegoat; God intends that Jesus be the final scapegoat; God requires an expiatory scapegoat to resolve the tension between God's own wrath and God's love. (3) The responsibility is now placed on God, not on the rebellious and violent powers of the world. The domination systems of the violent social order are merely pawns in a heavenly chess game. As Walter Wink describes it pointedly:

> The God whom Jesus revealed as no longer our rival, no longer threatening and vengeful, but unconditionally loving and forgiving, who needed no satisfaction by blood—this God of infinite mercy was metamorphosed by the church into the image of a wrathful God whose demand for blood atonement leads to God's requiring of his own son a death on behalf of us all. The nonviolent God of Jesus comes to be depicted as a God of unequaled violence, since God not only allegedly demands the blood of the victim who is closest and most precious to him, but also holds the whole of humanity accountable for a death that God both anticipated and required. Against such an image of God the revolt of atheism is an act of pure religion (Wink 1992, 149).

Simone Weil sets it in a terse proposition: the false god changes suffering into violence; the true God changes violence into suffering (Weil 1977, 384).

Girard's argument follows this same logic of the divine reversal:

> If Christianity were only one of many religions, then the basic mechanisms would have to be hidden, as in the other religions. The mechanism [of sacred violence] is actually nowhere more visible than in the gospels. Everything is written black on white, and in four different texts all at once. For the basic mechanism of violence to be effective, it must remain hidden. But here it is completely unmasked (Girard 1977, as quoted in Schwager 1987, 41).

And so, he concludes, "The gods of violence were disenfranchised when the God of Love was revealed. The machine has gone out of order. The mechanism of violence no longer works. The murderers of Christ acted in vain, or better yet; their deed was fruitful in that they helped Christ to record the objective truth of violence in the gospels" (Girard 1977, 54).

The violent stories of both the Hebrew and the Christian scriptures, troubling as they are, serve a transformative function. They increasingly expose the lie of the old myths. Their saving schemes are false. God is not appeased by violence, satiated by blood, or satisfied through sacrifice.

> The violence of the Bible is the necessary precondition for the gradual perception of its meaning. The scapegoat mechanism could have come to consciousness only in a violent society. The problem of violence could only emerge at the very heart of violence, in the most war-ravaged corridor on the globe, by a repeatedly scapegoated people unable to seize and wield power for any length of time. The violence of Scripture, so embarrassing to us today, became the means by which sacred violence was revealed for what it is: a lie perpetrated against victims in the name of a God who, through violence, was working to expose violence for what it is and to expose the divine nature as nonviolent (Wink 1992, 147).

Biblical history, a tragically violent history within an even more violent context, is surprisingly anti-violence when viewed through the lens of a new paradigm. Not until Jesus could it be called nonviolent, but the vision of beating swords into plowshares is old, is recurrent, is finally triumphant.

Blind Rage, Endemic Violence

We are creatures of passions, all too easily overcome by rage and anger. Anger is a recognizable human universal, regardless of culture or ethnicity. Rooted, as anger is, in the biological, its physiological and endocrinal components of arousal are similar across cultures. Rage blinds the human being; rage triggers paranoid thought; rage impels one to finger the enemy; rage leads to accusing the foe or the perpetrator of all that is evil. "The characteristics of anger are the ability to 'create' adversaries at will, to turn without cause upon others, and to vent itself upon any change object. Anger is blind towards the objects of its arousal" (Schwager 1987, 4). Being both powerful and blind, anger's power overwhelms reason and goodwill. Its blindness allows it to lose sight of its object and leap to another target. It can be tricked, manipulated, and diverted. It has a strange propensity to seize surrogate victims.

Sacrifice served this surrogate role. It offered a substitute object that, by controlled process, neutralized the process of mutual destruction. The victims were chosen from groups that could not continue the endless chain of recriminations and revenge, such as slaves, prisoners, captives taken in war, children (Girard 1977, 8).

Blinded by passion, mesmerized by the dramas of violence, humans repeated the senseless rituals of sacrifice and found temporary respite from the downward spirals of retaliation. The paranoid myths of rightness (we are just; they are unjust) could be sustained, the solidarity of the group reaffirmed. "Humans always find it distasteful to admit that the 'reasons' on both sides of a dispute are equally valid—which is to say that *violence operates without reason*" (Girard 1977, 46).

The process of mimetic desire, as Girard describes it, is visible in sibling rivalries and in other intense special relationships, but it is present in virtually all relationships on nonconscious levels (see figure 6.1). The process follows the following steps: Admiration draws person A toward model B. Admiration inspires imitation. Person B, the one admired, models desire for and attachment to some highly valued object, a highly desirable role, a much prized privilege, or an extremely attractive territory. Person A, in mimesis, chooses the same desirable object that is valued by

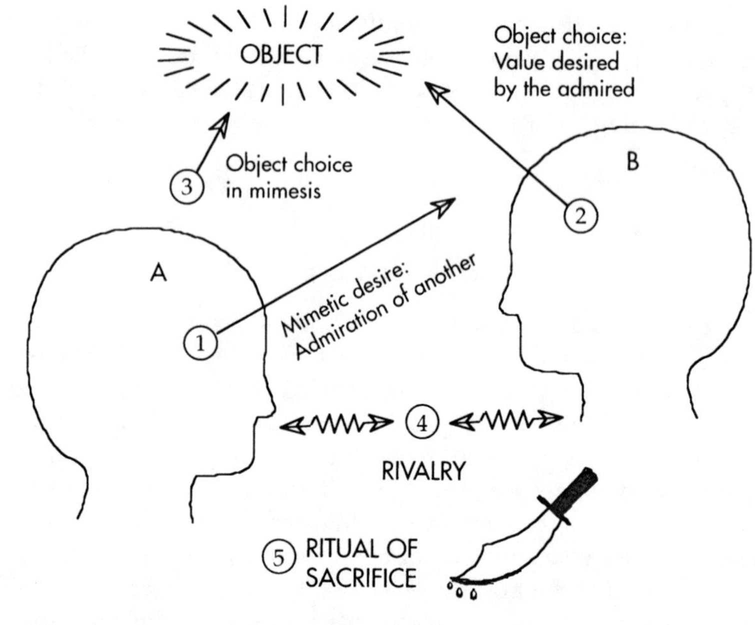

Figure 6.1

The Process of (Unconscious) Mimetic Desire

the admired person, model B. Eventually, rivalry ensues. Competition for the possession of the desired object is the inevitable outcome of mimetic social processes. All this leads to escalation of competition, the threat of violence, and the breakdown of the social fabric.

Only religion can save the situation, and the mechanism that resolves the impasse is the ritual of sacrifice. A social institution is created, which offers: (1) substitute pathways, (2) scapegoat candidates, and (3) surrogate release (4) in a ritual reenactment.

These steps are visible in virtually all the great myths, which offer us their uncritical narratives in celebration of redemptive violence that offers a sacrificial solution to human aggressions. Myth, by definition, is precritical literature that views violence in retrospect, from the perspective of salvific resolution. Concealment of the process is necessary for its salvific function to serve its substitutionary ends. Ritual, by definition, is a substitution for some prior event; it functions in society "to keep the conflictual mimesis from beginning afresh and escalating in recriminatory feuds and blood for blood cycles of defending honor through revenge. Substitution is necessary to break such cycles, or else they are an endless chain of eye-for-eye and life-for-life retaliation. The great religious rituals reenact the sacrifice of a surrogate, a defenseless victim who receives the aggression without continuing the cycle of destructiveness.

The Monstrous Double

Why is violence endemic? What causes rivalry and the vicious cycles of conflict?

The mechanism of mimetic desire creates the illusion of the enemy as a monster, and eventually when the illusion is full grown, it becomes the monstrous double to one's rage. This process of creating the illusion of enemy begins with desire. In this case desire does not arise from the desired object or its inherent values or beauty. The value of the desired object is created by the fact that another desires it. Desire is learned by imitation; it is desire for the object arising from desire to be like the other. But, as the imitator nears the object of desire, the imitated blocks or competes. The closer one comes to the desired object, the greater the hostility of the model. A double bind results. "Be like me: value the object, and you will have value," commands the model. When one reaches for the valued thing, the second command is heard, "Do not be like me. It's mine. You do not deserve it." And the third command fixes the double bind indelibly: "Don't recognize, don't name, don't end our rivalry." Just as individuals in conflict create their monstrous doubles in paranoid fear and projection, so societies finger the foe, name the enemy, and escalate the anxiety, fear, and rage.

Creation of the Double

Mimesis (mimetic desire) generates the creation of monstrous doubles through (1) the imitation of the admired model, (2) which creates desire for the object that the model desires, (3) thereby engendering rivalry for the desired object, (4) resulting in the creation of the monstrous double. The double is generated by the following process, charted in figure 6.2. Imitation, desire, rivalry, fear, and terror result, and the double, "the enemy" appears. As the projections escalate and the similarities in behavior interlock, the double becomes truly monstrous.

This process, concealed and denied in the individual, is unconcealable and undeniable in the society. As the monster is named, the society's reflection is revealed by the enemy chosen, the rhetoric employed, the metaphor utilized. For those caught up in its creation and destruction, the process seems inevitable and necessary; for the observer it seems impossible, then horrible and an ironic tragedy.

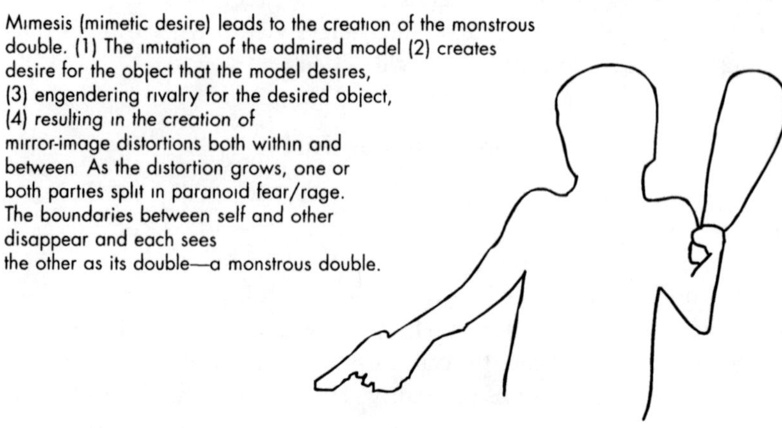

Mimesis (mimetic desire) leads to the creation of the monstrous double. (1) The imitation of the admired model (2) creates desire for the object that the model desires,
(3) engendering rivalry for the desired object,
(4) resulting in the creation of mirror-image distortions both within and between As the distortion grows, one or both parties split in paranoid fear/rage.
The boundaries between self and other disappear and each sees the other as its double—a monstrous double.

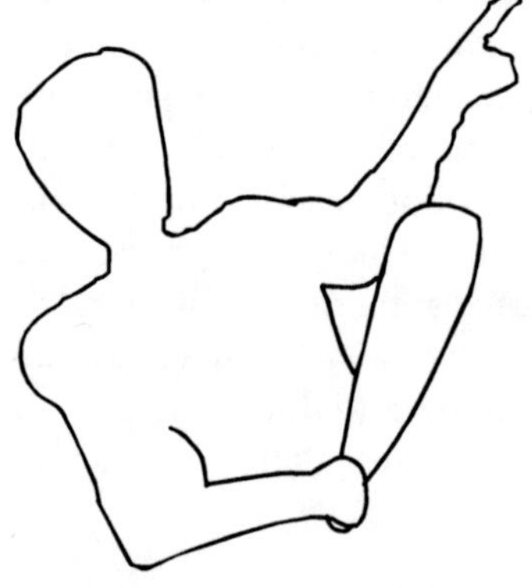

THE TRIUMPHANT RIVAL

BECOMES A SATAN, VILLAIN, HIDEOUS MONSTER

THE SELF

Splits:

1. My "contemptuous observer" becomes the angry "other within."
2. This "contemptuous observer" unites in hallucination with the "contemptible rival," "the other without."
3. My rage/evil added to that of the enraged rival becomes larger than life—as large as death. It is the "monstrous other."

THE MONSTROUS DOUBLE . . .

. . . is constructed by each, uniting the unconscious evil in the self with the visible evil in the other.

Figure 6.2
Creation of the Double

The desired model becomes the "monstrous double," in whom the society meets its own fears, desires, hates, and anxieties, mirrored and magnified. Such rivalry is inherent in all social relationships. As elemental as desire, as inevitable as modeling and mimetic learning, violence is the result of mimetic desire unless transformed by ritual. Rituals of sacrifice are instituted to provide a substitute for the demanded death of the evil monster. Aggression is redirected. Guilt is displaced. The arbitrary choice of the victim and its surrogate function are not acknowledged to protect the unity of the community. If it was forced to face the truth about itself, its tenuous peace would fracture, the social contract self-destruct (Girard 1977, 148).

In the creation of the monstrous double, the enemy is seen large, as the enemy of God no less. Such picturing releases us from any natural guilt at killing the other by converting the killing into a source of pride. Murder becomes an act of obedience, an expression of devotion. The enemy is transmogrified into devil or demon and as such is possessed by alien powers. Destroying such a foe is a sacred act; one need feel no remorse. It is a blow struck for truth and justice, an act of moral goodness. The warrior, doing battle for righteousness, may come to see his acts as a saving the enemy from the domination of evil by setting him free. The warrior becomes priest, the battle a holy war, the victory the salvation of both sides as righteousness prevails.

The monstrous double, exaggerated, becomes the demonic. When mimetic desire escalates to paroxysmal levels, the rival, who is now an idol, becomes the devil. This monster of evil takes on demonic stature and nature. The hallucination of the monstrous rival, now enlarged to grotesque proportions, takes over the subject. The evil rival, a captivating idol, now takes possession. If the personality possesses the predisposition to dissociation or detachment and overwhelming domination of a subpersonality, this possession by a demonic-monstrous double can paralyze the self and flood consciousness. The person experiences this as a loss of all personal power, responsibility, and ownership of the self and domination by an alien evil force, personality, or person. The phenomena multiply and intensify until both the person and observers conclude that an evil spirit is acting, moving, and speaking in an independent, bodily manifestation (Schwager 1987, 16).

The hideous rival capable of heinous crimes has now lost all human characteristics. The fearful fantasy is created by the kind of splitting familiar to us from the work of Klein or Kohut or other object-relations theorists. It runs along this familiar path: (1) I see that the desired object that I covet has been claimed by the triumphant rival. I am overwhelmed by my own rage. (2) Inside myself, my realistic self divides between the responsible self and "the contemptuous observer within," who can maintain a constant compound of hate, rage, and fear. This "contemptuous observer" becomes "the other within," which feels foreign to my self-image but is permitted as necessary by the crisis and threat. (3) Meanwhile the rival confronts me as "the other without," whose behavior seen through the eyes of my "contemptuous observer" within confirms my worst fears and justifies my extreme measures in self-defense. (4) Hallucination occurs: the two (the other within/the other without) merge. The other is now perceived as a compound of "my contemptuous other/the contemptible other." This merger of fears, hates, and rages creates a larger-than-life figure of truly monstrous proportions—a Stalin or Hitler out of a Qaddafi or a Hussein. As the image takes on a permanence in our perceptions, the monster is reality—things perceived to be real are real in their consequences. Mephistopheles has been revealed in full Lucifer armor.

> The contemptuous observer, the Other who is in me, constantly approaches the Other who is outside Me, the triumphant rival. On the other hand, this triumphant rival, the Other who is outside Me, whose desire I imitate and who imitates Mine, constantly approaches Me. As the inner division of the conscious is reinforced, the distinction between Me and the other disappears; the two movements converge and engender the "hallucination" of a double (Girard 1977, as quoted in Schwager 1987, 12).

The double is a mixture of the other with parts of one's own self which the desiring person then projects outside the self on the feared rival. The rival, in reality, is caught up in the same process and imitates the desire being directed toward and projected upon him or her. Mimesis creates enemies, enemies who are chained to each other. As the desire grows, the imitation intensifies, the bonding deepens, and the differences disappear. The mirror-image distortion, the polarized thinking response, the mote-beam mechanism, and the double-standard defense all flower from the same root.

One's double, monstrous in appearance, perceives one as monstrous too. Enemy creates enemy, other fears the other in progressive projection of the dark self (its fears, its potential violence, its hateful depths). The spiraling negativism has familiar components.

1. *The Mirror Image Distortion.* It is not uncommon for both parties to feel that they are innocent victims representing truth and justice while being evilly attacked. "I see you maliciously frustrating me, while I am only concerned about you and being honest, forthright, and faithful." Meanwhile, "You see me as deliberately hostile and spitefully critical, while you are simply stating the obvious" (mimetic perception).

2. *The Polarized Thinking Defense.* It is common for both to hold an oversimplified view of the conflict, in which everything "I" do is good, everything "you" do is bad. "I'm trying to work it out in a fair and mutual way, but you are just jealous. That's all" (mimetic cognition).
3. *Mote-Beam Mechanism Distortion.* It is common for one party to see all the vicious, underhanded acts of the other, but be blind to identical acts engaged in by the self. "Never mind the log in my eye, let me get the splinter out of yours," or "I'm sick and tired of your nagging, you are always cutting me down, you crank!" (mimetic projection).
4. *The Double-Standard Defense.* It is common, even when both are aware of identical acts, for both to yield to the tendency to feel that what is all right for oneself to do to the other, if one can, is not all right for the other to do to oneself. "I'm just being firm in a responsible way, but you are being obstinate, even pigheaded" (mimetic defense).

Repentance is the art of reversal. When mimesis is involved, the enemy becomes a sign, a revelatory gift for self-understanding. To understand one's own culture in depth, examine its enemies; to perceive the truth denied, see one's own group through the eyes of the alienated. As one listens with compassion to the rationale of the enemy, one can see more clearly the realities behind the rhetoric of one's own people. The way to self-knowledge leads through the enemy's world and then returns to one's own world with new eyes.

Omnipresent Mimesis

Mimesis is everywhere at work. Every blow cries out the invitation to be imitated. Imitation seduces into rivalry, and rivalry induces into violence. When the enemy appears, there are always legitimate reasons to accuse the other of initiating the evil and excuse the self of culpability. The responsibility and guilt of both sides has many levels—conscious and nonconscious, individual and systemic, and rarely can it be appropriately apportioned.

Mimesis casts its hypnotic spell. Rage responds to rage, evil demands repayment with evil, resentment replies to hostility, violence answers violence. All are locked into mimesis. The first blow is despicable, the second predictable as a counterblow, the third inescapable, and once the cycle of violence is established, the issue of who made the first move becomes moot.

Girard's analysis exposes the eternal spiral. Combating violence is continuing violence. Direct resistance inevitably seduces one to use similar means as the aggression one resists. The ethical demands of Jesus reveal the only possible interruption of enmities. "Whether the ethical demands of Jesus seem unrealistic or not, Girard's theory makes it abundantly clear that they indicate the only possible way to break through the circle of evil. Only where mimesis is neutralized is the spread of evil checked. That is why it is absolutely necessary not to resist evil with evil" (Schwager 1987, 173).

The radically hard sayings of Jesus on human negativity offer us no permissive moral difference between just and unjust violence. "Love of enemy," says Schwager, "is the Magna Charta of Christian ethics" (1987, 174). (Tolstoy wrote, "The difference between just violence and unjust violence is like the difference between cat shit and dog shit. They both smell the same.")

Hatred is not to be mirrored by hatred. Curses need not be echoed by curses. Blows do not have to be returned as blows. Kindness, blessings, and turning the other cheek are possibilities. Evil defines its own ultimate terms, but goodness can refuse them. This is the only authentic revolution, in fact, the original revolution, as John Howard Yoder has named the politics of Jesus (Yoder 1971).

In the history of human violence, the revolutionary teaching of Jesus on forgiveness stands out in gigantic proportions. Seen through the metaphoric lens of mimesis, it is the central action of Jesus' revolution, an act of immense significance that is central to all other elements of discipleship.

Only forgiveness can interrupt the cycles of evil at their vortex, at the core. The domination systems we have created throughout all human history have been one empire of violence succeeding another. The deceit of violence has held humankind hostage. Its roots run deep, into the most primary metaphors of life. Self-esteem is united with self-defense, and safety and security become the ultimate goods; we are saved by redemptive violence. The sociopsychological and sociotheological analyses of Jesus reveal the hopelessness and helplessness of violence and offer a new direction toward overcoming destructive mimetic violence. It is a direction all Christians face, just-war theorists and pacifists alike. All seek to limit violence, reveal its true nature, expose its deceit, reach toward peaceful solutions, or accept sacrificial resolutions. One unfortunate approach accepts mimesis as inescapable. The other rejects it as indefensible. Jesus is clearly on the side of the latter. He does not soften or accommodate his call to practice forgiving, reconciling, nonviolent love. So he teaches his disciples to forgive, even an offense repeated the metaphorical seven times in one day (Luke 17:4). In a clear allusion to the earliest teaching—the archetypal model of violent retribution—he asks for forgiving seventy-seven times (Matt. 18:22). The metaphor is from Lamech, the father of Noah (Gen. 4:23–24). Lamech articulates the harsh law of retribution with unlimited violence.

> I have killed a man for wounding me,
> a young man for striking me.
> If Cain is avenged sevenfold,
> truly Lamech seventy-sevenfold.

Lamech slays a boy for a slap and takes seventy-sevenfold retaliation. Jesus teaches a forgiveness that responds to any Lamech with his seventy-sevenfold revenge by offering a seventy-times-seven acceptance. Jesus sets no limits, draws no line in the sand, defines no point when forgiving love can capitulate to evil and offer reactive violence.

It is in this refusal of limits, this boundless and stubborn refusal to draw lines to define the intolerable, that we reflect the fullness of God's love.

> Externally forgiveness must never capitulate before the immoderation of the vengeful violence of others; internally, it has God's perfection for its norm. A forgiveness that outdoes not only the murder by Cain but also the extreme vindictiveness of a Lamech reveals the true essence of the forgiving love of the heavenly father. The positive boundlessness of perfect love takes on concrete form through overcoming the negative measurelessness of evil (Schwager 1987, 176).

So Then, to What Ends?

Caregiving, counseling, or mediating from a perspective influenced by the radical teaching of the New Testament holds up a startling mirror to human hate and resentment. The gospel does not impose the demand to love and forgive; it reveals the utter, inevitable, inescapable necessity for love and forgiveness for any reconstruction of life. Forgiveness offers hope; violence, despair. Jesus is this mirror of true humanity and window to divinity. As we grasp the awesome power of the innocent victim—not to glorify or tolerate victimization but to expose it for what it is—we turn its power back upon itself. Our caregiving and careful living reflect the many learnings that come from seeing the Jesus event in constantly renewing and repeatedly revelatory moments of encounter with Jesus' surprising God. This is a God who invites us to be unsatisfied with anything less than the mysterious inbreaking of odd reconciliations and strange reconnections.

A few of these spiritual surprises may be:

> *God refrains from all reprisals.* So we can seek reconciliation by exposing injury without inflicting further injury. No mimetic reprisals.

God refuses all redemptive violence. So we do not do evil that good may come, coerce that "our freedom" will be chosen. No mimetic strategies of utilitarian coercion.

God transforms violence into suffering. So we enter into suffering as a transformative process. We distrust all theology that is prepain (Soelle 1984, 90). No mimetic triumphalism.

God offers unconditional and unilateral renunciation of violence. So we commit ourselves to be unconditionally creative in the ways we participate in God's work. No mimetic regression.

God rejects the scapegoat ritual of sacrificing one for the release of other(s). So we reject the scapegoating processes of (1) naming the enemy, (2) placing blame, (3) ventilating rage, (4) inflicting pain, (5) destroying the monstrous double, (6) discharging violence, (7) celebrating our innocence, our release, our redemption, (8) denying—sacralizing the process. No mimetic ritualizations.

God offers freely extended healing love. So we face our hatred in order to perceive love, deal with our hatred in order to extend love, live repentantly with our hatred in order to experience the slow healing work of love. No mimetic flight from our shadows.

God invites us to experience this, not imitate it. So we give up mimetic reflection of the admired, and slowly allow the nonconscious to become conscious. We participate in the end of rivalry, the end of enmity, the beginnings of New Being. No mimetic discipleship.

The Killing Zone is a movie by thirty-year-old Quan Lelan, one of the first among his generation of Vietnamese-Americans to explore the complexity of forgiveness for those who are products of wartime Vietnam and postwar America. "I see myself as a bridge between the two cultures," says Lelan. "A few years younger and I would be too American, a few years older and I would be too Vietnamese."

The story he tells is set in Orange County's Little Saigon. One night an old Vietnamese man enters a bakery to buy a dessert for his granddaughter. He talks briefly with the Vietnamese waitress and exchanges glances with another man, an Anglo, a Vietnam veteran. The soldier, recognizing the old man as a North Vietnamese soldier whose unit ambushed his squad twenty years earlier, leaps from his chair and pulls a knife.

The old man, cornered, argues that he was only a farmer in Vietnam. To resolve the dispute, the American soldier demands that the old man cut a deck of cards; high card wins. If the old man outdraws the soldier, he goes free. If the soldier draws the high, the man dies.

They tie on the first draw. The old man makes a break for the door, but is tackled. "The war is over," the old man pleads, "can't we forget?" As they face each other, the Vietnamese waitress points a gun at both. She slowly turns it on the old man. "He's not getting away," she says.

At that moment, the old man's granddaughter enters the bakery and runs to her grandfather. Moved by the presence of the little girl, the waitress drops the gun and allows the old man to leave. Together the waitress and the soldier place the unturned card back in the deck.

When the movie was screened for the first time in Little Saigon, Lelan was startled when the audience applauded after the waitress let the old man go. And at the end when the unturned card was being returned to the deck, someone in the audience began yelling "Ace, Ace," the high card that would set the old man free. When the card was reinserted unturned, applause swept the room. "Forgiveness is something too dear for most people," Lelan says, "but for the future, we can't hold grudges forever" (Dunn 1993).

Toward a New Paradigm of Forgiveness

1. Aggression is elemental to human community. Violence is endemic. Religion has served to limit it by sacralizing the process of selecting a scapegoat to bear the community's collective wrath. But the ritual is a lie. Its solution is brief, its ultimate impact destructive.

2. The scapegoat mechanism, and with it the myth of redemptive violence, promises the resolution of a community's rage and the cessation of its hostilities, but it is powerless to effect such a result. We need the interjection of the new element called forgiveness.

3. True reconciliation requires that human violence be transformed into suffering; that the innocence of victims be recognized; that guilt and responsibility of violence be faced; and that repentance, reapproachment, and forgiveness be sought.

7

The Basis and Bias for Bridgebuilding

> The peacemaker is a bridge,
> A bridge is walked on by both sides,
> It is only as strong, as useful,
> as its attachment at both ends.
> —David Bosch

> She that cannot forgive others
> breaks the bridge over which
> she herself must pass
> for all have need to be forgiven
> —Thomas Fuller

It is told of Rabbi Akiba ben Joseph, who lived and died in the years of Israel's last revolt against the Roman oppression, that he recited his blessings three times. When asked why, he replied: "The first I ask for my family and myself, the second for my friends and my people, and the third for my enemies."

"Why should you wish to bless your enemies? They seek to destroy you. Why do you wish to sustain them?"

"There was a neighbor of our land who embittered my days by stoning stray sheep, dirtying the water from which our camels drank, sowing our fields with weeds and strewing them with his rocks. No pleas from my father, no tears or kind words from my mother, and no attempts to reason with him by the elders could stop this man from his evil ways.

"We suffered for many years, and when my parents died, I sold my lands and cattle for a meager amount and left Samaria. I could bear the treatment no longer. I took work with a Hebrew, Kalba Sabua, near the city of Jerusalem. There I met the love of my life, the daughter of that man, and through her I met the Lord of my life, by whose divine guidance I daily pray three blessings.

"Now I am a Rabbi, and I hear His voice in my heart and His commandments are in my soul. I spend my days in the teaching of the Torah and my nights in its study. And all this happiness I owe, not to a friend and not to a stranger, but to an enemy full of evil intent. Why should I not bless my enemy daily? He is a great spoke in the wheel of my life.

"So I say, love thy neighbor, for the neighbor is like you. Love thy neighbor no matter how evil, for the neighbor is in God, as are we all" (adapted from Runes 1961, 88).

Reconciliation as Base

Reconciliation is central to pastoral theology; reconciliation is primary in pastoral practice. The work of reconciling is the basic agenda of healing. It is a bias that the pastoral counselor brings to each encounter with broken or distant relationships.

Although not all relationships can or should be restored, the pastoral counselor brings the bias that connectedness is preferable to individualism; human solidarity is our goal rather than isolation; open communication systems more healthful than closed and cut-off relationships. A concern for healing, a hope for restoration, and a commitment to reconnection biases the pastoral therapist toward joining with others as both a model and a mentor in rebuilding severed relationships.

Neutrality concerning the particulars of the counselee's choices is a prerequisite for all effective therapy. It is the inevitable consequence of seeing the person as a volitional being who becomes authentic in the act of choosing and taking responsibility for the consequences. But neutrality in the therapist's orientation—the theoretical, ethical, and theological assumptions that undergird all practice—is not only undesirable, it is impossible. Every effective people helper operates from a philosophical position, acts according to an ethical code, treats on the basis of particular personality theories, and functions within a theological world of values.

Owning one's bias as well as one's basic assumptions in the therapeutic situation dispels the notion of the totally neutral participant observer. The therapist is recognized as not value-free, but as coercion-free; the therapist is for life, not death, for constructive relations, not destructive rupture. The commitment of the therapist in any marriage consultation, for example, is to three units, to each person as a center of dignity and integrity, and to the relationship as an entity of equal concern. As persons create their relationships, their worth, depth, and ability to keep faith are invested in them, but the person is prior to, superior to, and ultimately more important than the relationship covenanted. At the same time, the relationship has a life of its own in the familial-communal matrix; it must be taken with the profound seriousness of a social reality with substance, power, and enduring consequence. All three entities deserve equal focus, especially since, in stress, persons withdraw investment to protect selfhood.

In therapy, the counselor is committed not only to fostering openness in the persons but also to the facilitating of an open system: the counselor is biased not only toward the welfare of the persons and their right to authentic choices but also to the responsibilities to working through covenant without cutoffs (preemptory severing of contact and communication) or flight (distancing as a *means* rather than as a considered and accountable *end*).

Reconciliation as a Bias

It has become the operational assumption, in Western societies, that reconciliation is one of several possible outcomes to any dispute, and those standing alongside should have no bias, no prior intentions that could influence the outcome. Convergence or divergence may be equal options since the welfare of the individual takes precedence over the wholeness of the community or the integrity of the relationship. In contrast, sociocentric societies value the relationship above the individual, and the maintenance of harmony as far more crucial than the fulfillment of the person's needs. The biblical world is clearly such a society of social solidarity, and its understandings of reconciliation and forgiveness are communal, not individual. Its primary focus is on the web of human covenants and commitments that enable just and loving relationships.

The modern reader, standing in the post-Enlightenment tradition of individual identity, self-definition, and self-actualization, endows the biblical texts with a radically different set of definitions for even the most basic words. "Self" becomes not a reflexive reference to the person, but a discrete, individualized function of the personality and its ego-identity. In first-century usage, "self" referred to the person as a whole, not to the core "self" of the individual which is grounded in self-esteem and actualized in the search for self-fulfillment.

In the twentieth century, the self is a rational subject who views other and the world as object, and grows into an emancipated, autonomous individual with all final referents of value within the self—what one thinks, believes, chooses, actualizes in life. The teaching of Jesus stands in striking contrast to such assumptions of the primacy of the individual. His instructions are guides and goads toward reconciliation. His expressed concern is not about the inner peace of the person who forgives to find release from private feelings of guilt; his goal is the reestablishing of relationship, the restoring of harmony, the regaining of community.

Puzzling as it may be to postmodern individualists, this is the nature of the language of the biblical documents. The corporate sense of human personhood, the sense that sociocentric personalities live in interconnected balance, is present linguistically as well as sociologically. The frequency of plural forms that address the group, not the individual; the rarity of descriptions of solitary experience; and the absence of a sense of self as a discrete, autonomous entity all focus reconciliation on the person-in-community.

The examples in the Hebrew scriptures are unmistakable: the great prayer of Abraham for the forgiveness of the people of Sodom (Gen. 18:23–33); the plea for forgiveness of the idolatrous people of Israel offered by Moses (Ex. 32:30–32); the prayer of intercession for a people threatened with destruction which is central to the prophecy of Amos (Amos 7:1–9); the forgiveness that leads to union between God and the chosen people (Hos. 2:21–22). The language, the experience, the expressions of forgiving arise from solidarity and community.

Concerning this corporate character of biblical language, theologian Joseph Sittler wrote:

> Of the great Christian or Jewish words—God, love, sin, guilt, forgiveness, reconciliation—none is a definition. They are all relational statements. That is, love is not a thing; it is a relation. Guilt is not a thing; it is a relation. Sin, too, is not a thing, it is a relation. In reconciliation, the prefix *re-* means conciliation reestablished, or harmony once broken put back together. This is terribly important. When I say you cannot find a definition of love, I mean that love becomes clear and recognizable only when you behold a relationship (Sittler 1986, 80).

The communal-relational perspective of the biblical world, although decidedly uncommon in post-Enlightenment Christianity, is faithfully represented in Judaism. The Jewish perspective on forgiveness has an intrinsically communal basis, for "within Judaism one is not an autonomous moral agent, but a member of a covenanted community." This stands in sharp contrast to secularized Protestantism, which places great value on individual autonomy and the voluntary quasi-contractual nature of social and moral relations (Newman 1987, 169).

Words like *reconciliation* and *forgiveness,* although clearly communal concepts in the biblical documents, can so easily be torn from these contexts of social solidarity and reduced to contractual negotiations between solitary autonomous selves. The outcome of such reductionist reconciliation is seen as a satisfactory dispute resolution, not restoration of community. The nature of such forgiveness is an intrapsychic transaction that reduces internal stressors, resolves hostility, and facilitates acceptance of differences. It is not the regaining of sister or brother.

Be Solitary or Be in Solidarity

Krister Stendahl, in his much-quoted critique of reading a more recent psychology back into the thought of Paul, challenges our common assumptions about personal guilt and private forgiveness as central concerns of the New Testament epistles. The Protestant formula, that one is at the same time righteous and sinner, "may have some foundation in the Pauline writings, but this formula cannot be substantiated as the center of Paul's conscious attitude toward his personal sins" (Stendahl 1976, 82).

Paul does not have the type of introspective conscience with its general guilt orientation that the simultaneously sinner/righteous formula presupposes. This may explain why forgiveness "is the term for salvation which is used least of all in the Pauline writings." In contrast, "forgiveness is the term most used both in the pulpit and, more generally, in contemporary Western Christianity to describe the sum total, the fruit, and the effect of the deeds of Jesus Christ" (Stendahl 1976, 24).

Paul exhibits, not the troubled guilt orientation of his later interpreters, but "a rather robust conscience" that can affirm, "I have lived in all good conscience unto this day." Augustine "may well have been one of the first to express the dilemma of the introspective conscience, " which turned the New Testament meaning of justification from the corporate to the individual, from the need for forgiveness in community to the need for forgiveness for intrapsychic healing. "The Augustinian line leads into the Middle Ages and reaches its climax in the penitential struggle of an Augustinian monk, Martin Luther, and in his interpretation of Paul. . . . The West for centuries has wrongly surmised that the biblical writers were grappling with problems which no doubt are ours, but which never entered their consciousness" (Stendahl 1976, 85, 95).

Words like "love," "hate," and "forgiveness" are profoundly introspective terms for twenty-first-century humans, but in the first century they had little or no such content. To understand their meaning to the writers of the Gospels, one must enter a radically different social-psychological context. The following paragraphs will describe it, but it must be experienced to be understood.

First-century persons were sociocentric, not egocentric, in identity. They were group-oriented, not self-oriented. True human existence is found in solidarity with the community that gives one life, nurturance, guidance, and a place to belong. In our century, existence is defined by separating a self, defining a unique identity, achieving autonomy. They, in contrast, developed as persons within the kin group, the village community, the social class, the religious movement. Each person's sense of selfhood, awareness of conscience, and experience of integrity came from solidarity with the group. Others told them who they were; others defined their patterns of behavior; others participated in their extended and external conscience.

Control of their emotional and spiritual life issues was not internal, in "the self," but external, in "the group." Responsibility for choices and actions was lodged not primarily in "the inviolate individual" but in the solidarity of the community. This is difficult for Western, post-Enlightenment citizens to comprehend since they take internal control and internal responsibility as essential to and inseparable from healthy identity and view external control and external responsibility with suspicion of dysfunction or labels of pathology.

The familiocentric or sociocentric personality was neither psychological nor introspective. *Self* was a reflexive word, not the identification of an inner center of agency, responsibility, dignity, and volition. Words we understand as designating internal states, they used to define the appropriate expression in relationship and action in community.

Thus "to love God with all one's heart" means total attachment. "To love one's neighbor as oneself" is to be attached to the people in one's neighborhood as to one's own family (Matt. 22:37–40; Lev. 19:18). And, correspondingly, *hate* would mean "disattachment, nonattachment, indifference." Again, there may or may not be feelings of repulsion. But it is the inward feeling of nonattachment along with the outward behavior bound up with not being attached to a group and the persons that are part of that group that hate entails. In sum, Paul's famous triad in 1 Cor. 13:13 (faith, hope, love) might best be translated: "personal loyalty, enduring trust in another, group attachment," and, of course, "the greatest of these is group attachment" (Malina and Rohrbaugh 1992, 57).

Forgiveness, in biblical thought, is a relational process *between* disputants and *among* community members, which calls the participants into such solidarity that they are willing to forgive *within*, that is, "from the heart" (Matt. 18:35).

The word *reconciliation* ("to reconcile," *katallassein*) occurs only thirteen times in the Pauline writings. Three different dimensions of reconciliation are described: we are reconciled to God the Other, whom we perceived as Enemy; we are reconciled with others from whom we were alienated as enemies; and we are called to be reconcilers to do the work of conciliation between those who are alienated and in enmity.

We Are Reconciled to God the Other, the Enemy

Two central passages on reconciliation in the writings of Paul reveal why the bias toward the reunification of disunity is central to the message of Jesus.

> When we were reconciled to God by the death of his Son, we were still enemies; now that we have been reconciled, surely we may count on being saved by the life of his Son? Not merely because we have been reconciled but because we are filled with joyful trust in God, through our Lord Jesus Christ, through whom we have already gained our reconciliation (Rom. 5:10–11, JB).

> It is all God's work. It was God who reconciled us to himself through Christ and gave us the work of handing on this reconciliation. In other words, God in Christ was reconciling the world to himself, not holding men's faults against them, and he has entrusted to us the news that they are reconciled (2 Cor. 5:18–19, JB).

Something inexplicable happens in the death of Jesus. Classical theology has defined it as God reconciling us to Godself in a unilateral work of atonement. God initiates, performs, completes this action. Is this reconciliation or expiation? Does this address the healing issues of transforming enmity? Or does this add the contradiction of "redemptive violence" to the existing alienation? If God destroys the Son for some greater good—the salvation of humankind—what guarantee of God's steadfast love could ever be offered? What assurance of God as Abba—loving parent—could be believable to both our conscious and unconscious trust processes?

The healing word is the reverse of that classical view. Jesus "himself bore our sins in his body on the cross" (1 Peter 2:24), not to reconcile an angry God to us, as blood-atonement theories hold, but to reconcile us to God. This is "the God who comes into the world as the Innocent Victim and who defends and frees victims" (Williams 1991, 2). The meaning of the cross, in pastoral theology and in the individual therapeutic journey, is less a matter of reconciling God to us, as many atonement theories stress, than of reconciling us to God. God has refused ledger keeping; God makes no demands for repayment. The redemptive act of God is to break us from our bondage to rage, resentment, recrimination, and revenge. "God needs no reparation, but human beings must be extracted from their own prison if they are to be capable of accepting the pure gift of freely offered love. It is not God who must be appeased, but humans who must be delivered from their hatred" (Schwager 1987, 209).

The central imagery Paul uses to explain our relationship to God is enmity and friendship, alienation and reconciliation. While we were enemies, God acted in Christ to bring an end to enmity and create joyful trust. Four intriguing corollaries are essential to Paul's argument.

First, reconciliation begins with the victim. We are the reciprocal victims of one another's evil; we are the victims of evil in the whole contextual system—the social, political, economic, as well as moral system—that alienates us from each other and from which, as well as within which, we are alienated. If reconciliation begins with the victim, someone must rise from among the victimized to initiate the healing movement. Jesus appears from the poor, the powerless, the people under domination of an occupying army. He stands in solidarity with the abused, is arrested as a suspected subversive, charged as a revolutionary, condemned by religious leaders as disloyal to the Roman state, sentenced without demonstrated guilt, executed as another powerless victim. He is a spokesperson for justice to the oppressed, a voice for the voiceless. The reconciling movement comes from the Truly Human One.

Second, reconciliation comes from the victim, and paradoxically, profoundly—although we do not see it until we have been reconciled and our eyes are clear—God the Reconciler is the victim and we the perpetrators. God initiates and carries out the reconciliation by entering the victim world and being violated. In affirming the nature of reconciliation as victim-initiated, we are recognizing the proper subjects and objects of reconciliation. The victim is the subject, not the perpetrator, and the object is not the violent event, which may be inexcusable, but the offender who is still human in spite of inhumanity committed. In the act of violence, a perpetrator gives up a portion of his or her humanity, but a core of human character and possibility remain. In reconciliation, the subject, the violated, perceives the object, the violator, as cause of the injury yet as distinct from and more than the act of violation. As the injured is able to see the self as more than the injury, he or she becomes able to see the injurer as also being something more than the injury event and its consequences.

God takes the lead in reconciliation because only God can take the lead. As the One offended and as the One who has been present with all who are offended, God chooses to be the Innocent Victim at the center of history, thus initiating reconciliation.

The third corollary is that reconciliation begins with the victim, yet paradoxically, both parties are victims, both have been wronged, though often by others for whom the present victims are substitutes or surrogates. Both parties become participants in the reconciliation process as each perceives the self as having been victim or as now being or as to become victimized. Each is both subject and object of reconciliation. Rarely do parties in a dispute *not* feel some degree of self-justification, some measure of demonstrable self-righteousness, some claim to justice, some sense of being or having been wronged by someone, which motivates and reinforces even when it does not justify the hurtful action taken. (The complexity of the preceding sentence is deliberate since it reflects the ambiguity of the motivations in virtually any dispute.)

It is this sense of wrongedness, more than the sense of wrongness, which brings persons to the healing conversation. Our own experiences of loss, alienation, or injury connect us to the pain we see in others. The sympathy evoked or the empathy empowered link us to the injured or the offended. Both offender and offended bring this sense of wrongedness, diffuse as its sources may be, to the reconciliation situation. Both sides feel victimized, both feel some claim to justice.

Both parties participate in the estrangement and in the complex interweaving of hostility that results when two persons or parties are alienated. The rupture of the relationship involves both in the evil done: for the offender in the desire to aggress; for the offended in the wish to retaliate.

> The offended feels in the very entrails of his/her being the need to demand payment in kind. It seems that the damage done by sin can only be repaired by sinning against the one who sinned, except that the action taken against the offender appears as necessary according to the demands of justice. . . . [T]he ultimate sinfulness of sin itself and its greatest tragedy is that it converts the victim into a sinner (Elizondo 1986, 71).

The reflex of pain is to inflict pain. Whether passively by revealing the depth of the injury to invite guilt or actively in some form of retaliation, the human impulse to seek or seize justice is rooted in our earliest developmental layers.

The most painful insult of an injury is often the secondary one, the internal implosion of rage that takes us hostage, that elevates hatred and resentment to a dominant, even idolatrous, position in our inner court of justice.

> The greatest damage of an offense—often greater than the offense itself—is that it destroys my freedom to be me, for I find myself involuntarily dominated by the inner rage and resentment—a type of spiritual poison which permeates throughout all my being—which will be a subconscious but very powerful influence in most of my life. . . . I hate the offender for what he/she has done to me but in the very hatred of the other I allow them to become the Lord and Master of my life (Elizondo 1986, 70).

The victim-offender dynamic throws light on the divine-human encounter. The human experience of victimization, powerlessness, and despair turns us toward seeking reconciliation, but the encounter with God reveals that we are the offenders, not the offended. Moved by our pain, we turn toward God seeking reconciliation, only to discover that God has already moved toward us in reconciliation. God, in the innocent victim Jesus, has acted to enable our reconciliation, but this action is taken through the one who is truly one of us, one with us in our suffering and pain.

The fourth corollary of Paul's view of our relationship to God is that all our movement toward reconciliation is rooted in our having been reconciled by another's mercy and therefore empowered to be an agent of reconciliation. Reconciliation is not something we do, it is something we discover.

> First and foremost, the reconciliation that Christians have to offer in overcoming the enmity created by suffering is not something they find in themselves, but something they recognize as coming from God. Thus the question is not *How can I bring myself, as victim, to forgive those who have violated me and my society?* It is, rather, *How can I discover the mercy of God welling up in my own life, and where does that lead me?* Reconciliation, then, is not a process that we initiate or achieve, we discover it (Schreiter 1992, 43).

Reconciliation with God always comes as a discovery, not as an achievement. Later we shall reflect on how reconciliation between all offenders and offended is something to be discovered, not something to be done. In the relationship with God, we discover that God's action toward us not only precedes ours, it draws from us our own response.

This is true not only of divine forgiveness but of all human forgiveness, John Patton has argued. Forgiveness is not doing something but discovering something. I am able to forgive when I discover that I am in no position to forgive since I also need forgiveness. I am more like those who hurt me than I differ from them. Forgiveness is not an act of generosity or superiority but rather a discovery of similarity. It is the admission that it is all right to be like everyone else that at last sets us free (Patton 1985).

We Are Reconciled to One Another, No Matter How Other the Enemy

Another human being may be seen as the loved and needed other, as the other who attracts, complements, completes, and fulfills relationship and creates community. Or, in hostility, the other may be seen as a foreign object, dissimilar and discontinuous with the self, unknowable, undesirable, unforgivable. The other is an "I" that is not my "I"; the other is a center of experience that I cannot experience in the mode through which I experience myself. The other is a separate I—experiencing, interpreting, feeling the world in a noninterchangeable way, in an inaccessible manner. And the other is experiencing me. I am also being experienced, interpreted, and perceived with deep feelings by the other. I am something in the other's unique world of experience; I exist in another's frame of reference; I exist in that person's world; I am seen in another's perceptions, perhaps with radical clarity, perhaps with projected distortion. I am not the only "I," for I exist in relationships; I am not the sole autonomous actor in my story; I must be in relationship to the I that exists in another's perceptions. The other has knowledge of me and perception of my way of being which contest my experience and conflict with my assessments. The other is not interchangeable with me, not reducible to my perceptions; the other is a challenge to my claims of autonomy (Farley 1990, 35–36).

Reconciliation between self and other requires meeting—the meeting of worlds of experience and perception. These encounter each other while remaining other, make peace with each other without absorbing or melting into the other. Each party can see the stranger as friend or enemy. Schreiter suggests seven common ways of perceiving the other. We can *demonize* the other as evil to be eliminated. We can *romanticize* the other as a superior to be emulated. We can *colonize* the other as an inferior to be pitied and used. We can *generalize* the other as nonindividual and generic. We can *trivialize* the other by stereotyping and ignoring. We can *homogenize* the other by denying and assimilating. We can *vaporize* the other by blinding ourselves to the other's existence, by making the oppressed invisible (Schreiter 1992, 32–33).

Or we can *recognize* and *empathize*. These are the two basic actions that enable us to authentically encounter the other as other. They allow us to see both the similarities (what we recognize as familiar) and the differences (what we must empathize to appreciate). Seeing our common experience, frailty, and failures evokes compassion; empathizing with what is foreign, fearsome, even repugnant invites us to engage and be engaged by what we do not perceive within ourselves because of its absence or our lack of insight.

The most celebrated passages of the Pauline epistles addressing our being reconciled to the other—enemy, stranger, or outsider—are Eph. 2:11–16 and Col. 1:22–23. The thematic elements lifted from the text are

> Do not forget, then, that there was a time when you . . . were excluded from membership . . . aliens with no part . . . immersed in this world, without hope and without God. But now in Christ Jesus, you that used to be so far apart from us have been brought very close. . . . For he is the peace between us, and has made the two into one and broken down the barrier which used to keep them apart, actually destroying in his own person the hostility. . . . This was to create one single [prototype of the new humanity] . . . restoring peace . . . to unite them both . . . and reconcile them with God. In his own person he killed the hostility (extracted from Eph. 2:11–16, JB).

> Not long ago, you were foreigners and enemies, in the way that you used to think and the evil things that you did; but now he has reconciled you, by his death . . . (Col. 1:21–22, JB)

In reconciling us to Godself, God has reconciled us to each other. Something is essentially, radically different about the human situation—the sinner and the sinned against, the oppressor and the oppressed are now in a new situation. The good news of the gospel is that I and my enemy are no longer in two irreconcilable camps. God has drawn a new map of the universe in the "kin-dom" of God. We are no longer on opposite sides; we both stand, together, in need of reconciliation and are the beneficiaries of the same reconciling act on God's part. My enemy and I are one.

Embracing the enemy is not a desirable option, it is the optimum goal of reconciliation. This is a hard word. A more immediate and less demanding resolution seems far more desirable—a hasty peace is preferable to most of us. The cost of working toward true liberation seems too great. The attractiveness of turning it over to professionals who practice a scientific process of resolving disputes through perceptual adjustment, cognitive redefinition, and behavioral modification tempts us to discard this hard work of confronting and coming to terms with our enemies.

When reconciliation is seen as a hasty peace, it seeks to deal with a history of violence by suppressing the memory, denying the injury, and rewriting the violent reality with the rationale of beginning afresh. Perpetrators welcome a hurried forgiveness that lets bygones be bygones. Such reconciliation trivializes and ignores the oppressive situation by ignoring its causes.

When reconciliation is seen as an alternative to liberation, it utilizes the call to forgiveness, to love of enemies, to the union of opposites to cover continuing injustices.

> Put simply, liberation is not an alternative to reconciliation; it is the prerequisite for it. Thus, we do not call for reconciliation instead of liberation; we call for liberation in order to bring about reconciliation. Not liberation *or* reconciliation. Reconciliation can only come about if the nature of the violence perpetrated is acknowledged, and its conditions for continuing or reciprocating are removed (Schreiter 1992, 22).

When reconciliation is confused with conflict mediation, the balancing, negotiating, need-meeting process becomes a way of managing the differences toward resolution. The resemblance to authentic reconciliation may be striking, but the differences are crucial. Dispute resolution, with its neutrality, its concern for the legitimate interests of each side, maintains a sense of dignity for both parties and promises enough mutual satisfaction to reduce the likelihood of recurrence of the conflict.

> But reconciliation as a managerial process falls short of the Christian understanding of reconciliation in significant ways. First of all, we do not bring about reconciliation, it is God who reconciles. Second, reconciliation is not a skill to be mastered, but rather,

> something discovered—the power of God's grace welling up in one's life. Third, to see reconciliation as a form of technical rationality, a skill or know-how, is to reduce reconciliation to the form it takes in one kind of culture . . . and to devalue it in other cultures (Schreiter 1992, 26–27).

This last point, subtle yet crucial, is an antidote to the toxicity of technology. As Western culture devotes its technology-rich resources to the study of conflict resolution, it comes to prize reconciliation processes as the highest form of rationality, the crowning scientific process of transcending human differences through deciphering the dynamics of human needs and interests. As reconciliation is reduced to skill formation in the technical-rational, it is given ultimate value in one culture while being devalued in another. Reconciliation remains mystery, art, grace, and act of God in each and in all cultures (Augsburger 1992).

We Are Reconcilers for One Another, for the Enmity between Enemies

If genuine reconciliation seems a rare event, it is because authentic love is uncommon as well. Love, when it is true *agapē,* is an equal regard that includes love of enemy. In the situation of alienation, the other is an opponent, at enmity and therefore the enemy. *Agapē* refuses that definition and sees the other as estranged but not excluded. The nature of *agapē* is inclusion.

If the goal of genuine reconciliation is joining with the other, then the movement toward concord may begin with sharpening discord. Peacemaking may be at first conflictmaking. This does not feel "christian" since it does not allow for the degree of denial, accommodation, and "niceness" necessary to "christian" behavior. Confrontation with clear differentiation precedes union with authentic connection.

The truth will set you free, but first it sets you right side up, and that is often the reverse of the position one is defending in a dispute. One must return from self-defensive withdrawal and reapproach the opponent; one must reverse both the self-justifications and the accusations against the offender by risking openness and practicing empathy. The necessary union of empathy and exploration—for disputants and those who mediate—offers the two faces of respect. Respect has two aspects, empathy for the other's feelings, perspectives, and capacities, and a challenge to fully responsible behavior.

> Respect is a moral connection that discloses how empathy and certain ways of being confrontative require each other. Respectful

> considerate confrontation goes hand in hand with empathy. . . . Respectful confrontation communicates in essence, "Having gained some understanding of you, I now trust you to deal openly with some things you have not considered." That is, for all their differences, there is no fundamental contradiction when ministers who are empathic are also confrontational, so long as there is respect (Underwood 1985, 90).

Genuine respect for the alienated sister or brother requires the exploration of truth. The truth will set free, but first it makes uncomfortable.

Paul's third dimension of reconciliation invites us to serve one another in love by being agents of reconciliation by bridging enmity and reapproaching the enemy. We are called to do the work of conciliation between those who are alienated and in enmity. "God has enlisted us in this service of reconciliation" (2 Cor. 5:19). "If anyone is detected in a transgression, you who have received the Spirit should restore such a one in a spirit of gentleness" (Gal. 6:1). Other passages (Col. 3:12–16; Rom. 12:1–21; Phil. 4:1–3) offer examples of the form this reconciliation takes as the practice of love.

The proper location for the work of reconciliation is within community, in Paul's thought. "If one of your number has a dispute with another, has he the face to take it to pagan law-courts instead of to the community of God's people? . . . If therefore you have such business disputes, . . . can it be that there is not a single wise man among you able to give a decision in a brother-Christian's cause? Must brother go to law with brother?" (1 Cor. 6:1, 4, 5, NEB). The indisputable sign of Christian integrity is the willingness to submit a dispute to the community. Christianity is participation in community, not individualized religious experience. The willingness to trust the community with one's conflict and accept the outcome the community prescribes is rare among twentieth-century Christians, but a basic assumption for first-century believers. For the contemporary person in our litigious society, filing a suit is a grand assertive gesture. We would rather fight for vindication (what we call justice) than make peace. In spite of our cynicism—with satirist Ambrose Bierce, we define a lawsuit as "something you go in a pig and come out a sausage"—we continue to sue rather than pursue a mediated settlement. The central issues of relationship—anger, trust, and intimacy—are outside the competence of the court yet they fill our courtrooms. It is in mediation that they are addressed and the real injuries of relationship can be redressed.

The Reconciling Community

A significant group of Christian thinkers are translating the gospel directly into relevant social decision making. Since conservative theology long ago married conservative politics and economics, and liberal theology and liberal politics and economics have been sterilely cohabiting, these thinkers have pointed out that authentically biblical theology is an equal challenge to all of the above.

The most provocative leader in this movement is John Howard Yoder, who argues in *The Politics of Jesus* that Jesus himself is the norm for Christian ethics, and the perfection in love set forth in the life and teaching of Jesus is fully relevant to all human existence. It is nonsense to insist that we must compromise Jesus as the true norm of our ethical behavior in order to be "effective" or to reach utilitarian goals. It is equally empty to seek to withdraw from the world and its dilemmas to maintain our own consistence. Obedience to Jesus' way is inevitably and inescapably relevant to the historical process, not a retreat or flight from it.

For Yoder, we can be sure of our moral judgments as they reject evil means such as violence. In every case where we are presented with a violent means toward any end, no matter how good it appears, we are to reject it. We can be absolute in rejection of evil means while open to conversation on a longer hermeneutic path in discerning our way through other ethical dilemmas.

In Matthew's Gospel, the process of community in resolving differences—unilateral actions of injury or the mutual loss of relationship—is outlined as a positive, hopeful search for reconciliation.

"If your brother [or sister] sins against you, go and tell them their fault . . . if they will hear you, you have regained your brother [or sister]" (Matt. 18:15) is Jesus' counsel. His focus is on regaining or re-creating relationships, not with appearing morally right, defending one's own position as superior, or vindicating one's actions and attitudes.

The other—the offender—is a brother whose unbrotherly behavior has torn the fabric of community. It is the task of community to reknit that fabric, and those closest to the torn edges act first. If their efforts to reconnect are refused, the adjoining persons accompany them, and if necessary, the entire community becomes active participants.

It is assumed at the outset that there is within the community a decided commitment to seek reconciliation. The entire chapter 18 of Matthew's Gospel addresses the commitment to forgive, and within the chapter lies a process for reconciliation. For Jesus, the steps toward reconciliation and the stances toward wrongdoing are on the pathway toward forgiveness that seeks to regain the brother or sister. As John Howard Yoder observes,

> Twice in Matthew's Gospel Jesus is reported to have assigned to his disciples the authority "to bind and to loose." . . . [B]inding and loosing means what we have called "practical moral reasoning."
>
> What is said to the disciples by Jesus strikes one as presumptuous, if not preposterous or even blasphemous. "What you bind on earth shall be considered as bound in heaven." A transcendent

> moral ratification is claimed for the decisions made in the conversation of two or three or more, in a context of forgiveness and in the juridical form of listening to several witnesses.
>
> Every fragment of the previous sentence matters. The context, . . . the conversation, . . . the commitment, the process, . . . the confrontation (Yoder 1984, 26–27).

The process of reconciliation outlined is a conversation between the immediate parties involved. This conversation is broadened gradually and only as essential to the goal of reconciliation. This offers a process for practical moral reasoning in a situation of conflict which is seen in a context of forgiveness, not revenge or retaliation. The intention of the process is not exclusion, excommunication, reprimand, or punishment but reconnection and reconciliation. As Yoder concludes,

> Every element noted in the passage cited from Matthew 18 has something to say to the way we think today about decision-making in the context of faith.
>
> Most discussions of practical moral reasoning do not ask whether the intention of those doing the reasoning is to reconcile.
>
> Most treatments of this subject do not concretize the decision about issues in the form of a conversation between persons who differ on the issues.
>
> Most discussions of practical moral reasoning do not concretize that conversation by seeing it as surrounded by a church (i.e., a locally gathered body) which ultimately will ratify either the reconciliation or the impossibility of reconciliation.
>
> Most guides to practical moral reasoning do not have the nerve to claim that the discernment reached will stand ratified in heaven (Yoder 1984, 27).

The heart of this passage, Matt. 18:15–20, defines the steps: (1) interaction of the offender/offended; (2) inclusion of two or three witnesses; (3) involvement of the community; (4) recognition of success or failure of the process. It is climaxed by:

> "I tell you solemnly, whatever you bind on earth shall be considered bound in heaven; whatever you loose on earth shall be considered loosed in heaven.
>
> "I tell you solemnly again, if two of you on earth agree to ask anything at all, it will be granted to you by my father in heaven. For where two or three meet in my name, I shall be there with them" (Matt. 18:18–20, JB).

The two statements are parallel: what is bound on earth is bound in heaven; what two or three on earth agree to ask is granted in heaven. What does this equating of divine and human processes mean for us?

It is the meeting of disputants "in the name of Christ," which Jesus promises to attend. He is in the midst of a group gathered in the name of the Reconciler, for the purpose of reconciliation, in a process consistent with his self-giving love. This is the heart of Matthew's forgiveness message. "If you go about it in an open context, where both parties are free to speak, where additional witnesses provide objectivity and mediation, where reconciliation is the intention and the expected outcome is a judgment God himself can stand behind, then the rest of the practical moral reasoning process will find its way" (Yoder 1984, 28).

It is noteworthy that the word of forgiveness can be spoken at any point in the process where repentance—mutual repentance or unilateral amends—is perceived as genuine, but the binding work of moral judgment is done only by the community. The individual has no right to such judgment here. The authority of the community comes through prayer, not through its pretensions to perfection, and the goal is to "win back" the offender, not to maintain a "pure community."

Here, in the conciliation process, the presence of Christ is actual, it is pledged in his own guarantee. It is in discernment and moral reasoning that we are promised God's response and support. (The implication being that regardless of the accuracy of the prayer or the perfection of the judgment, God honors the process. Is God more concerned that community, coresponsibility, and collaboration in ethical discernment take place than God is concerned about the particulars of the judgment reached?) Practical reason as it occurs in moral discernment in Christian community should parallel how it unfolds within the individual Christian conscience. The community develops and delegates functions to persons who demonstrate particular gifts that serve the whole (even as the person comes to trust certain subpersonalities as ways of coping effectively, behaving productively, being authentically).

Practical reason in ethical-relational life is not a disembodied process of abstract values, ideals, and principles, it is a community going about discerning boundaries and defining its virtues and goals. The gifts that give persons roles include

> Agents of vision—the charisma of prophecy that sees the particular situation in the community's story, its history and tradition, and its trajectory towards its ideals.
>
> Agents of memory—the charisma of recollection which collects and recalls "the store of memorable identity—confirming acts of faithfulness praised and of failure repented." This includes scripture, its past interpretations, and tradition with its meanings and guidelines.
>
> Agents of linguistic self-consciousness—the charisma of steering a community with the rudder of language. Such persons, real-

izing at once the power and danger of language to use verbal distinctions or purely verbal solutions to "solve" substantial problems, will guide the community in moral discourse.

Agents of order and due process—the charisma of leadership which oversees and directs the community. These persons insure that everyone is heard and that the conclusions reached are genuinely consensual (adapted from Yoder 1984, 30–33).

The reconciling community may contain or may gather people with such gifts—the prophet's vision, the historian's sense of continuity and precedent, the linguist's knowledge of semantics, syntactics, and pragmatics (meaning, use, and relationships in language), and the facilitator's concern for due process, clarity, and justice. In the individual counseling setting, the therapist is required to perform all four functions: to explore hope, memory, meaning, and process, and to maintain balance and order as the client discerns values and takes the risks of responsible moral behavior.

The reconciling community is a community of bridge builders. The building of bridges calls for many skills. No one person possesses all the gifts required. No one is sufficient to create the links, the long or short connections needed to join the many relationships of diverse character across multiple rifts and clefts. Each member, no matter how unnoteworthy or unnoticed, has a gift to contribute.

One can build bridges and make peace, or one can get the credit for it. But one cannot do both. When there is a choice, one should choose to bridge and be bridged. It is our only hope.

Elias Chacour, Palestinian Arab Christian pastor of a congregation in Ibillin in Galilee, a village thirty minutes from Nazareth, found his village rent by long histories of conflict—conflict that set blood brothers against each other in deep enmity. Nothing, not even the death of their mother, drew them together, or even allowed common entry into the others' homes.

But the tradition of Easter invariably brought them all into the church where they sat far from one another, unmoved, unflinching, without the least contact, even of the eyes.

At the end of a stiff and painful Palm Sunday service, Chacour, having given the most unimpassioned sermon of his life, seeing the congregation even more divided and indifferent, invited all to stand and receive the benediction. As he lifted his hand, something tightened within him, then exploded. He dropped his hand, strode to the back doors—the only doors—drew them shut, pulled the heavy chain through the handles, and snapped the padlock. "Sitting in this building does not make you a Christian," he said. "You are a people divided, arguing, hating, spreading malicious lies. What does the

Moslem community around us think? Surely that our religion is false. If we cannot love the brother we see, how can we love God whom we cannot see? For many months I've tried in vain to unite you. I've failed. There is someone who can bring you together, Jesus Christ. So I will be quiet and allow him to give you the power to forgive. If you will not forgive, we will stay locked in here. You can kill each other and I will provide your funerals gratis."

Silence hung. Tight lipped, fists clenched, all glared as if carved in stone. Long minutes passed. Outside, the sound of a donkey boy clattered on the pavement. Chacour knew he was finished as priest.

Then Abu Maubib, the toughest of the brothers, the village police officer, rose, faced the congregation. "I am the worst one of all. I've hated my own brothers. Hated them so much I wanted to kill them. More than any of you I need forgiveness."

Then he turned to the pastor, "Can you forgive me, too, Abuna?" (*Abuna* means "our father," a term of deep affection and respect, the first warm greeting Chacour had ever heard in that circle.)

"Come," said Chacour, and they embraced, giving the double kiss of peace. "Now go and greet your brothers." And as his brothers came to meet him, a chaos of embracing and tears broke out. Cousins who had not spoken to each other in years wept openly. Confessions were offered. Invitations to Arab hospitality were renewed, and people at last left arm in arm. A lifeless body—the church—was returning from the dead (adapted from Chacour 1984, 169–74).

Toward a New Paradigm of Forgiveness

1. A bias toward reconciliation, a commitment to work toward the renewal and rejoining of alienated parties or groups, is foundational to Christian theology and practice.

2. Reconciliation begins with the victim, but the identification of the victim is not simple or easy. All participants are, to a surprising degree, victims of violence in general and victimized by the particular occurrence. We stand on more level ground than we know; we are all in need of being reconciled and forgiven.

3. The forgiving community exists within the story of God's forgiveness, lives by the stories of its own participation in forgiveness, and serves as it acts as an agent of forgiveness. To be a participant in a reconciling community is our highest experience of being human and the one undeniable evidence that God is in our midst.

Epilogue

Probes and Pointers toward a New Paradigm

The concluding propositions from each of the chapters, which reach toward a renewed paradigm of forgiveness, are reprinted here in a continuous series of probes and pointers for reflection.

1. Accepting and forgiving are different processes. We accept persons for the good that they *are* or *do*. We forgive persons for the evil that they did or caused.
2. Excusing and forgiving are different processes. We excuse people when we no longer hold them accountable. We forgive people when we hold them accountable but do not excuse.
3. Tolerating and forgiving are different processes. We tolerate what another has done when we overlook or ignore. We forgive what we cannot tolerate, will not overlook or ignore.
4. Forgetting and forgiving are different processes. We do not need to forgive if we can simply forget—forgetting is passive, avoidant, repressive; it denies, detaches, dismisses. We do not forget when we forgive, but the meaning of the memory changes—forgiving is active and aware; it is recognizing the injury, owning the pain, and reaching out to reframe, re-create, restore, reconstruct, rebuild, reopen what can be opened.
5. Forgiveness is not an arbitrary, unilateral act of mercy that the offender experiences as a stroke of good fortune. Such "forgiveness" requires no moral response and offers no truly moral contact (Kraus 1987, 238).

6. Forgiveness is not a moral victory for the offended; it is not a self-serving mercy that controls, obligates, or morally judges the offender; rather it transforms the relationship.
7. Authentic reconciliation requires movement by both sides, the offender and the offended. Both contribute, both grow, both reopen the future.
8. Forgiving and forgrieving are parallel, alternating, often cyclical processes. One must forgrieve the loss or injury in order to forgive the offender and the offense.
9. Forgiveness that takes place within interlocking, intimate systems or interrelationships of invisible loyalties calls for a special clarity and connection, an "I-position" and a "Thou respect" that are stubbornly "centered."
10. An authentic apology, differing from either giving an account or offering appeasement, is a balanced position of responsibility and integrity which enables the one who apologizes to pull up to a clearer "I-position" of maturity.
11. Both love and justice, and reconciliation and reconstruction take place at the midpoint between union and separation, connectedness and individuation. Love is maximum closeness with minimum threat; it is contact without control; it is union that protects separateness.
12. The capacity to grieve, feel the loss of relationship, and make reparations to those we have injured is learned early and rooted deeply in childhood development. It is essential to our humanness and progressive in maturation.
13. The movement from the paranoid position (when hate, rage, blaming, and judgment are used to cope with frustration) to the depressive position (when grieving and regret lead to reparations and reconciliation) is the crucial passage of childhood and the ongoing challenge of adulthood. In stress, we all regress. But regression only to the depressive level, not to the paranoid level, is evidence of maturing.
14. Adult reparations and adult mourning are possible when the objects within (both good and bad internalized identifications) are accepted; then others who act evilly (external bad objects) can be seen with empathy and compassion.

15. Forgiveness is the extension of empathy to become mercy, and the capacity to experience and express empathy is profoundly shaped by the experiences of deprivation or adequate parental "gleam" (affirmation) in infancy and childhood.

16. Forgiveness or each person's capacity for forgiving is shaped by the wounds to the self-structure, the splitting utilized to cope with threat, the overwhelming power of shame, and the defensive emergence of the grandiose self.

17. Forgiveness, as an interpersonal bridge, requires adult skills; achieving adulthood requires resolving the unresolved dilemmas of childhood, strengthening of self-structures, and developing mature narcissistic capacities and abilities.

18. Forgiveness limits but does not eliminate resentment; it directs it from obsessive resenting to realistic resenting; it becomes a profound passion for justice, social transformation, and ultimately reconciliation.

19. Forgiveness, to be at all meaningful, requires an ethical context. Without norms, values, mores, and moral categories, forgiveness is formless and meaningless. In a permissive context, it is reduced to tolerance or indulgence.

20. Forgiveness is the virtue that enables the practice of reconciliation. It becomes a true virtue as it embodies and extends the narrative of a community that draws persons together, bridges breaches, and invites reconciliation.

21. We need to embrace our communities or create new communities that prize and retell communal stories, and strengthen their connection to larger stories that unite us, reconciling us with each other across all boundaries.

22. Aggression is elemental to human community. Violence is endemic. Religion has served to limit it by sacralizing the process of selecting a scapegoat to bear the community's collective wrath. But the ritual is a lie. Its solution is brief, its ultimate impact destructive.

23. The scapegoat mechanism, and with it the myth of redemptive violence, promises the resolution of a community's rage and the cessation of its hostilities, but it is powerless to effect such a result. We need the interjection of the new element called forgiveness.

24. True reconciliation requires that human violence be transformed into suffering; that the innocence of victims be recognized; that guilt and responsibility of violence be faced; and that repentance, reapproachment, and forgiveness be sought.

25. A bias toward reconciliation, a commitment to work toward the renewal and rejoining of alienated parties or groups, is foundational to Christian theology and practice.

26. Reconciliation begins with the victim, but the identification of the victim is not simple or easy. All participants are, to a surprising degree, victims of violence in general and victimized by the particular occurrence. We stand on more level ground than we know; we are all in need of being reconciled and forgiven.

27. The forgiving community exists within the story of God's forgiveness, lives by the stories of its own participation in forgiveness, and serves as it acts as an agent of forgiveness. To be a participant in a reconciling community is our highest experience of being human and the one undeniable evidence that God is in our midst.

Appendix

Visualizing Healing

When forgiveness seems impossible, visualization of new ways of seeing the binding situation can clear the eyes. Our eyes are unable to refocus, to see reality again. Our mental pictures have become still shots, in black and white, freeze frame in resentment. Visualization can initiate the process of forward movement, the flow of pictures with fluidity, color, richness, and the ongoing sequence of new forms and vitality.

Imagination, the eye of the soul, is filled with images, with mental pictures that allow us to reconstruct what we have known and construct what we wish for, desire, hope for, what we create.

If you pause now, close your eyes, relax, and think of someone or someplace you love, you will find your mind exploring mental pictures. Images emerge to give life to your memories or color to your creative thoughts. The old images that gave form to our perceptions may be phobic, or paranoid, or perfectionist, or repetitious, or simply distorted. Growth comes as we discover alternate images.

Our images combine to create our guiding metaphors. These basic propositions compressed into a trigger word are the nodal points that connect whole units of behavior. When we recognize the faulty metaphors and change the images that give meaning to them, our behavior changes.

Visualizing a new image, seeing a different picture, choosing a fresh metaphor can thaw frozen emotions and set us more free. The following exercises are examples of such visualization that have proven useful as guided imaging in the therapeutic process.

Visualization 1

1. Visualize your own journey toward forgiveness as a movement toward the light. From the darkness of abuse, injury, invasion, exclusion,

devaluation, hatred, hot resentment, or cold bitterness, see yourself slowly moving toward the light of acceptance and healing. Allow the warmth of the light to stream over you, to welcome you in love, to embrace you in the arms of divine love.

2. Now visualize the other—the offender, the attacker, the abuser, the rejecter—as also moving toward that same light, in that person's own strange, meandering, circuitous way, perhaps. With advances and retreat, with stubborn insistence on taking her or his own path, but nevertheless, inching toward the light. It is enough to simply visualize the person on that journey, whatever the status or progress. In time you may visualize yourself reaching out to support, to encourage, to accept the other in prayer. Do not rush or press the process. We do not hurry the light, it draws us by its own power.

Visualization 2

1. Visualize a dear friend who through some blind choice has hurt another deeply. Think of listening until the story has been fully, freely told. Think of caring until the other feels cared for in spite of the wrongdoing done. Think of inviting the other to make a fresh start.

2. Visualize a dear friend who through some blind choice has hurt *you* deeply. Think of suspending your anger for a while and seeking to understand the other's motives, choices, actions from within. Think of setting yourself beside the other and helping him or her to make a new beginning.

3. Visualize an enemy, who through some malice has injured someone you love. Think of bracketing your anger for a period and choosing to hear what the enemy hears, see what he sees, feel what she feels, and make some degree of sense from within. Think of offering compassion for the other's confusion, distortion, or failure.

4. Visualize an enemy who through the worst of motives has injured you. Do not think of yourself reaching out as a friend; no, instead, visualize God as the most patient of friends, the most understanding of listeners, the most caring conversationalist before whom no evasion is possible or necessary, who, knowing the worst, the most gross or monstrous wrongs, yet takes a position firmly by the side of the enemy and invites a new beginning.

Visualization 3

1. Visualize a situation in which another's action has lowered your esteem in the eyes of others or attacked your self-esteem.

2. Reflect on Simone Weil's observation "It is impossible to forgive whoever has done us harm if that harm has lowered us. We have to think that it has not lowered us but revealed our true level."

3. Visualize the other's put-down as simply highlighting your worst but not speaking to your best; consider it a comment on the lowest common denominator, of which you might be capable, but not addressing the higher motives or actions that express your true intentions. Visualize strengthening your own security to the point that you can own a wide range of ambivalent feelings, motives, expressions. Affirm your own complexity, appreciate your own inner diversity, accept both the good and the bad in yourself.

4. Visualize addressing the person who has put you down. Instead of defending yourself, tell of an even more serious failure, a time when you experienced your darkest side. Can you own your own humanity, frailty, fallibility, whether or not the other's charges were accurate? Do you find that this draws the pain from the sting?

Visualization 4

This visualization employs the use of "time projection," of moving into the future and then looking back on present pain from the vantage point of six months or a year later.

1. Visualize yourself at the end of the month, perhaps two weeks in the future. Present tasks have all been completed, new opportunities open. Now go further into future time, six months first, then one year. Look back at your present pain, sadness, anger, resentment. What do you see? What do you feel?

2. Looking back on losses from the present, one asks, Was it my fault? Did I fail miserably? Was I wronged? How could I let myself be caught in such a situation? These questions trigger a chain reaction. Now go forward a year in time. Place yourself in a new situation. Look back from a position of freedom. Visualize yourself as having let go of the resentments, of releasing the demands on the other person to undo what was done. Picture yourself as filled with new, rewarding concerns that satisfy the deep needs of your soul.

3. Move into the future in time projection and allow yourself to feel pleasure again, to experience joy again, to welcome new intimacy, to celebrate deep happiness. Explore its feelings, its beliefs, its way of perceiving the world. Which of these can you find present in your life—to some extent—now? Can you nourish them?

4. Can you give yourself permission, from the projected vantage point of the future, to be truly happy? Abraham Lincoln, after years of chronic depression, concluded: "Most folks are about as happy as they make up their minds to be."

5. By visualizing yourself at the horizon of the future, you look back on the unfolding landscape of your life. Forgiveness comes from the horizon,

theologian Karl Rahner has suggested. "God is the horizon of all experience." God is always at the edges of human awareness just as the horizon is at the edges of visual perception. The horizon is the invisible backdrop against which we see everything else. When we visualize ourself, with God, on the horizon looking back at our present standpoint, we can revisualize our life, see it illuminated by the rising sun, see it in the new light of hope.

Visualization 5

The one great commandment with the promise of opening us to living long and well is that which governs relationship with one's parents. It can be translated:

> Forgive your parents that you may live long
> in the land which the Lord your God giveth you.

1. Reflect on John Warkentin's words:

> To the degree I have forgiven my parents,
> to that degree I am useful as a therapist.
>
> To the degree that I have outlived my childhood bitterness and pouting,
> to that degree I am valuable as a therapist.
>
> (Warkentin 1972, 261)

2. Focus on two unfinished resentments toward a parent. Let them fill you. Exaggerate. Release emotional feelings to well up into the pictures that form. Now turn your attention on yourself. What has this done to your sense of self? How old are you in this picture? Are you still a child? What sense of childishness is comforting, satisfying? What feelings of childishness are embarrassing, obsolete?

3. Visualize growing up again, move slowly through the years and let go of the childhood bitterness, release the little girl/little boy resentments, give up the pouting by seeing it for what it is.

4. Reflect, with humor (forced, if necessary), on Warkentin's ironic words:

> Neurosis is a large remnant of childhood attitudes
> plus too much pride.
>
> Psychosis is neurosis plus a great determination to make the parents suffer for "what they did wrong."
>
> (Warkentin 1972, 258)

Bibliography

Arendt, Hannah. 1958. *The Human Condition.* Chicago: University of Chicago Press.

Arnett, Ronald G. 1986. *Communication and Community.* Carbondale: Southern Illinois University Press.

Atkinson, David. 1982. "Forgiveness as a Personality Development." *Thirdway.* Nov. 18–22.

Augsburger, David W. 1981. *Caring Enough to Forgive.* Ventura, Calif.: Regal Books.

———. 1986. *Pastoral Counseling across Cultures.* Philadelphia: Westminster Press.

———. 1992. *Conflict Mediation across Cultures.* Louisville, Ky.: Westminster/John Knox Press.

Austin, J. L. 1962. *How to Do Things with Words.* Cambridge, Mass.: Harvard University Press.

Bondi, Richard. 1986. "Character." In James F. Childress and John Macquarrie, eds., *The Westminster Dictionary of Christian Ethics.* Philadelphia: Westminster Press.

Bonhoeffer, Dietrich. 1949. *The Cost of Discipleship.* New York: Macmillan Co.

Bowen, Murray. 1978. *Family Therapy in Clinical Practice.* Northvale, N.J.: Jason Aronson.

Brakenhielm, Carl-Reinhold. 1993. *Forgiveness.* Translated by Thor Hall. Minneapolis: Augsburg Fortress.

Bristol, Goldie, and Carol McGinnis. 1982. *When It's Hard to Forgive.* Wheaton, Ill.: Victor Press.

Browning, Don. 1976. *The Moral Context of Pastoral Care.* Philadelphia: Westminster Press.

———. 1983. *Religious Ethics and Pastoral Care.* Philadelphia: Fortress Press.

———. 1987. *Religious Thought and the Modern Psychologies.* Philadelphia: Fortress Press.

Brueggemann, Walter. 1991. *Interpretation and Obedience.* Philadelphia: Fortress Press.

Burkert, Walter. 1983. *Homo Necans.* Berkeley, Calif.: University of California Press.

Burkert, Walter, René Girard, and Jonathan Z. Smith. 1987. *Violent Origins.* Stanford, Calif.: Stanford University Press.

Burkhart, Louise M. 1989. *The Slippery Earth.* Tucson: University of Arizona Press.

Butler, Joseph. 1726. *Fifteen Sermons.* London (n.p.). London: J. and P. Knapton, 1749.

———. 1896. *The Works of Joseph Butler.* Oxford: Clarendon Press.

Cannon, Katie G. 1985. *God's Fierce Whimsy.* New York: Pilgrim Press.

———. 1988. *Black Womanist Ethics.* Atlanta: Scholars Press.

Chacour, Elias. 1984. *Blood Brothers.* Grand Rapids: Zondervan Publishing House.

Chessick, Richard C. 1985. *Psychology of the Self and the Treatment of Narcissism.* Northvale, N.J.: Jason Aronson.

Claassen, Ron. 1988. "Victim Offender Reconciliation Program." *VORP News.* VORP of the Central Valley, 2529 Willow Avenue, Clovis, CA 93612.

Collins, David. 1991. "Easter's Gift." *The Vintage Voice.* New York: Episcopal Church Fund of Family Beneficiaries.

Collins, Scott. 1994. "Cityscapes." *Los Angeles Times,* Sept. 24, sec. B, pp. 1–8.

———. 1994b. "On road to ruin, teenager gets help making a U-turn." *Los Angeles Times,* September 24, 1994, B1.

Cone, James H. 1975. *God of the Oppressed.* New York: Seabury Press.

Courlander, Harold, and Wolf Leslau. 1950. *Fire on the Mountain and Other Ethiopian Stories.* New York: Holt, Rinehart & Winston.

Cox, Harvey. 1967. *On Not Leaving It to the Snake.* New York: Macmillan Co.

Daniel, Valentine. 1984. *Fluid Signs: Being a Person the Tamil Way.* Berkeley: University of California Press.

Davies, Robertson. 1988. *The Lyre of Orpheus.* New York: Penguin Books.

DeSpain, Pleasant. 1993. *Thirty-three Multicultural Tales to Tell.* Little Rock, Ark.: August House Publishers.

Dolbee, Sandi. 1994. "Looking Past the Hurt." *The San Diego Union-Tribune.* Friday, December 9, sec. E, pp. 1–4.

Dostoyevsky, Fyodor. [1880] 1957. *The Brothers Karamazov.* New York: Signet Classics.

Dunn, Ashley. 1993. "Bridging the Vietnamese and American cultures." *Los Angeles Times,* April 19, 1993, F1.

Dyck, Arthur. 1973. "A Unified Theory of Virtue and Obligation." *Journal of Religious Ethics,* vol. 1, no. 1, pp. 37–52.

Eilbert-Schwartz, Howard. 1990. *The Savage in Judaism.* Bloomington: Indiana University Press.

Elizondo, Virgil. 1986. "I Forgive but I Do Not Forget," in Casiano Floristan and Christian Duquoc, *Forgiveness.* Edinburgh: T. & T. Clark.

Farley, Edward. 1990. *Good and Evil: Interpreting a Human Condition.* Minneapolis: Fortress Press.

Fenichel, Otto. 1945. *The Psychoanalytic Theory of Neurosis.* New York: W. W. Norton & Co.

Frazer, James G. 1963. *The Golden Bough.* Vol. 1. New York: Macmillan Co.

French, Peter, et al., eds. 1988. *Ethical Theory: Character and Virtue.* Midwest Studies in Philosophy, vol. 13. Notre Dame, Ind.: Notre Dame University Press.

Friedman, Edwin H. 1985. *Generation to Generation.* New York: Guilford Press.

Friedman, Maurice. 1983. *The Conformation of Otherness.* New York: Pilgrim Press.

Gandhi, M. K. 1965. *The Collected Works of Mahatma Gandhi.* New Delhi: Delhi Publication Division, Government of India.

Gil, Eliana. 1988. *Treatment of Adult Survivors of Childhood Abuse.* Walnut Creek, Calif.: Launch Press.

Girard, René. 1977. *Violence and the Sacred.* Baltimore: Johns Hopkins University Press.

———. 1986. *The Scapegoat.* Baltimore: Johns Hopkins University Press.

Glover, E. 1968. *The Birth of the Ego.* New York: International University Press.

Golding, Martin. 1984. "Forgiveness and Regret." *Philosophical Forum* 16, nos. 1–2 (winter/fall).

Haber, Joram Graf. 1991. *Forgiveness.* Savage, Md.: Rowman & Littlefield.

Hamerton-Kelly, Robert G. 1992. *Sacred Violence: Paul's Hermeneutic of the Cross.* Minneapolis: Fortress Press.

Hauerwas, Stanley. 1974. *Vision and Virtue.* Notre Dame, Ind.: Fides Publishers.

———. 1975. *Character and the Christian Life.* San Antonio, Tex.: Trinity University Press.

———. 1977. *Truthfulness and Tragedy.* Notre Dame, Ind.: University of Notre Dame Press.

———. 1981. *A Community of Character.* Notre Dame, Ind.: University of Notre Dame Press.

———. 1983. *The Peaceable Kingdom.* Notre Dame, Ind.: University of Notre Dame Press.

———. 1988. *Christian Existence Today.* Durham, N.C.: Labyrinth Press.

———. 1989. *Resident Aliens.* Nashville: Abingdon Press.

———. 1991. *After Christendom?* Nashville: Abingdon Press.

Hauerwas, Stanley, and Alasdair MacIntyre, eds. 1983. *Revisions: Changing Perspectives in Moral Philosophy.* Notre Dame, Ind.: University of Notre Dame Press.

Hunter, R.C.A. 1978. "Forgiveness, Reconciliation and Paranoid Reactions." *Canadian Psychiatry Journal* 23:190–98.

James, William. [1902] 1958. *The Varieties of Religious Experience.* New York: Mentor Books.

Jung, Carl G. 1977. "Transformation Symbolism in the Mass." In *Psychology and Religion: East and West.* The Collected Works of C. G. Jung, vol. 11. Princeton, N.J.: Princeton University Press.

Kaufman, Gershen. 1985. *Shame: The Power of Caring.* Cambridge, Mass.: Schenkman Publishing Co.

Keen, Sam. 1986. *Faces of the Enemy.* San Francisco: Harper & Row.

Kerr, Michael E., and Murray Bowen. 1988. *Family Evaluation: An Approach Based on Bowen Theory.* New York: W. W. Norton & Co.

Kierkegaard, Søren. 1954. *Fear and Trembling.* Garden City, N.Y.: Doubleday & Co.

Klassen, William. 1984. *Love of Enemies.* Philadelphia: Fortress Press.

Klein, Melanie. 1948. *Contributions to Psychoanalysis.* London: Hogarth.

———. 1957. *New Directions in Psychoanalysis.* New York: Basic Books.

———. 1962. *Love, Hate and Reparation.* London: Hogarth Press.

———. 1975a. *Envy, Gratitude and Other Works.* New York: Delacorte Press.

———. 1975b. *Love, Guilt and Reparation and Other Works 1921–1945.* New York: Delacorte Press.

Klein, Melanie, et al. 1953. *Development in Psycho-Analysis.* London: Hogarth Press.

Kohut, Heinz. 1974. "Narcissism and Narcissistic Rage." In *The Psychoanalytic Study of the Child,* vol. 27. Edited by Ruth S. Eissler. New York: Quadrangle.

———. 1978. *The Search for the Self.* Edited by P. Ornstein. New York: International Universities Press.

———. 1984. *How Does Analysis Cure?* Edited by Arnold Goldberg and Paul Stepansky. Chicago: University of Chicago Press.

Kraus, C. Norman. 1987. *Jesus Christ Our Lord: Christology from a Disciple's Perspective.* Scottdale, Pa.: Herald Press.

Kuhn, Thomas S. 1970. *The Structure of Scientific Revolutions.* 2d ed. Chicago: University of Chicago Press.

Lambert, Jean C. 1985. *The Human Action of Forgiving.* Lanham, Md.: University Press of America.

Lapsley, James. 1967. "Character." In James F. Childress and John Macquarrie, eds., *The Westminster Dictionary of Christian Ethics.* Philadelphia: Westminster Press.

Lasch, Christopher. 1979. *The Culture of Narcissism.* New York: W. W. Norton & Co.

Lea, Henry C. [1896] 1968. *A History of Auricular Confession and Indulgences in the Latin Church.* New York: Greenwood Press.

Lebacqz, Karen. 1985. *Professional Ethics.* Nashville: Abingdon Press.

Leehan, James. 1989. *Pastoral Care for Survivors of Family Abuse.* Louisville, Ky.: Westminster/John Knox Press.

Lord, Richard P. 1991. "Do I Have to Forgive?" *Christian Century,* Oct. 9, 902–3.

MacDonald, Margaret Read. 1992. *Peace Tales: World Folktales to Talk About.* Hamden, Conn.: Linnet Books.

MacIntyre, Alasdair. 1975. "How Virtues Become Vices: Medicine and Social Context." In *Evaluation and Explanation in the Biomedical Sciences.* Edited by H. Tristram Engelhardt, Jr., and Stuart F. Spicker. Boston: D. Reidel.

———. 1981. *After Virtue.* Notre Dame, Ind.: University of Notre Dame Press.

———. 1984. *Marxism and Christianity.* Notre Dame, Ind.: University of Notre Dame Press.

———. 1986. "Positivism, Sociology and Practical Reasoning: Notes on Durkheim's *Suicide.*" In *Human Nature and Natural Knowledge.* Edited by A. Donagan et al. Dordrecht: D. Reidel.

Malina, Bruce, and Richard J. Rohrbaugh. 1992. *Social Science Commentary on the Synoptic Gospels.* Minneapolis: Fortress Press.

Marcus, Paul, and Alan Rosenberg. 1989. *Healing Their Wounds: Psychotherapy with Holocaust Survivors and Their Families.* New York: Praeger Publishers.

Mayeroff, Milton. 1971. *On Caring.* New York: Harper & Row.

McClendon, James W., Jr. 1986. *Ethics.* Systematic Theology, vol. 1. Nashville: Abingdon Press.

Melville, Herman. 1922. *Moby-Dick, or The Whale.* London: Constable.

Miller, Alice. 1981. *Prisoners of Childhood.* New York: Basic Books. (Published as *The Gifted Child,* 1994.)

———. 1983. *For Your Own Good.* New York: The Noonday Press.

Mouw, Richard J. 1989. *Distorted Truth.* New York: Harper & Row.

Murdoch, Iris. 1987. "The Sovereignty of Good over Other Concepts." In *The Virtues,* edited by Robert Kruschwitz and Robert C. Roberts. Belmont, Calif.: Wadsworth Publishing Co.

Murphy, Jeffrie. 1982. "Forgiveness and Resentment." In *Social and Political Philosophy.* Midwest Studies in Philosophy, 7, pp. 90–99. Edited by Peter French et al. Notre Dame, Ind.: Notre Dame University Press.

Murphy, Jeffrie G., and Jean Hampton. 1988. *Forgiveness and Mercy*. New York: Cambridge University Press.

Neill, Stephen. 1959. *A Genuinely Human Existence*. Garden City, N.Y., and London: Doubleday & Co./Constable.

Newman, Louis E. 1987. "The Quality of Mercy: On the Duty to Forgive in the Judaic Tradition." *Journal of Religious Ethics* 15 (fall 1987): 155–72.

Niebuhr, Reinhold. 1941. *An Interpretation of Christian Ethics*. London: SCM Press.

Outka, Gene. 1973. *Agape: An Ethical Analysis*. New Haven, Conn.: Yale University Press.

Patton, John. 1985. *Is Human Forgiveness Possible?* Nashville: Abingdon Press.

Phillips, Derek L. 1987. "Authenticity or Morality?" In *The Virtues*, ed. Robert B. Kruschwitz and Robert C. Roberts. Belmont, Calif.: Wadsworth Publishing Co.

Rieff, Philip. 1966. *The Triumph of the Therapeutic*. New York: Harper & Row.

Ross, W. D. 1930. *The Right and the Good*. Oxford: Clarendon Press.

Runes, Dagobert. 1961. *Lost Legends of Israel*. New York: Philosophical Library.

Schreiter, Robert J. 1992. *Reconciliation*. Maryknoll, N.Y.: Orbis Books.

Schwager, Raymond. 1987. *Must There Be Scapegoats?* San Francisco: Harper & Row.

Segal, Hanna. 1964. *Introduction to the Work of Melanie Klein*. New York: Basic Books. New enl. ed., London: Hogarth Press, 1973.

Shriner, Donald. 1962. *Forgiving and Therapeutic Community*. Th.D. dissertation. Harvard University, Cambridge, Mass.

Sipe, A. W. Richard, and Clarence J. Rowe. 1984. *Psychiatry, Ministry and Pastoral Counseling*. Collegeville, Minn.: Liturgical Press.

Sittler, Joseph. 1986. *Gravity and Grace*. Minneapolis: Augsburg Publishing House.

Smith, Jonathan Z. 1982. *Imagining Religion, from Babylon to Jonestown*. Chicago: University of Chicago Press.

Soelle, Dorothee. 1984. *To Work and to Love*. Philadelphia: Fortress Press.

Solomon, Robert. 1976. *The Passions*. Garden City, N.Y.: Doubleday & Co., Anchor Press.

Stackhouse, Max. 1992. "Alasdair MacIntyre: An Overview and Evaluation." *Religious Studies Review*, vol. 18, no. 3, July, pp. 203–8.

Stendahl, Krister. 1976. *Paul among Jews and Gentiles*. Philadelphia: Fortress Press.

Strawson, P. F. 1974. *Freedom and Resentment, and Other Essays*. London: Methuen & Co.

Tavuchis, Nicholas. 1991. *Mea Culpa: A Sociology of Apology and Reconciliation.* Stanford, Calif.: Stanford University Press.

Thomas, Michele Berhard. 1992. *An Introduction to Marital and Family Therapy.* New York: Merrill Publishing Co. (Macmillan).

Tolstoy, Leo. [1873] 1954. *Anna Karenina.* London: Penguin Books.

Truax, Charles, and Robert Carkhuff. 1967. *Toward Effective Counseling and Psychotherapy.* Chicago: Aldine Publishing Co.

Tyler, Anne. 1991. *Saint Maybe.* New York: Ivy Books (Ballantine Books).

Underwood, Ralph L. 1985. *Empathy and Confrontation in Pastoral Care.* Philadelphia: Fortress Press.

Van der Post, Laurens. 1970. *The Seed and the Sower.* New York: William Morrow & Co.

Wainwright, Geoffrey. 1980. *Doxology: The Praise of God in Worship, Doctrine, and Life.* New York: Oxford University Press.

Warkentin, John. 1972. "The Paradox of Being Alien and Intimate," in *Twelve Therapists: How They Live and Actualize Themselves.* San Francisco: Jossey-Bass.

Weil, Simone. 1977. *The Simone Weil Reader.* Edited by George A. Panichas. New York: David McKay Co.

Wiesenthal, Simon. 1972. *The Sunflower.* London: W. H. Allen.

Williams, James G. 1991. *The Bible, Violence and the Sacred.* San Francisco: HarperCollins.

Willimon, William H. 1991. Quoted in Michael Goldberg, *Against the Grain,* pp. 81–98 (Valley Forge, Pa.: Trinity Press International, 1993).

Wink, Walter. 1992. *Engaging the Powers.* Minneapolis: Fortress Press.

Winnicott, D. W. 1955. "The Depressive Position in Normal Development." *British Journal of Medicine and Psychology* 28.

Wittgenstein, Ludwig. 1952. *Philosophical Investigations.* New York: Macmillan Co.

Yancey, Philip. 1991. "An Unnatural Act." *Christianity Today,* April 8, pp. 36–39.

Yoder, Elizabeth G., ed. 1992. *Peace, Theology and Violence against Women.* Elkhart, Ind.: Institute of Mennonite Studies.

Yoder, John Howard. 1971. *The Politics of Jesus.* Grand Rapids: Wm. B. Eerdmans Publishing Co.

———. 1984. *The Priestly Kingdom: Social Ethics as Gospel.* Notre Dame, Ind.: University of Notre Dame Press.

Acknowledgments

Grateful acknowledgment is made to the following for the use of copyrighted material:

The Christian Century Foundation, from Richard Lord, "Do I Have to Forgive?" copyright 1991 Christian Century Foundation. Reprinted by permission from the October 9, 1991 issue of *The Christian Century.*

Henry Holt and Company, from *Fire on the Mountain and Other Ethiopian Stories,* by Harold Courlander and Wolf Leslau. Copyright © 1950. Reprinted by permission of Henry Holt and Company, Inc.

Oxford University Press and SCM Press, from *Doxology,* by Geoffrey Wainwright, © 1980 by Geoffrey Wainwright. Published by Oxford University Press, New York, and Epworth Press, London.

LaVergne, TN USA
31 August 2010
195287LV00004B/4/A